QSAR and Molecular Modeling

Other Titles of Interest

Books

A Selection of Prime Ayurvedic Plant Drugs: Ancient-Modern Concordance
SUKH DEV

Bioactive Marine Natural Products
D.S. BHAKUNI AND D.S. RAWAT

Chemical Kinetics and Reaction Dynamics
SANTOSH K. UPADHYAY

New Trends in Green Chemistry (2/E)
V.K. AHLUWALIA AND M. KIDWAI

Organic Spectroscopy
L.D.S. YADAV

Recent Trends in Fuel Cell Science and Technology
SUDDHASATWA BASU (ED.)

Journal

Indian Chemical Engineer
QUARTERLY JOURNAL OF INDIAN INSTITUTE OF CHEMICAL ENGINEERS

QSAR and Molecular Modeling

S.P. Gupta

CONSISTING OF KNOWLEDGE

Anamaya Publishers
New Delhi

Prof. S.P. Gupta
Department of Pharmaceutical Technology
Meerut Institute of Engineering and Technology
Meerut - 250 005, India
Formerly, Department of Chemistry
Birla Institute of Technology and Science
Pilani - 333 031, India

ANAMAYA PUBLISHERS
F-154/2, Lado Sarai, New Delhi - 110 030, India
E-mail: anamayapub@vsnl.net

Copublished, sold and distributed in North, Central and South America by Springer, 233 Spring Street, New York, USA and in all other countries, except India, by Springer, P.O. Box 322, 3300 AH Dordrecht, The Netherlands.

ISBN 978-81-89927-09-7

Published by Manish Sejwal for Anamaya Publishers
F-154/2, Lado Sarai, New Delhi - 110 030. Printed in India.

To

My parents who gave me birth

and

My wife, Kanak, who adorned my life

Preface

Quantitative structure-activity relationships (QSAR) and molecular modeling has now become a highly active area of research in medicinal chemistry. Therefore, it has become essential that all medicinal chemists have some basic understanding of this field. The research in this area is highly software-dependent and, hence, it is also referred to as *Computer-Aided Drug Design* (CADD). While a large number of softwares have been developed, these are used without much understanding of the basics of the field by the users. As a result the interpretation of results becomes very difficult. The objective of this book is to acquaint the readers with the fundamentals of QSAR and molecular modeling. The area is very vast and, hence, it is not easy to cover all its facets in one single book. Nevertheless, an attempt has been made to cover the most essential aspects starting from simple Hansch analysis, a two-dimensional (2D) approach, to some important three-dimensional (3D) methodologies.

The book begins with a brief introduction of QSAR in Chapter 1 and then discusses in detail in Chapter 2 the different physicochemical parameters that can govern the biological activity of compounds. Chapter 3 presents an eloquent discussion of drug-receptor interactions, mentioning the type of receptors and forces involved in drug-receptor interactions. Various models used for QSAR analysis are vividly described in Chapter 4. These models particularly include 2D-approaches, such as multiple linear regression analysis (Hansch approach), Free-Wilson analysis, Kubinyi's bilinear model, principal component analysis, partial least-square method, discriminant analysis, neural networks, etc. Chapter 5 presents some very popular 3D methodologies, such as pharmacophore mapping, *de novo* ligand design, structure-based ligand design, molecular docking, comparative molecular field analysis (CoMFA), hologram QSAR, hypothetical active site lattice (HASL) approach, 3D molecular similarity and QSAR, etc.

For a drug molecule it is not sufficient to only study its interaction with the receptor, but it is also essential to study its absorption, distribution, metabolism, excretion, and toxicity (ADMET) properties. Chapter 6 describes some methodologies of ADMET studies. Finally, Chapter 7 embodies a brief discussion of high-throughput screening (HTS), which is the screening of a large number of diverse chemical compounds to identify candidates *hits* rapidly and accurately. It has greatly facilitated drug discovery and has become the backbone of the drug industry.

At the end of each chapter some important references have been cited to enable the readers to go into the detail of any topic of their interest. Additionally, at the end of the book, some more literature have been cited for further reading. The book will be interesting and useful for those interested in QSAR. It is not intended to write a treatise on QSAR and, therefore, the book has lot of scope for further addition. Any useful suggestions for addition of any more chapters and even for improvement in the present chapters will be highly welcome and will be taken care of in future editions of the book.

At the end, I would like to express my sincere thanks to some of my graduate students, namely Mallari A. Naik, V.S.A. Kumar Satuluri, and Jyostna Seelam, who have greatly helped me in preparing the manuscript through word-processing and drawing many structures and figures. I also thank all those copyright owners who kindly granted me the permission to reprint certain figures, tables, structures, etc., from their literature. Lastly, I express my gratitude to all my Ph.D. students who showed immense love for QSAR and inspired me to write this book.

S.P. GUPTA

Contents

QSAR and Molecular Modeling

1 Introduction

The term "Drug Design" introduced in pharmaceutical and medicinal chemistry represents the efforts to develop new drugs on a rational basis so as to decrease the trial and error factor and predict the biological activity of compounds before their synthesis. These rational efforts have drastically reduced the cost and time to bring a drug from a laboratory to a patient's bed and thus the ratio of output to input has significantly increased.

Long ago it was proposed that the biological activity of a compound is a function of its chemical structure. The development of a mathematical relation between structure and the activity of compounds led to coin the word "quantitative-structure activity relationships (QSAR)" and the discipline of QSAR was initiated by the pioneering work of Carwin Hansch on growth-regulating phenoxy acetic acids. He laid the foundations of QSAR (1962-1964) by three important contributions: the combination of several physicochemical parameters in one regression equation, the definition of *lipophilicity* (or *hydrophobicity*) *parameter* π, and the formulation of the parabolic model for nonlinear lipophilicity-activity relationships. Now QSAR derives models which not only describe the structural dependence of biological activities on physicochemical parameters but also on several indicator variables and three-dimensional molecular property profiles of the compounds.

Drugs exert their biological effects through interaction with a specific target which can be an enzyme, a receptor, an ion channel, a nucleic acid, or any other biological macromolecule. This interaction is determined by intermolecular forces which are mainly hydrophobic, electrostatic, polar, and steric in nature, and for an effective interaction a drug molecule must have a three-dimensional structure, which in an arrangement of its functional groups and surface properties is more or less complimentary to a binding site in the target. This is warranted because the better are the steric fit and the complementarity of the surface properties of a drug molecule to its binding site, the higher would be its affinity to binding site and consequently the higher would be its biological effect.

However, while the fit of the three-dimensional structure and the complementarity of the surface properties of a drug are established as the necessary conditions for its biological effects, the foremost condition before that is that the drug must reach its binding site, which is controlled by lipophilicity and the ionization of the drug in a biological system. Even in a simple *in vitro* system, e.g., the inhibition of an enzyme in aqueous medium, the surrounding water molecules can reduce the affinity of a drug by competing to form the hydrogen bonds with the binding site as well as with the functional groups of drug molecules. However, notwithstanding all such requirements, the 2D QSAR models do not consider the three-dimensional arrangements of functional groups, which then become a domain of 3D QSAR approaches.

The objective of this book is, therefore, to provide an introduction of both 2D and 3D QSAR methodologies to those interested in drug design. Writing a book on QSAR is a difficult task, since QSAR in the present time is a highly active area of research, developing various methodologies, such that it has become almost impossible for an individual, or even for a small group of people, to attain a mastery over all the methodologies. Even keeping a track of the development of newer and newer parameters has become a difficult task. Nonetheless, an attempt has been made to cover the maximum of this area with particular emphasis on the fundamentals. Since the area of QSAR has grown on a theoretical platform where the computer has played an enormous role, this area is also known as Computer-Aided Drug Design (CADD). To facilitate understanding of the area, interested readers may also refer to some more literature [1-3].

References

[1] Hansch, C., Sammes, P.G. and Taylor, J.B. (Eds.), Ramsden, C.A. (Series Ed.), *Comprehensive Medicinal Chemistry, Vol. 4: Quantitative Drug Design*, Pergamon Press, Oxford (1990).

[2] Kubinyi, H., *QSAR: Hansch Analysis and Related Approaches*, VCH, Weiheim, New York (1993).

[3] Hansch, C. and Leo, A., *Exploring QSAR: Fundamental and Applications in Chemistry and Biology*, American Chemical Society, Washington, D.C. (1995).

2

Parameters

To derive any type of QSAR model the most basic requirement is to have biological activity data of compounds in terms of numerical parameters and then the physicochemical or structural parameters that control the biological activity. The former are called *biological parameters* and are used as *dependent variables* and the latter are called *structural parameters* or *molecular descriptors* and are used as *independent variables*. A description of both is given here separately.

2.1 Biological Parameters

The biological data that are mostly used in the QSAR studies are usually kinetic or pharmacokinetic data such as substrate or receptor binding constants (affinity data), association or dissociation constants which are basically related to rate constants, Michaelis-Menten constants, enzyme inhibition constants, K_i or IC_{50} (molar concentration of compounds leading to 50% inhibition of the enzyme), absorption rate constants, rate constants of metabolic degradation, and elimination rate constants. Some *in vitro* biological activity data that are related to the inhibition of growth of bacteria, fungi, and other cell cultures are also used. Some pharmacodynamic or toxic activity measurements *in vivo* are also used as biological parameters.

All the above-mentioned biological data can be used in QSAR studies if they are in the appropriate form and in the right scale: e.g., for the inhibition of the enzyme either K_i (the inhibition constants) or IC_{50} should be used and not the % inhibition and they should be transformed to logarithmic scale, i.e., they should be used as pK_i ($-\log K_i$) and pIC_{50} ($-\log IC_{50}$). The K_i or IC_{50} values are preferred to % inhibition because they are related to free energy term ΔG in the form as

$$K = \exp[-\Delta G/RT] \qquad (2.1)$$

where K is the equilibrium constant of a reaction. The inhibition constant K_i is the inverse of the equilibrium constant of the reaction between an inhibitor I and an enzyme E

$$E + I \underset{k_{-1}}{\overset{k_1}{\rightleftharpoons}} E\,I \tag{2.2}$$

and is related to the concentrations of enzyme and inhibitor at equilibrium as shown by the equation

$$K_i = k_{-1}/k_1 = ([E] - [EI])/[EI] \tag{2.3}$$

Sometimes, the inhibitor's binding constant K_b is used which is defined as

$$K_b = \mathrm{IC}_{50}/(1 + C/K_d) \tag{2.4}$$

where C is the concentration of the radioligand used and K_d is the apparent dissociation constant of the radioligand-receptor complex.

The use of biological data in terms of logarithmic scale is desired because all the physicochemical parameters that are used to describe them are linear free energy-related values (and that is why Hansch approach is also called "*linear free energy-related approach*" or "*extra thermodynamic approach*") and so the biological data should also be in the form which has a linear relationship with free energy and Eq. 2.1 suggests that it is possible if it is transformed to the form

$$-\ln K = \Delta G/RT \tag{2.5}$$

or

$$\log(1/K) = \Delta G/2.303\ RT \tag{2.6}$$

If the value of the gas constant R is taken equal to 8.314 $\mathrm{JK^{-1}\ mol^{-1}}$ and T is taken equal to 300 K (approximately the room temperature), Eq. 2.6 becomes

$$\log(1/K) = (1.74 \times 10^{-4}\ \mathrm{mol\ J^{-1}})\ \Delta G \tag{2.7}$$

When ΔG is taken in J $\mathrm{mol^{-1}}$, the right hand term becomes dimensionless and so becomes left hand term.

Another reason of using particularly $\log(1/C)$ term is that the drug-receptor interactions usually involve first-order kinetics, where the concentration of the reactant is linearly related to the rate constant k, which controls the end results (Eq. 2.8).

$$\log(1/C) = \log(1/C_0) + (1/2.303)\ kt \tag{2.8}$$

Further, the use of logarithmic terms gives larger values for more active compounds and provides normal distribution of the experimental error in the dependent variable, which is a condition for the application in the regression analysis.

Sometimes data like mg/kg can also be used if the compounds are in narrow molecular weight range. Similarly, % effect can be used if there is a wide span in the data. However, in good QSAR analysis they are usually not used. In fact, for good QSAR results there should be a wide span in the biological data as well as in the values of descriptors used.

2.2 Structural Parameters

The biological activities depend on the structural features of the compounds which can be described by a variety of physicochemical and topological parameters. The biological activities can quantitatively be correlated with these parameters. Of them, the physicochemical parameters are of special importance since they are directly related to the intermolecular forces involved in the drug-receptor interactions as well as to the transport and distribution properties of the drugs. Thus, they include specifically hydrophobic, polar, electronic and steric parameters. There are also polarizability parameters but they are synonymous to some steric parameters, such as molar refractivity, molar volume, and parachor, which of course may have different significance in different situations in drug-receptor interactions.

The topological parameters are single valued molecular descriptors that are calculated from 2D graph representation of the molecules. They characterize the shape, size, and the degree of branching in the molecules. The best known and the most useful topological parameters are the molecular connectivity indices, first described by Randic [1] and subsequently developed by Kier and Hall [2].

In addition to physicochemical and topological parameters, there are indicator variables, also called dummy variables. They are used for the structural features that affect the activity but cannot be parameterized by any physicochemical or topological parameters. These indicator variables are arbitrarily assigned two values: 1 to indicate the presence of a specific structural feature and zero to indicate its absence. If the entire series of congeners is divided into two sets, one with and one without the specific structural feature, two equations, almost parallel, would be obtained, with a difference only in their intercepts. Thus, an indicator variable can be pictured simply as a constant that adjusts two parallel equations into one.

Now a detailed description is presented of all physicochemical parameters and some important topological parameters in the following sections. For a quick survey of some of these parameters, readers may refer to Table 2.1 [3].

Table 2.1. Linear free energy related parameters (reprinted with permission from [3]. Copyright 1987 American Chemical Society)

Parameter	Name	Description
P	Partition coefficient	log P taken as a measure of the hydrophobicity of the molecule; for measuring P, an octanol-water system preferred
π	Hydrophobic constant	$\pi = \log P_X - \log P_H$, where P_X is the partition coefficient of the substituted compound and P_H that of the unsubstituted reference compound
R_M	Hydrophobic constant from chromatography	log P linearly related to R_M as $\log P = R_M +$ constant
k'	Hydrophobic constant from high-pressure liquid chromatography (HPLC)	log P linearly related to log k' as $\log P = \log k'$ + constant
$\sigma(\sigma_m, \sigma_p)$	Hammett constant	Defined only for meta and para substituents to represent electronic character; positive value of σ denotes electron-withdrawing character and negative value of σ denotes electron-donating character; parameter may represent effects of ionization, hydrogen bonding, and charge-charge or charge-dipole interactions of compounds with the receptor
σ_0	Apparent Hammett constant for ortho substituents	Unreliable and rarely used; hydrogen bonding to solvent decreases π so covariance may occur
σ^+, σ^-	Hammett constants	Used, respectively, when substituents donate electrons to a positive site or withdraw from a negative site by direct resonance interaction
σ^*	Taft constant	Measure of the electronic effect produced by aliphatic substituents
σ_I	Inductive constant	Related to σ^* as $\sigma_I = 6.43\ \sigma^*$
R, F	Resonance and field constants	σ involves resonance effect and field (inductive) effect (F) of a substituent, i.e., $\sigma = aR + bF$, where a and b are constants depending upon the type of σ (σ_m, σ_p); R and F more indicative of intrinsic resonance and field effects of a substituent; sign of R and F would indicate the sign of the charge that the substituents would place on the ring
pK_a	Ionization constant	$pK_a = -\log K_a$, K_a being the ionization constant of an acid
$Q(Q^\sigma, Q^\pi)$	Charge of an atom	Positive charge indicates interaction of atom with a negative center of the receptor; negative charge indicates interaction of the atom with a positive center of the receptor; Q^σ stands for the σ charge and Q^π for the π charge, calculated by quantum mechanical methods

Contd.

Table 2.1. Continued

Parameter	Name	Description
f_r^E, f_r^N	Electrophilic and nucleophilic frontier orbital densities	Quantum mechanical parameters used to discuss the electrophilic and nucleophilic reactions at a particular center in the molecule
S_r^E, S_r^N	Electrophilic and nucleophilic superdelocalizabilities	Incorporate the concept of charge-transfer capabilities along with an orbital charge at a particular atom
E_{HOMO}	Energy of the highest occupied molecular orbital	Quantum mechanical parameter that corresponds to the energy of the ionization potential of the molecule
E_{LEMO}	Energy of the lowest empty molecular orbital	Quantum mechanical parameter that corresponds to the electron affinity of the molecule
E_s	Taft steric constant	Related to the acid-catalyzed hydrolysis of α-substituted acetates (XCH_2COOR) and represents the steric effect, signifying intramolecular and intermolecular hindrance to the reaction or binding
MR	Molar refractivity	MR = $[(n^2 - 1)/(n^2 + 2)]$ *MW/d*, where n is the refractive index for the sodium D line, MW is the molecular weight, and d is the density of the compound; *MR* can be used as a steric parameter in the absence of E_s; measures the electronic effect also and may reflect the dipole-dipole interaction at the active site
MV	Molar volume	MV, V_w, r, R, L and B, MW, etc., have also been used as steric parameters
V_w	Van der Waals volume	
r	Van der Waals radius	
R	Interatomic distance	
L	Length parameter	
B	Width parameter	
MW	Molecular weight	
χ	Molecular connectivity index	Topological parameter defined to account for the effects of kinds of atoms, bonding type, adjacency environment, branching pattern, unsaturation, and heteroatom content in a molecule on its reactivity or activity

2.2.1 Physicochemical Parameters

(a) Electronic Parameters

Hammett Constants

The first electronic parameter, denoted as σ, was defined by Hammett [4] to describe the effect of substituents on the ionization of the benzoic acid. It was related to the ionization constant of the substituted benzoic acid K_X, and that of unsubstituted benzoic acid K_H, as

$$\sigma = \log K_X - \log K_H \tag{2.9}$$

In place of the ionization constants, one can also use the rate constants k_X and k_H and write the equation in a modified form as

$$\log k_X = \rho\sigma + \log k_H \tag{2.10}$$

where the slope ρ (referred to as the reaction constant) is a measure of the sensitivity of such a reaction to the electronic effect of the substituents [5]. This σ is now known as *Hammett constant* and its positive value represents the electron-withdrawing and the negative value the electron-donating ability of the substituents relative to *H*.

Although the Hammett equation was basically written for benzoic acid, it was postulated that it could also be used for other similar reaction systems and in fact it works best also in other reaction systems when the reaction center is insulated from resonance interaction with the aromatic ring (e.g. $X\text{-}C_6H_4CH_2Q$, where *Q* is the reaction center). The σ values, however, have been estimated only for meta- and para-substituents and not for ortho-substituents since the latter may also have the steric effect on the ionization.

Hammett's simple σ constants, however, can also not be used when substituents are in direct conjugation with the reaction center as in phenols. An electron-withdrawing substituent such as NO_2 can have a resonance effect as shown in Fig. 2.1 (a, b), which upon ionization will have resonating structures as shown in Fig. 2.2 (a, b).

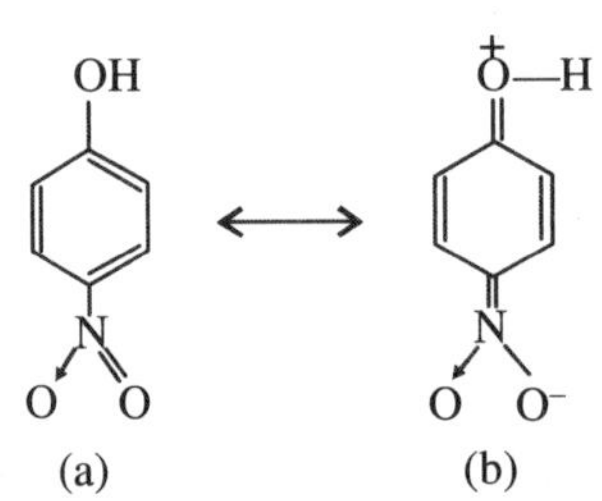

Fig. 2.1

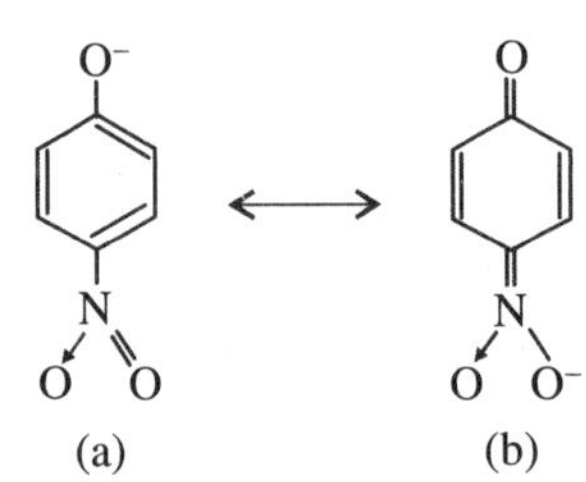

Fig. 2.2

This kind of observation for electron-withdrawing substituents led to define σ^- parameter which was derived from phenols or anilines for para-substituents. Similarly, σ^+ was formulated for electron-donating substituents that could delocalize a positive charge.

Since the direct resonance effect on the reaction center of the meta-substituents is not very significant, the σ^-, σ^+, and σ^0 are essentially the same as σ^m. The σ^0 constant has been formulated for few strong electron-donating substituents, like NH_2, OH, etc., that have the resonating effect on the carboxylic group in the benzoic acid (Fig. 2.3 (a, b)), while the Hammett's σ constants have been defined for the situations where the reaction center is insulated from the interaction with the aromatic ring. The σ^0 values

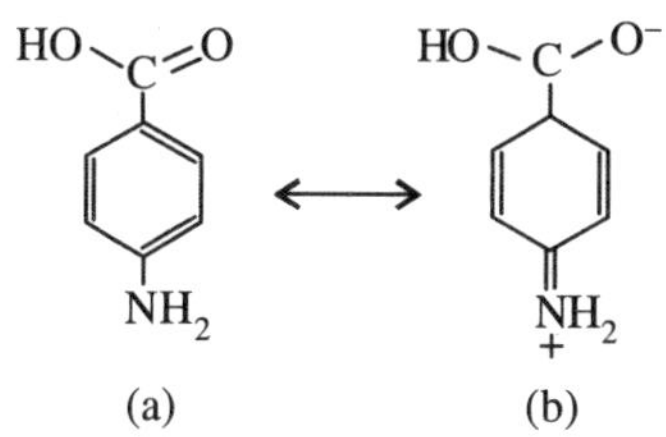

Fig. 2.3

have been evaluated either from the ionization of phenylacetic acids [6] or hydrolysis of substituted phenyl acetates [7], or from a statistical procedure [8].

Inductive and Resonance Parameters

The Hammett σ constants were found to incorporate two kinds of electronic effects: the field-inductive effect and the resonance effect, where the former was also regarded as being made up of two components: a through-the-bonds effect of substituents on the reaction center, referred to as the static inductive effect (I_s), and a direct through-solvent-space electrostatic effect of the substituents on the reaction center, referred to as the field effect (D). Since the field effect was found to be dominant [9] and since it could not be possible to separate the two effects, both I_s and D were lumped together to be termed only as field-inductive or simply inductive effect (I). Thus, if the inductive effect and the resonance effect are referred to by the parameters σ_I and σ_R, respectively, the Hammett constants may be expressed as [10]

$$\sigma = \sigma_I + \sigma_R \tag{2.11}$$

where for para-substituents, the major contribution is of σ_R.

The ionization of bicycloctane carboxylic acids (Fig. 2.4) was assumed to provide an unambiguous system for defining a field or inductive effect, because in this rigid system the substituent X is held firmly in its place and there is little possibility of resonance or polarization effect of it on COOH function [11]. Consequently, the only way the X can affect the ionization of carboxylic group was assumed to be through the space (the predominant field effect) and through the intervening σ bonds (the inductive effect). Using this system, electronic parameter σ' was defined as

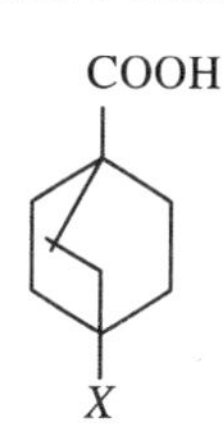

Fig. 2.4

$$\sigma' = \log K_X - \log K_H \tag{2.12}$$

Swain and Lupton [12] considered this σ' to be a good descriptor of their field-inductive effect F, which according to them was a component in both σ_m and σ_p of Hammett and thus they proposed that F can be evaluated by the equation

$$F = \sigma' = a\sigma_m + b\sigma_p + c \tag{2.13}$$

where the coefficients *a*, *b* and *c* were to be determined by the least squares method. However, the *F* values determined in this way (using σ') were not on the scale of Hammett's constants. Hansch et al. [13] accomplished this by defining $F = \sigma'/1.65$ and thus using the values of σ' as determined by Holtz and Stock [14], Hansch et al. formulated

$$F = \sigma'/1.65 = 1.369\ (\pm\ 0.186)\ \sigma_m - 0.373\ (\pm\ 0.142)\ \sigma_p - 0.009\ (\pm\ .038)$$
$$n = 14,\ r = 0.992,\ s = 0.042 \tag{2.14}$$

where the intercept is almost zero.

Equation 2.14 was reformulated by Hansch et al. [15] using σ' values for 38 substituents and a slightly modified scaling factor [16]. This reformulated equation (Eq. 2.15) was then used to evaluate the values of *F* and *R* (Swain and Lupton's resonance parameter) for 500 substituents. To evaluate the values of *R*, Swain and Lupton had proposed Eq. 2.16.

$$F = 1.297\ (\pm\ 0.147)\ \sigma_m - 0.385\ (\pm\ 0.089)\ \sigma_p + 0.033\ (\pm\ 0.026)$$
$$n = 38,\ r = 0.968,\ s = 0.046 \tag{2.15}$$

$$\sigma_p = \alpha\ F + R \tag{2.16}$$

These *F* and *R* parameters of Swain and Lupton were found to be well correlated with Ehrenson et al.'s σ_I and σ_R parameters [16] (Eqs. 2.17 and 2.18) [5].

$$F = 0.852\ (\pm\ 0.07)\ \sigma_I + 0.051\ (\pm\ 0.029)$$
$$n = 24,\ r = 0.981,\ s = 0.038 \tag{2.17}$$

$$R = 0.980\ (\pm\ 0.011)\ \sigma_R + 0.011\ (\pm\ 0.036)$$
$$n = 24,\ r = 0.971,\ s = 0.076 \tag{2.18}$$

For the use in saturated compounds, an inductive (polar) parameter σ^* was defined by Taft [17] (Eq. 2.19) which had greatly facilitated the QSAR analysis. In Eq. 2.19, k_X and k_H are the rate constants for the hydrolyses of

$$\sigma^* = (1/2.48)\ [\log(k_X/k_H)_B - \log(k_X/k_H)_A] \tag{2.19}$$

substituted acetates ($X\text{-}CH_2COOR$, where R = Me or Et) and unsubstituted acetate ($H\text{-}CH_2COOR$), respectively. The subscripts *A* and *B* refer to acidic and basic conditions, respectively.

All the above described electronic parameters are non-quantum mechanical parameters which can be empirically determined. For a very large set of substituents, the values of some such parameters were compiled by Hansch et al. [15] and are reproduced here in Table 2.2. In addition to these electronic parameters, the dipole moment (μ), dielectric constant (D),

Table 2.2. Hammett and modified Swain-Lupton constants.[a,b] Reprinted with permission from [16]. Copyright 1991 American Chemical Society

No.	Substituent	σ_m	σ_p	*F*	*R*
1	BF_2	0.32	0.48	0.26	0.22
2	Br	0.39	0.23	0.45	– 0.22
3	$GeBr_3$	0.66	0.73	0.61	0.12
4	$SiBr_3$	0.48	0.57	0.44	0.13
5	Cl	0.37	0.23	0.42	– 0.19
6	HgCl	0.33	0.35	0.33	0.02
7	SO_2Cl	1.20	1.11	1.16	(– 0.05)
8	SCl	0.44	0.48	0.42	0.06
9	ICl_2	1.10	1.11	1.03	0.08
10	$P(O)Cl_2$	0.78	0.90	0.70	0.20
11	PCl_2	0.54	0.61	0.50	0.11
12	$P(S)Cl_2$	0.70	0.80	0.63	0.17
13	$GeCl_3$	0.71	0.79	0.65	0.14
14	$SiCl_3$	0.48	0.56	0.44	0.12
15	F	0.34	0.06	0.45	– 0.39
16	HgF	0.34	0.33	0.35	– 0.02
17	SOF	0.74	0.83	0.67	0.16
18	SO_2F	0.80	0.91	0.72	0.19
19	IF_2	0.85	0.83	0.82	0.01
20	POF_2	0.81	0.89	0.74	0.15
21	PF_2	0.49	0.59	0.44	0.15
22	GeF_3	0.85	0.97	0.76	0.21
23	SF_3	0.70	0.80	0.63	0.17
24	SiF_3	0.54	0.69	0.47	0.22
25	IF_4	1.07	1.15	0.98	0.17
26	PF_4	0.63	0.80	0.54	0.26
27	SF_5	0.61	0.68	0.56	0.12
28	I	0.35	0.18	0.42	– 0.24
29	IO	0.58	0.62	0.55	0.07
30	IO_2	0.68	0.78	0.61	0.17
31	NO	0.62	0.91	0.49	0.42
32	NO_2	0.71	0.78	0.65	0.13
33	ONO_2	0.55	0.70	0.48	0.22
34	$N{\equiv}N^+$	1.76	1.91	1.58	0.33
35	$N{\equiv}N^+(BF_4)^-$	1.65	1.79	1.48	0.31
36	NNO_2	0.00	– 0.43	0.20	– 0.63
37	N_3	0.37	0.08	0.48	– 0.40
38	O^-	– 0.47	(– 0.81)	– 0.26	(– 0.55)
39	SO_2	– 0.02	– 0.05	0.03	– 0.08
40	SO_3	0.30	0.35	0.29	0.06
41	S^-	– 0.36	– 1.21	0.03	– 1.24
42	AsO_3H^-	0.00	– 0.02	0.04	– 0.06
43	H	0.00	0.00	0.03	0.00
44	$NHNO_2$	0.91	0.57	0.99	– 0.42
45	OH	0.12	– 0.37	0.33	– 0.70

Contd.

Table 2.2. Continued

No.	Substituent	σ_m	σ_p	F	R
46	S(O)OH	– 0.04	– 0.07	0.01	– 0.08
47	PO_3H^-	0.20	0.26	0.19	0.07
48	OPO_3H^-	0.29	0.00	0.41	– 0.41
49	SH	0.25	0.15	0.30	– 0.15
50	$B(OH)_2$	– 0.01	0.12	– 0.03	0.15
51	NH_2	– 0.16	– 0.66	0.08	– 0.74
52	NHOH	– 0.04	– 0.34	0.11	– 0.45
53	SO_2NH_2	0.53	0.60	0.49	0.11
54	$PO(OH)_2$	0.36	0.42	0.34	0.08
55	PH_2	0.06	0.05	0.09	– 0.04
56	$B(OH)_3^-$	– 0.48	– 0.44	– 0.42	– 0.02
57	GeH_3	0.00	0.01	0.03	– 0.02
58	$NH3^+$	0.86	0.60	0.92	– 0.32
59	$NHNH_2$	– 0.02	– 0.55	0.22	– 0.77
60	SiH_3	0.05	0.10	0.06	0.04
61	CBr_3	0.28	0.29	0.28	0.01
62	$CClF_2$	0.42	0.46	0.40	0.06
63	5-chloro-1-tetrazolyl	0.60	0.61	0.58	0.03
64	COCl	0.51	0.61	0.46	0.15
65	$N{=}CCl_2$	0.21	0.13	0.26	– 0.13
66	CCl_3	0.40	0.46	0.38	0.09
67	$OCCl_3$	0.43	0.35	0.46	– 0.11
68	COF	0.55	0.70	0.48	0.22
69	OCF_2O	0.36	0.36	0.36	0.00
70	CF_3	0.43	0.54	0.38	0.16
71	$HgCF_3$	0.29	0.32	0.29	0.03
72	$HgSCF_3$	0.39	0.42	0.38	0.04
73	$I{=}NSO_2CF_3$	1.30	1.35	1.20	0.15
74	$N{=}NCF_3$	0.56	0.68	0.50	0.18
75	OCF_3	0.38	0.35	0.39	– 0.04
76	$SOCF_3$	0.63	0.69	0.58	0.11
77	$SeOCF_3$	0.81	0.83	0.76	0.07
78	SO_2CF_3	0.83	0.96	0.74	0.22
79	SeO_2CF_3	1.08	1.21	0.97	0.24
80	OSO_2CF_3	0.56	0.53	0.56	– 0.03
81	SCF_3	0.40	0.50	0.36	0.14
82	$SeCF_3$	0.44	0.45	0.43	0.02
83	HgCN	0.28	0.34	0.27	0.08
84	CN	0.56	0.66	0.51	0.15
85	NC	0.48	0.49	0.47	0.02
86	$CN(BBr_3)$	0.61	0.48	0.64	– 0.16
87	$CN(BCl_3)$	0.95	0.86	(0.93)	(– 0.05)
88	$CN(BF_3)$	0.72	0.66	(0.71)	(– 0.05)
89	N=C=O	0.27	0.19	0.31	– 0.12
90	OCN	0.67	0.54	0.69	– 0.15
91	SO_2CN	1.10	1.26	0.97	0.29

Contd.

Table 2.2. Continued

No.	Substituent	σ_m	σ_p	*F*	*R*
92	N=C=S	0.48	0.38	0.51	– 0.13
93	SCN	0.51	0.52	0.49	0.03
94	SeCN	0.61	0.66	0.57	0.09
95	N=NCN	0.71	1.03	0.56	0.47
96	N(O)=NCN	0.78	0.89	0.70	0.19
97	$C(NO_2)_3$	0.72	0.82	0.65	0.17
98	5-azido-1-tetrazolyl	0.54	0.54	0.53	0.01
99	CO_2^-	– 0.10	0.00	– 0.10	0.10
100	$CHBr_2$	0.31	0.32	0.31	0.01
101	$CHCl_2$	0.31	0.32	0.31	0.01
102	$OCHCl_2$	0.38	0.26	0.43	– 0.17
103	CHF_2	0.29	0.32	0.29	0.03
104	$OCHF_2$	0.31	0.18	0.37	– 0.19
105	$SOCHF_2$	0.54	0.58	0.51	0.07
106	SO_2CHF_2	0.75	0.86	0.67	0.19
107	$SCHF_2$	0.33	0.37	0.32	0.05
108	$S(O)(=NH)CF_3$	0.72	0.84	0.64	0.20
109	$NHSO_2CF_3$	0.44	0.39	0.45	– 0.06
110	CHI_2	0.26	0.26	0.27	– 0.01
111	NHCN	0.21	0.06	0.28	– 0.22
112	1-(1*H*)-tetrazolyl	0.52	0.50	0.52	– 0.02
113	5-(1*H*)-tetrazolyl	0.64	0.56	0.65	– 0.09
114	5-hydroxy-1-tetrazolyl	0.39	0.33	0.41	– 0.08
115	5-mercapto-1-tetrazolyl	0.45	0.45	0.44	– 0.01
116	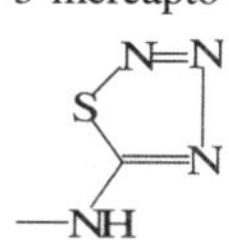	0.30	0.19	0.35	– 0.16
117	CHO	0.35	0.42	0.33	0.09
118	COOH	0.37	0.45	0.34	0.11
119	CH_2Br	0.12	0.14	0.14	0.00
120	CH_2F	0.11	0.12	0.13	– 0.01
121	CH_2Cl	0.25	0.08	0.33	– 0.25
122	OCH_2Cl	0.12	0.11	0.15	– 0.04
123	OCH_2F	0.20	0.02	0.29	– 0.27
124	SCH_2F	0.23	0.20	0.25	– 0.05
125	CH_2F	0.10	0.11	0.12	– 0.01
126	NHCHO	0.19	0.00	0.28	– 0.28
127	$CONH_2$	0.28	0.36	0.26	0.10
128	$CSNH_2$	0.25	0.30	0.24	0.06
129	CH=NOH-*t*	0.22	0.10	0.28	– 0.18
130	$3,4\text{-N=CHNH}^-$	– 0.15	– 0.15	– 0.10	– 0.05
131	$N(O)=NCONH_2$	0.59	0.63	0.56	0.07
132	OCH_2O^-	– 0.16	– 0.16	– 0.11	– 0.05
133	Me	– 0.07	– 0.17	0.01	– 0.18
134	CH_2SO_2R	0.15	0.17	0.16	0.01

Contd.

Table 2.2. Continued

No.	Substituent	σ_m	σ_p	F	R
135	$SiMeCl_2$	0.31	0.39	0.29	0.10
136	$SiMeF_2$	0.29	0.23	0.32	– 0.09
137	HgMe	0.43	0.10	(0.55)	(– 0.45)
138	$NHCH_2SO_3^-$	– 0.10	– 0.57	0.12	– 0.69
139	$NHCONH_2$	– 0.03	– 0.24	0.09	– 0.33
140	$N(Me)NO_2$	0.49	0.61	0.43	0.18
141	$NHCSNH_2$	0.22	0.16	0.26	– 0.10
142	OMe	0.12	– 0.27	0.29	– 0.56
143	CH_2OH	0.00	0.00	0.03	– 0.03
144	SOMe	0.52	0.49	0.52	– 0.03
145	S(OMe)	0.21	0.17	0.24	– 0.07
146	$OS(=O)CH_3$	0.44	0.45	0.43	0.02
147	S(O)OMe	0.50	0.54	0.47	0.07
148	SO_2Me	0.60	0.72	0.53	0.19
149	SSO_2Me	0.43	0.54	0.38	0.16
150	OSO_2Me	0.39	0.36	0.40	– 0.04
151	SMe	0.15	0.00	0.23	– 0.23
152	SSMe	0.22	0.13	0.27	– 0.14
153	SeMe	0.10	0.00	0.16	– 0.16
154	NHMe	– 0.21	– 0.70	0.03	– 0.73
155	CH_2NH_2	– 0.03	– 0.11	0.04	– 0.15
156	$NHSO_2Me$	0.20	0.03	0.28	– 0.25
157	$CH_2NH_3^+$	0.59	0.53	0.59	– 0.06
158	$N(COF)_2$	0.58	0.57	0.57	0.00
159	$HgOCOCF_3$	0.50	0.52	0.48	0.04
160	$COCF_3$	0.63	0.80	0.54	0.26
161	$SCOCF_3$	0.48	0.46	0.48	– 0.02
162	$OCOCF_3$	0.56	0.46	0.58	– 0.12
163	$N(CF_3)C{=}O(F)$	0.50	0.50	0.49	0.01
164	$CF_2OCF_2^-$	0.81	0.81	0.77	0.04
165	OCF_2CF_3	0.47	0.52	0.44	0.08
166	$SO_2CF_2CF_3$	0.48	0.28	0.55	– 0.27
167	$SO_2CF_2CF_3$	0.92	1.08	0.81	0.27
168	SCF_2CF_3	0.44	0.48	0.42	0.06
169	$N(CF_3)_2$	0.40	0.53	(0.35)	0.18
170	$S(CF_3){=}NSO_2CF_3$	1.18	1.28	1.07	0.21
171	$SO(CF_3){=}NSO_2CF_3$	1.23	1.40	1.09	0.31
172	$P(CF_3)_2$	0.61	0.83	0.50	0.33
173	$N(SO_2CF_3)_2$	0.60	0.69	0.55	0.14
174	$P(CN)_2$	0.82	0.90	0.75	0.15
175	C≡CH	0.21	0.23	0.22	0.01
176	OCF_2CHFCl	0.35	0.28	0.38	– 0.10
177	$NHCOCF_3$	0.30	0.12	0.38	– 0.26
178	$CH{=}NSO_2CF_3$	0.76	1.00	0.63	0.37
179	OCF_2CHF_2	0.34	0.25	0.38	– 0.13
180	SCF_2CHF_2	0.38	0.47	0.35	0.12

Contd.

Table 2.2. Continued

No.	Substituent	σ_m	σ_p	*F*	*R*
181	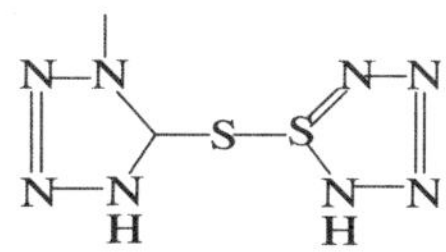	0.63	0.64	0.60	0.04
182	SC≡CH	0.26	0.19	0.30	– 0.11
183	SCH=CHCl	0.31	0.24	0.34	– 0.10
184	SeCH=CHCl	0.28	0.26	0.30	– 0.04
185	CH_2CF_3	0.12	0.09	0.15	– 0.06
186	CH_2SOCF_3	0.25	0.24	0.27	– 0.03
187	$CH_2SO_2CF_3$	0.29	0.31	0.29	0.02
188	CH_2SCF_3	0.12	0.15	0.13	0.02
189	CH_2CN	0.16	0.18	0.17	0.01
190	$CH{=}CHNO_2$-*t*	0.32	0.26	0.35	(– 0.09)
191	$CHOCO_2^-$	0.07	– 0.16	0.19	– 0.35
192	CH_2SCN	0.12	0.14	0.14	0.00
193	$CH{=}CH_2$	0.06	– 0.04	0.13	– 0.17
194	$NHCOCH_2Cl$	0.17	– 0.03	0.27	– 0.30
195	$N(Me)SO_2CF_3$	0.46	0.44	0.46	– 0.02
196	$HgOCOCH_3$	0.39	0.40	0.39	0.01
197	$C(Me)(NO_2)_2$	0.54	0.61	0.50	0.11
198	oxiranyl	0.05	0.03	0.09	– 0.06
199	$OCH{=}CH_2$	0.21	– 0.09	0.34	– 0.43
200	COMe	0.38	0.50	0.33	0.17
201	SCOMe	0.39	0.44	0.37	0.07
202	OCOMe	0.39	0.31	0.42	– 0.11
203	COOMe	0.37	0.45	0.34	0.11
204	2-thiacyclopropyl	0.04	0.01	0.08	– 0.07
205	$SCH{=}CH_2$	0.26	0.20	0.29	– 0.09
206	$SeCH{=}CH_2$	0.26	0.21	0.29	– 0.08
207	1-aziridinyl	– 0.07	– 0.22	0.03	– 0.25
208	2-aziridinyl	– 0.06	– 0.10	– 0.01	– 0.09
209	N-methyl-3-oxaziridinyl	0.09	0.12	0.10	0.02
210	NHCOOMe	– 0.02	– 0.17	0.07	– 0.24
211	NHCOMe	0.21	0.00	0.31	– 0.31
212	CONHMe	0.35	0.36	0.35	– 0.01
213	CH=NOMe	0.37	0.30	0.40	0.10
214	CH_2CONH_2	0.06	0.07	0.08	– 0.01
215	NHCSMe	0.24	0.12	0.30	– 0.18
216	CSNHMe	0.30	0.34	0.29	0.05
217	$CH{=}NNHCSNH_2CONH_2$	0.45	0.40	0.46	– 0.06
218	$OCH_2CH_2O^-$	– 0.12	– 0.12	– 0.08	– 0.04
219	Et	– 0.07	– 0.15	0.00	– 0.15
220	$CH{=}NNHCONHNH_2$	0.22	0.16	0.26	– 0.10
221	OCH_2CH_3	0.10	– 0.24	0.26	– 0.50
222	CH(OH)Me	0.08	– 0.07	0.16	– 0.23
223	CH_2OMe	0.08	0.01	0.13	– 0.12

Contd.

Table 2.2. Continued

No.	Substituent	σ_m	σ_p	*F*	*R*
224	SO_2Et	0.66	0.77	0.59	0.18
225	SEt	0.18	0.03	0.26	– 0.23
226	$P(Cl)NMe_2$	0.38	0.56	0.31	0.25
227	$CH_2SC(NH_2)_2^+$	0.13	0.15	0.14	0.01
228	$SiClMe_2$	0.16	0.21	0.16	0.05
229	$SiFMe_2$	0.12	0.17	0.12	0.04
230	NHEt	– 0.24	– 0.61	– 0.04	– 0.57
231	$N(Me)_2$	– 0.16	– 0.83	0.15	– 0.98
232	$N(Me)SO_2Me$	0.21	0.24	0.21	0.03
233	SO_2NMe_2	0.51	0.65	0.44	0.21
234	$N(SO_2Me)_2$	0.47	0.49	0.45	0.04
235	$SN(Me)_2$	0.12	0.09	0.15	– 0.06
236	$N{=}NNMe_2$	– 0.05	– 0.03	– 0.02	– 0.01
237	$N(Me)N^+{=}(Me)N^-$	1.17	1.17	1.10	0.07
238	$P(O)Me_2$	0.43	0.50	0.40	0.10
239	$PO(OMe)_2$	0.42	0.53	0.37	0.16
240	PMe_2	0.03	0.06	0.05	0.01
241	S^+Me_2	1.00	0.90	0.98	– 0.08
242	$S^+(Me)_2$tosyl	1.06	0.96	1.04	– 0.08
243	$CH_2CH_2NH_3^+$	0.23	0.17	0.27	– 0.10
244	$SiH(Me)_2$	0.01	0.04	0.03	0.01
245	$1\text{-}(1,7(BH)_{10}\text{-}C_2H)$	0.25	0.33	0.23	0.10
246	$2\text{-}(1,7(BH)_{10}\text{-}C_2H)$	0.14	0.15	0.16	– 0.01
247	$4\text{-}(1,2(BH)_{10}\text{-}C_2H)$	– 0.02	0.02	0.00	0.02
248	$1\text{-}(1,2(BH)_{10}\text{-}C_2H)$	0.49	0.43	0.50	– 0.07
249	$3\text{-}(1,2(BH)_{10}\text{-}C_2H)$	0.20	0.19	0.22	– 0.03
250	$C{\equiv}CCF_3$	0.41	0.51	0.37	0.14
251	$CF{=}CFCF_3$-*t*	0.39	0.46	0.36	0.10
252	$N{=}C(CF_3)_2$	0.29	0.23	0.32	– 0.09
253	$CF_2CF_2CF_3$	0.44	0.48	0.42	0.06
254	$CF(CF_3)_2$	0.37	0.53	(0.31)	0.22
255	$SO_2CF_2CF_2CF_3$	0.92	1.09	0.81	0.28
256	$SO_2CF(CF_3)_2$	0.92	1.10	0.80	0.30
257	$SCF_2CF_2CF_3$	0.45	0.48	0.43	0.05
258	$SCF(CF_3)_2$	0.48	0.51	0.46	0.03
259	$TeCF_2CF_2CF_3$	0.46	0.48	0.45	0.03
260	$C(OH)(CF_3)_2$	0.29	0.30	0.29	0.01
261	$CH(SCF_3)_2$	0.44	0.44	0.43	0.01
262	$CH(CN)_2$	0.53	0.52	0.52	0.00
263	$CH{=}CHCF_3$-*c*	0.16	0.17	0.18	0.01
264	$CH{=}CHCF_3$-*t*	0.24	0.27	0.24	0.03
265	$CH{=}CHSO_2CF_3$	0.31	0.55	0.22	0.33
266	$CH{=}CHCN$	0.24	0.17	0.28	– 0.11
267	$C{\equiv}CMe$	0.21	0.03	0.29	– 0.26
268	$N(Me)COCF_3$	0.41	0.39	0.41	– 0.02
269	$CH{=}CHCHO$	0.24	0.13	0.29	– 0.16

Contd.

Table 2.2. Continued

No.	Substituent	σ_m	σ_p	F	R
270	cyclopropyl	– 0.07	– 0.21	0.02	– 0.23
271	$C(Me)=CH_2$	0.09	0.05	0.13	– 0.08
272	CH=CHMe-*t*	0.02	– 0.09	0.09	– 0.18
273	$CH_2CH=CH_2$	– 0.11	– 0.14	– 0.06	– 0.08
274	$C(Et)(NO_2)_2$	0.56	0.64	0.51	0.13
275	$OCH_2CH=CH_2$	0.09	– 0.25	0.25	– 0.50
276	COEt	0.38	0.48	0.34	0.14
277	COOEt	0.37	0.45	0.34	0.11
278	CH_2OCOMe	0.04	0.05	0.07	– 0.02
279	CH_2CH_2COOH	– 0.03	– 0.07	0.02	– 0.09
280	$SCH_2CH=CH_2$	0.19	0.12	0.23	– 0.11
281	$SeCH_2CH=CH_2$	0.21	0.12	0.26	– 0.14
282	$CH_2CH_2CH_2^-$	– 0.26	– 0.26	– 0.20	– 0.06
283	N(Me)COMe	0.31	0.26	0.34	– 0.08
284	$CH_2NHCOMe$	0.05	– 0.05	0.12	– 0.17
285	NHCOOEt	0.11	– 0.15	0.23	– 0.38
286	$C(NO_2)Me_2$	0.18	0.20	0.19	0.01
287	$OCH_2CH_2CH_2O^-$	0.00	0.00	0.03	– 0.03
288	isopropyl	– 0.04	– 0.15	0.04	– 0.19
289	$CH_2CH_2CH_3$	– 0.06	– 0.13	0.01	– 0.14
290	$N^+(Me)=CHN(Me)^-$	1.11	1.11	1.05	0.06
291	NHCONHEt	0.04	– 0.26	0.19	– 0.45
292	NHCSNHEt	0.30	0.07	0.40	– 0.33
293	$OCHMe_2$	0.10	(– 0.45)	0.34	(– 0.79)
294	$OCH_2CH_2CH_3$	0.10	– 0.25	0.26	– 0.51
295	$CH_2CH(OH)Me$	– 0.12	– 0.17	– 0.06	– 0.11
296	$C(OOH)Me_2$	0.06	– 0.14	0.17	– 0.31
297	$SCHMe_2$	0.23	0.07	0.30	– 0.23
298	CH_2NMe_2	0.00	0.01	0.03	– 0.02
299	$GeMe_3$	0.00	0.00	0.03	– 0.03
300	$N^+(Me)_3$	0.88	0.82	0.86	– 0.04
301	$CH_2NH^+(Me)_2$	0.40	0.43	0.39	0.04
302	$Si(Me)_2OMe$	0.04	– 0.02	0.09	– 0.11
303	$OSiMe_3$	0.13	– 0.27	0.31	– 0.58
304	$SiMe(OMe)_2$	0.04	0.10	0.05	0.05
305	$Si(OMe)_3$	0.09	0.13	0.10	0.03
306	P^+Me_3	0.74	0.73	0.71	0.02
307	$SiMe_3$	– 0.04	– 0.07	0.01	– 0.08
308	$SnMe_3$	0.00	0.00	0.03	– 0.03
309	$1\text{-}(1,2(BH)_{10}\text{-}C_2Me)$	0.50	0.65	0.43	0.22
310	$CH_2\text{-}1\text{-}(1,7(BH)_{10}\text{-}C_2H)$	0.00	0.01	0.03	– 0.02
311	$CH_2\text{-}1\text{-}(1,2(BH)_{10}\text{-}C_2H)$	0.12	0.12	0.14	– 0.02
312	$1\text{-}(1,2(BH)_{10}\text{-}C_3H_3CH_3)$	0.86	0.85	0.82	0.03
313	2-(hydroxymethy)carboran-1-yl	0.38	0.49	0.34	0.15
314	$I(OCOCF_3)_2$	1.28	1.34	1.18	0.16
315	cyclo-C_4F_7	0.48	0.53	0.45	0.08

Contd.

Table 2.2. Continued

No.	Substituent	σ_m	σ_p	F	R
316	$COCF_2CF_2CF_3$	0.63	0.79	0.55	0.24
317	$C(CF_3)_3$	0.55	0.55	0.53	0.02
318	$(CF_2)_3CF_3$	0.47	0.52	0.44	0.08
319	$SO_2C(CF_3)_3$	0.96	1.13	0.84	0.29
320	$SC(CF_3)_3$	0.51	0.58	0.47	0.11
321	$C(SCF_3)_3$	0.51	0.53	0.49	0.04
322	$SeC(CF_3)_3$	0.49	0.54	0.46	0.08
323	$C(CN)_3$	0.97	0.96	0.92	0.04
324	cyclo-1-(OH)C_4F_6	0.36	0.37	0.36	0.01
325	$CH{=}C(CN)_2$	0.66	0.84	0.57	0.27
326	2-(5-bromofuryl)	0.15	0.00	0.23	– 0.23
327	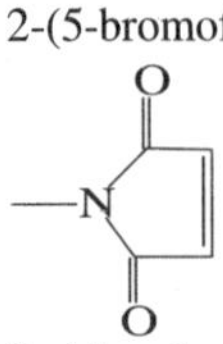	0.33	0.27	0.36	– 0.09
328	3-chloro-l-pyrroline-2,5-dione	0.47	0.46	0.47	– 0.01
329	3-pyridazinyl	0.28	0.48	0.21	0.27
330	3,4-CH=CHCH=CH⁻	0.04	0.04	0.07	– 0.03
331	$C(Me)(CN)_2$	0.60	0.57	0.59	– 0.02
332	4-pyrimidinyl	0.30	0.63	0.18	0.45
333	2-pyrimidinyl	0.23	0.53	0.13	0.40
334	5-pyrimidinyl	0.28	0.39	0.25	0.14
335	2-furyl	0.06	0.02	0.10	– 0.08
336	2-thienyl	0.09	0.05	0.13	– 0.08
337	3-thienyl	0.03	– 0.02	0.08	– 0.10
338	2-selenienyl	0.06	0.04	0.10	– 0.06
339	2-tellurienyl	0.06	0.03	0.10	– 0.07
340	1-pyrryl	0.47	0.37	0.50	– 0.13
341	l-pyrroline-2,5-dione	0.34	0.31	0.36	– 0.05
342	CH=CHCOMe	0.21	– 0.01	0.31	– 0.32
343	$I(OCOMe)_2$	0.85	0.88	0.80	0.08
344	$N(COMe)_2$	0.35	0.33	0.36	– 0.03
345	cyclobutyl	– 0.05	– 0.14	0.02	– 0.16
346	$COCHMe_2$	0.38	0.47	0.35	0.12
347	$(CH_2)_4$	– 0.48	– 0.48	– 0.40	– 0.08
348	$NHCOCH(Me)_2$	0.11	– 0.10	0.21	– 0.31
349	$C(Me)_3$	– 0.10	– 0.20	– 0.02	– 0.18
350	CH(Me)Et	– 0.08	– 0.12	– 0.02	– 0.10
351	$CH_2CH(Me)_2$	– 0.07	– 0.12	– 0.01	– 0.11
352	$(CH_2)_3CH_3$	– 0.08	– 0.16	– 0.01	0.15
353	$O(CH_2)_3CH_3$	0.10	– 0.32	0.29	– 0.61
354	$CH_2C(OH)Me_2$	– 0.16	– 0.17	– 0.11	– 0.06
355	$C(OMe)_3$	– 0.03	– 0.04	0.01	– 0.05
356	$AsEt_2$	0.22	0.00	0.32	– 0.32
357	$As(O)Et_2$	0.57	0.44	0.60	– 0.16

Contd.

Table 2.2. Continued

No.	Substituent	σ_m	σ_p	*F*	*R*
358	$As(S)Et_2$	0.52	0.44	0.54	– 0.10
359	$NH(CH_2)CH_3$	– 0.34	– 0.51	– 0.21	– 0.30
360	$N(Et)_2$	– 0.23	– 0.72	0.01	– 0.73
361	$PO(Et)_2$	0.37	0.47	0.33	0.14
362	$N{=}NPO(OEt)_2$	(0.16)	0.74	(– 0.05)	(0.79)
363	$PO(OEt)_2$	0.55	0.60	0.52	0.08
364	$P(Et_2)$	0.10	0.13	0.11	0.02
365	$P(S)Et_2$	0.39	0.46	0.36	0.10
366	$CH_2N(Me)_3^+$	0.40	0.44	0.38	0.06
367	$CH_2CH_2NH(Me)_2^+$	0.24	0.14	0.29	– 0.15
368	$CH_2OSi(CH_3)_3$	– 0.04	– 0.05	0.00	– 0.05
369	$CH_2Si(Me)_3$	– 0.16	– 0.21	– 0.09	– 0.12
370	$PO(N(Me)_2)_2$	0.30	0.40	0.27	0.13
371	$P(N(Me)_2)_2$	0.18	0.25	0.17	0.08
372	2-(Methylcarbonyl)carboran-1-yl	0.40	0.63	0.31	0.32
373	2-[(carbonyloxy)methyl]carboran-1-yl	0.70	0.74	0.66	0.08
374	CH_2-1-(1,2-$(BH)_{10}$-C_2Me	0.10	0.11	0.12	– 0.01
375	$C(CN){=}C(CN)_2$	0.77	0.98	0.65	0.33
376	2-(5-cyanofuryl)	0.25	0.10	0.32	– 0.22
377	2-(5-formylfuryl)	0.22	– 0.05	0.34	– 0.39
378	2-pyridyl	0.33	0.17	0.40	– 0.23
379	3-pyridyl	0.23	0.25	0.24	0.01
380	4-pyridyl	0.27	0.44	0.21	0.23
381	2-(4,6-dimethyl-*s*-triazinyl)	0.25	0.39	0.21	0.18
382	1-cyclopentenyl	– 0.06	– 0.05	– 0.03	– 0.02
383	CH=CHCOOEt	0.19	0.03	0.27	– 0.24
384	cyclopentyl	– 0.05	– 0.14	0.02	– 0.16
385	$COC(Me)_3$	0.27	0.32	0.26	0.06
386	$C(Et)(Me)_3$	0.06	– 0.05	0.13	– 0.18
387	$CH_4C(Me)_3$	– 0.06	– 0.18	0.03	– 0.21
388	$NHCO_2(CH_2)_3$	– 0.05	– 0.17	0.03	– 0.14
389	$(CH_2)_4CH_3$	– 0.08	– 0.15	– 0.01	– 0.14
390	$O(CH_2)_4CH_3$	0.10	(– 0.34)	0.29	(– 0.63)
391	$CH_2PO(OEt)_2$	0.12	0.06	0.17	– 0.11
392	$CH_2CH_2N(Me)^{3+}$	0.16	0.13	0.19	– 0.06
393	$CH_2CH_2Si(Me)_3$	– 0.16	– 0.17	– 0.11	– 0.06
394	$Si(Me)_2OSi(Me)_3$	0.00	– 0.01	0.04	– 0.05
395	C_6Cl_5	0.25	0.24	0.27	– 0.03
396	C_6F_5	0.26	0.27	0.27	0.00
397	$P(O)(C_3F_7)_2$	0.95	1.10	0.84	0.26
398	$OP(O)(C_3F_7)_2$	0.66	0.56	0.67	– 0.11
399	$NHP(O)(C_3F_7)_2$	0.28	0.18	0.33	– 0.15
400	$CH_2Co(CN)_5^{3-}$	– 0.53	– 0.68	– 0.39	– 0.29
401	$CH_2Mn(CO)_5$	– 0.14	– 0.44	0.02	– 0.46
402	C_6H_2-2,4,6-$(NO_2)_3$	0.26	0.30	0.26	0.04
403	C_6H_4-3-Br	0.09	0.08	0.12	– 0.04

Contd.

Table 2.2. Continued

No.	Substituent	σ_m	σ_p	F	R
404	C_6H_4-4-Br	0.15	0.12	0.18	– 0.06
405	C_6H_4-3-Cl	0.15	0.10	0.19	– 0.09
406	C_6H_4-4-Cl	0.15	0.12	0.18	– 0.06
407	C_6H_4-3-F	0.15	0.10	0.19	– 0.09
408	C_6H_4-4-F	0.12	0.06	0.17	– 0.11
409	OC_6H_4-4-F	– 0.08	– 0.10	– 0.03	– 0.07
410	C_6H_4-3-I	0.13	0.06	0.18	– 0.12
411	C_6H_4-4-I	0.14	0.10	0.18	– 0.08
412	C_6H_4-3-NO_2	0.21	0.20	0.23	– 0.03
413	C_6H_4-4-NO_2	0.25	0.26	0.26	0.00
414	SC_6H_4-4-NO_2	0.32	0.24	0.36	– 0.12
415	SOC_6H_4-4-NO_2	0.58	0.60	0.55	0.05
416	2-benzotriazolyl	0.49	0.51	0.47	0.04
417	C_6H_5	0.06	– 0.01	0.12	– 0.13
418	$N(O){=}NSO_2C_6H_5$	0.69	0.79	0.62	0.17
419	$N{=}NC_6H_5$	0.32	0.39	0.30	0.09
420	OC_6H_5	0.25	– 0.03	0.37	– 0.40
421	SOC_6H_5	0.50	0.44	0.51	– 0.07
422	2-(5-acetylfuryl)	0.24	0.08	0.31	– 0.23
423	2-(6-methylpyronyl)	0.38	0.43	0.36	0.07
424	$SO_2C_6H_5$	0.62	0.68	0.58	0.10
425	$OSO_2C_6H_5$	0.36	0.33	0.37	– 0.04
426	SC_6H_5	0.23	0.07	0.30	– 0.23
427	NHC_6H_5	– 0.02	– 0.56	0.22	– 0.78
428	$HNSO_2C_6H_5$	0.16	0.01	0.24	– 0.23
429	$SO_2NHC_6H_5$	0.56	0.65	0.51	0.14
430	2-(5-ethylfuryl)	0.09	– 0.13	0.20	– 0.33
431	1-(2,5-dimethylpyrryl)	0.49	0.38	0.52	– 0.14
432	1-cyclohexenyl	– 0.10	– 0.08	– 0.07	– 0.01
433	cyclohexyl	– 0.05	– 0.15	0.03	– 0.18
434	$N(C_3H_7)_2$	– 0.26	– 0.93	0.06	– 0.99
435	$(CH_2)_4NMe_2$	– 0.08	– 0.16	– 0.01	– 0.15
436	$PO(isopropyl)_2$	0.37	0.41	0.36	0.05
437	$P(isopropyl)_2$	0.02	0.06	0.04	0.02
438	$P(O)(OPr)_2$	0.38	0.50	0.33	0.17
439	$Ge(Et)_3$	0.00	0.00	0.03	– 0.03
440	$(CH_2)_3N(Me)^{3+}$	0.06	– 0.01	0.12	– 0.13
441	$Si(OEt)_3$	0.02	0.08	0.03	0.05
442	$P(Et)^{3+}$	0.99	0.98	0.94	0.04
443	$Sn(Et)_3$	0.00	0.00	0.03	– 0.03
444	$P(=NSO_2CF_3)(C_3F_7)_2$	1.24	1.37	1.11	0.26
445	$Si(NMe_2)_3$	– 0.04	– 0.04	0.00	– 0.04
446	2-benzoxazolyl	0.30	0.33	0.30	0.04
447	2-benzthiazolyl	0.27	0.29	0.27	0.02
448	COC_6H_5	0.34	0.43	0.31	0.12
449	$OCOC_6H_5$	0.21	0.13	0.26	– 0.13

Contd.

Table 2.2. Continued

No.	Substituent	σ_m	σ_p	*F*	*R*
450	$COOC_6H_5$	0.37	0.44	0.34	0.10
451	$N{=}CHC_6H_5$	− 0.08	− 0.55	0.14	− 0.69
452	$CH{=}NC_6H_5$	0.35	0.42	0.33	0.09
453	$NHCOC_6H_5$	0.02	− 0.19	0.13	− 0.32
454	$CONHC_6H_5$	0.23	0.41	0.17	0.24
455	C_6H_4-4-Me	0.06	− 0.03	0.12	− 0.15
456	$CH_2C_6H_5$	− 0.08	− 0.09	− 0.04	− 0.05
457	$N{=}NC_6H_3$-5-Me-2-OH	0.27	0.31	0.26	0.05
458	C_6H_4-O-Me	0.05	− 0.08	0.13	− 0.21
459	$CH(OH)C_6H_5$	0.00	− 0.03	0.05	− 0.08
460	$CH_2OC_6H_5$	0.06	0.07	0.08	− 0.01
461	$CH_2SO_2C_6H_5$	0.15	0.16	0.17	− 0.01
462	$C(Et)_3$	− 0.07	− 0.20	0.02	− 0.22
463	$(CH_2)_6CH_3$	− 0.07	− 0.16	0.00	− 0.16
464	$SiMe(OSi(Me)_3)_2$	− 0.02	− 0.01	0.01	− 0.02
465	$CF_2CF_2C_6H_4$-4-F	0.34	0.39	0.32	0.01
466	$C{\equiv}CC_6H_5$	0.14	0.16	0.15	0.01
467	$CH{=}NCOC_6H_5$	0.39	0.51	0.34	0.17
468	$CH{=}CHC_6H_5$	0.03	− 0.07	0.10	− 0.17
469	$CH_2Fe(CO)_2(\pi\text{-}C_5H_5)$	− 0.26	− 0.49	− 0.11	− 0.38
470	$CH{=}NNHCOC_6H_5$	0.39	0.51	0.34	0.17
471	$N{=}CHC_6H_4$-4-OMe	− 0.07	− 0.54	0.15	− 0.69
472	$NHCOC_6H_4$-4-OMe	0.09	− 0.06	0.17	− 0.23
473	$SCH{=}NSO_2C_6H_4$-4-Me	0.65	0.70	0.61	0.09
474	C_6H_4-4-Et	0.07	− 0.02	0.13	− 0.15
475	$CH_2CH_2C_6H_5$	− 0.07	− 0.12	− 0.01	− 0.11
476	$N{=}C(Me)NHC_6H_5$	0.29	0.08	0.38	− 0.30
477	$Si(C_6H_5)(Me)_2$	0.04	0.07	0.06	0.01
478	$S(Me){=}NSO_2C_6H_4$-4-Me	0.65	0.70	0.61	0.09
479	2,4,6-trimethylpyridinium	0.62	0.58	0.61	− 0.03
480	$PO(CMe_3)_2$	0.31	0.41	0.28	0.13
481	$PO(C_4H_9)_2$	0.35	0.49	0.30	0.19
482	$PO(OC_4H_9)_2$	0.41	0.57	0.35	0.22
483	$P(CMe_3)_2$	0.01	0.15	− 0.01	0.16
484	$C_6H_5Cr(CO)_3$	0.29	0.14	0.36	− 0.22
485	2-benzo-4-thiopyronyl	0.34	0.35	0.34	0.01
486	2-benzothiopyronyl	0.48	0.45	0.48	− 0.03
487	2-benzo-1,4-pyronyl	0.41	0.40	0.41	− 0.01
488	$CH{=}CHCOC_6H_4$-4-NO_2	0.15	0.05	0.21	− 0.16
489	$CH_2Mo(CO)_3(C_5H_5)$	− 0.21	− 0.45	− 0.07	− 0.38
490	$CH{=}CHCOC_6H_5$	0.18	0.05	0.25	− 0.20
491	C_6H_4-4-$CHMe_2$	0.08	0.01	0.13	− 0.12
492	$Si(OSiMe_3)_3$	− 0.09	− 0.01	− 0.08	0.07
493	ferrocenyl	− 0.15	− 0.18	− 0.09	− 0.09
494	ferricenium	0.29	0.29	0.30	− 0.01
495	ferrocenonium	0.05	0.29	− 0.01	0.30
496	C_6H_4-4-CMe_3	0.07	0.01	0.12	− 0.11

Contd.

Table 2.2. Continued

No.	Substituent	σ_m	σ_p	F	R
497	1-adamantyl	– 0.12	– 0.13	– 0.07	– 0.06
498	1-dibenzarsenyl	0.19	0.13	0.23	– 0.10
499	1-dibenzoarsoxyl	0.17	0.09	0.22	– 0.13
500	1-dibenzoarsazinyl	0.14	0.09	0.18	– 0.09
501	$As(C_6H_5)_2$	0.03	0.09	0.04	0.05
502	$AsO(C_6H_5)_2$	0.54	0.64	0.49	0.15
503	$P(C_6H_5)_2(BCl_3)$	0.67	0.72	0.62	0.10
504	$N(C_6H_5)_2$	0.00	– 0.22	0.12	– 0.34
505	$PO(C_6H_5)_2$	0.38	0.53	0.32	0.21
506	$P(C_6H_5)_2$	0.11	0.19	0.10	0.09
507	$PS(C_6H_5)_2$	0.29	0.47	0.23	0.24
508	$P(N(C_3H_7)_2)C_6H_4$-3-F	0.20	0.24	0.20	0.04
509	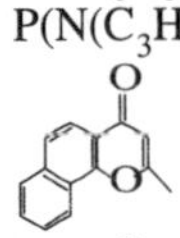	0.37	0.38	0.37	0.01
510	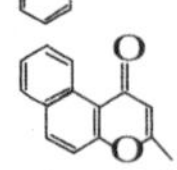	0.38	0.38	0.38	0.00
511	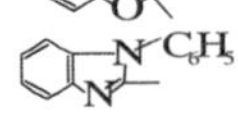	0.17	0.21	0.17	0.04
512	$CH(C_6H_5)_2$	– 0.03	– 0.05	– 0.05	– 0.06
513	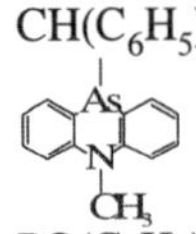	0.12	0.07	0.07	– 0.09
514	$PO(C_6H_5)C_6H_4$-4-Me	0.13	0.30	0.09	0.21
515	$CH_2PO(C_6H_5)_2$	0.14	0.01	0.21	– 0.20
516	$PS(C_6H_5)C_6H_4$-4-Me	0.09	0.30	0.03	0.27
517	$P^+(Me)(C_6H_5)_2$	1.13	1.18	1.04	0.14
518	$Si(Me)(C_6H_5)_2$	0.10	0.13	0.11	0.02
519	$COOCH(C_6H_5)_2$	0.36	0.56	0.28	0.28
520	$PO(C_6H_4\text{-4-Me})_2$	0.17	0.30	0.14	0.16
521	$PS(C_6H_4\text{-4-Me})_2$	0.20	0.23	0.20	0.03
522	$P^+(Me)(C_6H_5)(C_6H_4\text{-4-Me})$	1.09	1.11	1.02	0.09
523	$P^+(Me)(C_6H_4\text{-4-Me})$	1.13	1.18	1.04	1.14
524	$Ge(C_6H_5)_3$	0.05	0.08	0.07	0.01
525	2-methyl-4,6-diphenylpyridinium	0.65	0.70	0.61	0.09
526	$N{=}P(C_6H_5)_3$	– 0.33	– 0.77	– 0.10	– 0.67
527	$Si(C_6H_5)_3$	– 0.03	0.10	– 0.04	0.14
528	$Sn(C_6H_5)_3$	(0.53)	(0.27)	(0.62)	(– 0.35)
529	$C(C_6H_5)_3$	– 0.01	0.02	0.01	0.01
530	2,4,6-triphenylpyridinium	0.34	0.33	0.35	– 0.02

[a]Values in parentheses are not definite.
[b]Substituents are arranged by molecular formula C_xH_y

ionization constants (pK_a), and NMR chemical shifts (δ) are also used in the correlations.

Quantum Mechanical Parameters

Quantum mechanical parameters provide more accurate and detailed description of electronic effects than empirical parameters. Several reviews [18-24] can be referred to for verifying this fact. The development of high speed computers and the efficient algorithms have greatly facilitated the quantum mechanical calculations even for very large molecules. These calculations provide a large number of electronic parameters and geometric properties of molecules, which greatly help describe the drug-receptor interactions [25, 26]. Quantum mechanical methods are also employed to exclusively calculate the drug-receptor interaction energies.

When the computers were not so developed, the most popular and simple quantum mechanical (molecular orbital) method was Hückel molecular orbital (HMO) method [27]. Though this method was very crude, it was found to be very useful for dealing with the π-electron systems, and even today it has not lost its importance. A somewhat refined method to be excessively used was extended Hückel theory (EHT) approach [28]. However, over the last several decades, a number of refined methods have been developed; the most popular of them are: CNDO (complete neglect of differential overlap) [29, 30], INDO (intermediate neglect of differential overlap) [31], MINDO (modified INDO) [32], MNDO (modified neglect of differential overlap) [33], AM1 (Austin model 1) [34], and PM3 (parametric model 3) [35]. All these methods are, however, semi-empirical methods in which some parameters are determined using certain experimental data. Of these methods, the CNDO is the simplest (and most approximate) method, that neglects both diatomic and single-atom atomic orbital overlaps. Depending upon the two different ways to evaluate the essential parameters in it, it has been given two names CNDO/1 [29] and CNDO/2 [30].

The INDO and MINDO methods are slightly better in that they neglect only the diatomic atomic orbital overlaps and retain the single-atom (one-center) atomic orbital overlaps. MNDO, AM1, and PM3 are the methods that are based on the correct inclusion of one-center overlaps. Of all these semi-empirical methods, AM1 method has been found to provide a better description of molecular systems even for anions and hydrogen-bonded systems [34, 36].

A number of *ab initio* methods were developed to provide a complete representation of all non-relativistic interactions between the nuclei and the electrons in a molecule [36], but their use was found to be severely limited by the types of atoms and size of the molecules [37]. Further, most of the *ab initio* methods are extremely time consuming and require large CPU memories and are therefore impractical for the calculation of extended sets of relatively large molecules (i.e. more than 10 atoms). Thus, in comparison to any *ab initio* method, the semi-empirical AM1 method was found to be more practicable as its calculations are obtained more rapidly. In a QSAR study on toxicity [38], a preference was established for the AM1 derived descriptors. Further, it was demonstrated that AM1 method can be used to calculate the electronic effects which are difficult to be described by *ab initio* methods [37].

For all the semi-empirical methods, it has been observed that results produced by different methods are generally not comparable, but they do often exhibit similar trends, for example, the net electronic charges calculated by AM1, MNDO, and INDO methods largely differ in their absolute values, but are consistent in their trends. The variation in the molecular orbital indices is generally for AM1 and diminishes in the order AM1 > MNDO > INDO [39]. Now some of the important quantum mechanical parameters that are most often used in QSAR are briefly discussed below with their significance in drug-receptor interactions.

Q^+ and Q^-: Q^+ and Q^- are net positive and net negative charges on an atom, respectively. The positive charge on an atom defines its ability to have an electrostatic interaction with a negatively charged site of the receptor. Similarly, negative charge on an atom defines its ability to have an electrostatic interaction with a positively charged site of the receptor.

f^E and f^N: f^E and f^N are the electrophilic and nucleophilic frontier orbital densities of an atom, respectively, which signify the ability of an atom to interact with an electrophilic or a nucleophilic site of the receptor, respectively [40].

S^E and S^N: S^E and S^N are electrophilic and nucleophilic superdelocalizabilities of an atom, respectively. These indices incorporate a consideration of the charge-transfer capabilities of an atom to a charged receptor site. The S^E defines the capability of an atom to donate the electron to a positively charged site of the receptor and S^N defines the ability of an atom to accept the electron from the negatively charged site of the receptor [41].

E_{HOMO}: This parameter stands for the energy of the highest occupied molecular orbital and corresponds to the ionization potential of the molecule. It measures the ability of the whole molecule to participate in a charge-transfer phenomenon, where it can donate the electron [25, 42, 43].

E_{LUMO}: E_{LUMO} stands for the energy of the lowest unoccupied molecular orbital in a molecule and corresponds to the electron affinity of the molecule. It measures the ability of the whole molecule to participate in a charge-transfer phenomenon, where it can accept the electron [25, 42, 43].

For several other quantum mechanical parameters, readers may refer to the review by Karelson and Lobanov [26].

(b) Lipophilicity or Hydrophobicity Parameters

The actual breakthrough in QSAR, in fact, came when Hansch et al. [44, 45] assumed that the biological effect of a drug is basically controlled by two processes: the journey of drug from its point of entry into the body to the site of action (pharmacokinetics) and the interaction of the drug with the specific site of the receptor (pharmacodynamics). Hansch surmised that the diffusion of the drug from the extracellular phase to the reaction site in the cell involved a random walk (Fig. 2.5) which is a relatively slow process and depends on the molecular structure of the drug.

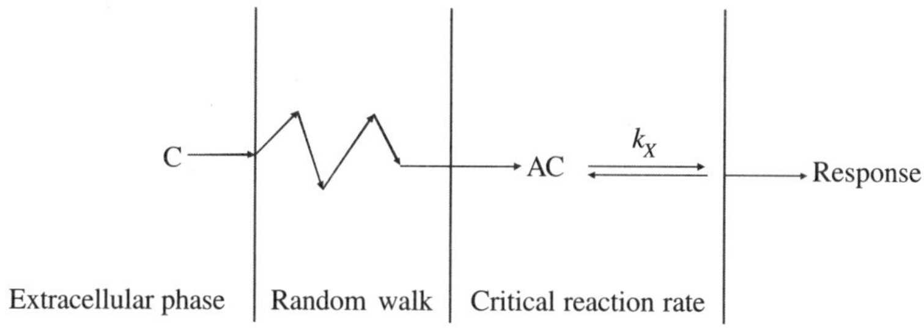

d(response)/*dt* = AC k_X
A: Probability of molecules
C: Concentration of drug applied

Fig. 2.5. The random walk of the drug from the extracellular phase to the critical reaction site in the cell.

The drug reaches the site of action by facing two different environments, lipophilic (e.g., membranes) and aqueous (the exobiophase, such as cytoplasm). All living cells are surrounded by lipophilic (nonaqueous) phase, membranes. These membranes protect the cells from water soluble substances, form a surface to which enzymes and other proteins can attach in order to produce a localization and structural organization, and separate the solutions of different electromechanical potentials (e.g., as in nerve conduction). One of the most important membranes is the one that surrounds the capillaries of the circulatory system in the brain and protects it from passive diffusion of undesirable chemicals from the bloodstream. This membrane is called *blood-brain barrier*. This is an important prophylactic boundary, but it can also block the delivery of the central nervous system drugs to their site of action.

The Hansch group then assumed that the first factor controlling the drug activity would be the probability of the drug molecules to cross this blood-brain barrier and reach the site of action [44, 46] and they proposed that this probability (*A*) can be estimated as a first approximation by the ability of the compound to partition between 1-octanol (that simulates a lipid membrane) and water (the aqueous phase). 1-Octanol has a long saturated alkyl chain and a hydroxyl group for hydrogen bonding, and it dissolves water to the extent of 1.7 M (saturation). This combination of lipophilic chains, hydrophilic groups, and water molecules gives 1-octanol properties very close to those of natural membranes.

Being aware of Collander's work [47] that rate of transport of many organic compounds through the cellular material of *Nitella* cells was proportional to their partition coefficient (*P*) between an organic solvent and water, Hansch et al. [48] surmised that the probabilities of the drug molecules reaching the critical site of the action may be related with the partition coefficient in a Gaussian manner as

$$A = f\,(\log P) = a\,\exp[-\,(\log P - \log P_0)^2/b] \tag{2.20}$$

where a and b are constants to be determined and $\log P_0$ is the value of $\log P$ corresponding to the maximum (mode) of the distribution (Fig. 2.6).

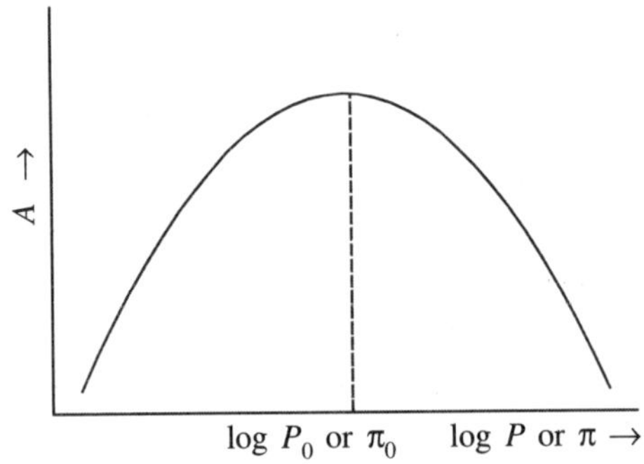

Fig. 2.6. Probability distribution for drug molecules of varying lipophilicity.

Then Hansch and Fujita [45] proposed that the rate of any biological response of any drug may be given by

$$\frac{d\,(\text{response})}{dt} = kAC \tag{2.21}$$

where C is the applied concentration (dose) of the drug and k is the rate constant when the drug reacts with critical reaction site. Now combining Eqs. 2.20 and 2.21, one can write

$$\frac{d\,(\text{response})}{dt} = k.a\,\exp[-\,(\log P - \log P_0)^2/b]C \tag{2.22}$$

If C is measured as a compound concentration necessary to cause a particular constant response (e.g., 50% inhibition of a given enzyme) in a fixed time interval, d(response)/dt can be taken as a constant. Consequently, taking logarithms (first natural and then converting to decadic) and collecting constants, Eq. 2.22 can be written, with some adjustments, as

$$\log(1/C) = \lambda_1(\log P_0)\,(\log P) - \lambda_2(\log P)^2 - \lambda_3(\log P_0)^2 + \log k + \lambda_4 \tag{2.23}$$

Taking $\log P_0$ also a constant and using Hammett equation (Eq. 2.10) for $\log k$, Eq. 2.23 can be written as

$$\log(1/C) = a_1 \log P - a_2(\log P)^2 + a_3\sigma + a_4 \tag{2.24}$$

Now this equation suggests that as the lipophilicity of the compounds would increase the activity would go to a maximum and then fall off to go to zero and, indeed, in *in vivo* system, it has been so observed. This is because as the log P increases ($P > 1$) the probability of the drug molecule reaching the critical reaction site, crossing the lipid phase membrane, increases and goes to a maximum, but the extremely lipophilic drug molecules may be so trapped in the lipid phase that nothing reaches the aqueous-phase to be transported to the reaction site and A may fall to zero.

One of the most important contributions of Hansch group at this time was the discovery that partition coefficient is an additive constitutive parameter [46], just like many other molecular properties, such as Hammett's constant σ. *Additive* means that the effect of multiple substituents can be equal to the sum of the effect of the individual substituents. *Constitutive* indicates that the effect of a substituent may differ depending on the molecule to which it is attached or on its environment. A lipophilicity parameter π was then defined in the same manner by Eq. 2.25 [46] as the Hammett constant σ was defined by Eq. 2.10. In Eq. 2.25, P_X refers to the partition coefficient of the compound with the substituent X and P_H to that of parent

$$\pi = \log P_X - \log P_H \tag{2.25}$$

compound ($X = H$). Since lipophilicity is synonymously also called hydrophobicity, π is also most popularly called hydrophobicity or hydrophobic constant.

Calculation of log *P*

From Eq. 2.25, it is obvious that $\pi_H = 0$. Thus, for many log P calculations, the following simple relation can be used

$$\log P_{X\text{-}R\text{-}Y} = \log P_{H\text{-}R\text{-}H} + \pi_X + \pi_Y \tag{2.26}$$

An example would be [5]

$$\begin{aligned} \log P[NO_2 - (C_6H_4) - CH_3] &= \log P_{C_6H_6} + \pi_{NO_2} + \pi_{CH_3} \\ &= 2.13 - 0.28 + 0.56 \\ &= 2.41 \text{ (obsd = 2.45)} \end{aligned}$$

It is to be pointed out, however, that log P should not be taken as the sum of π-values, but π-values of substituents should be added to the log P of the parent compound.

The calculation of log P manually is not so easy as it is affected by so many electronic and structural parameters. Nonetheless, a fragment method was suggested by Hansch and Leo [49] in which the log P of a solute can be expressed as a linear sum of fundamental structural constants known as fragments f and factors F that affect the partitioning equilibrium (Eq. 2.27). Experimentally determined log P values (1-octanol-water system) were often found to be reproduced by this approach. The computerization of the method has greatly facilitated the calculation of

$$\log P = \sum_{i}^{n} a_n f_n + \sum_{i}^{m} b_m F_m \qquad (2.27)$$

log P [50]. This method of Hansch and Leo for calculating log P is known as constructionist approach or synthetic method. Some other approaches for calculating log P are also described in a review by Leo [51]. The values of π for some selected substituents are given in Table 2.3.

Experimental Determination of log *P*

Different experimental methods such as shake-flask method [52], high performance liquid chromatography (HPLC) method [53], etc., have been suggested to determine the log P values. By far the most extensive and useful log P values were obtained by the shake-flask method just by simply shaking a solute with two immiscible solvents and then analyzing the solute concentration in one or both phases. The ratio of concentrations in two phases gave a true value of P only at saturation. However, measuring P from this shake-flask method is not as easy as it appears. So many practical problems arise, for example, highly polar, highly lipophilic, or compounds with small impurities may drastically distort the experimental values [54].

An alternative and slightly more reliable method is then reversed-phase thin-layer chromatography [55-58]. From this method, the chromatographic parameter R_f is determined, which is converted to a parameter R_M by Eq. 2.28. This R_M is supposed to be a true measure of lipophilicity. If R_M values are properly determined, they are found to be closely related to log P

$$R_M = \log(1/R_f - 1) \qquad (2.28)$$

values [56-58], e.g., for a very large set of quite heterogeneous compounds (n = 415), the two were found to be correlated with a value of r = 0.933 [57].

The determination of R_M values offers many important advantages as compared to the measurement of log P values, e.g., compounds need not be pure, only traces of material are required, a wide range of hydrophilic and lipophilic congeners can be investigated, the measurement of practically insoluble analogs poses no problems, no quantitative method for concentration determination is needed, and several compounds can be investigated simultaneously [54]. However, this method also has certain drawbacks. It lacks precision and reproducibility and uses different organic solvent systems, which pose the problems in derivation of π or factor f. Further, the chromatographic method is not an equilibrium process and thus produces deviations in the case of charged compounds. Therefore, a preference was

Table 2.3. Experimental π values from benzene system. Reprinted with permission from [5]. Copyright 1995 American Chemical Society

No.	Substituent	π value
1	$+N(CH_3)_3$	– 5.96
2	SULFITE ANION	– 4.76
3	CO_2	– 4.36
4	$+NH_3$	– 4.19
5	$(CH_2)_3N(CH_3)_3$	– 4.15
6	$CH_2NH_3^+$	– 4.09
7	OXIDE ANION-O^-	– 3.87
8	IO	– 3.74
9	$C{=}NH(NH_2)HCl$	– 3.72
10	$(CH_2)_4N(CH_3)_3^+$	– 3.65
11	$CH_2CH(NH_3^+)CO_2^-$	– 3.56
12	IO_2	– 3.46
13	MALTOSYL	– 3.27
14	O-β-GLUCOSYL	– 2.84
15	C≡C-CYCLOPROPYL-CO_2	– 2.74
16	$CONHNHCONH_2$	– 2.63
17	$AS(O)(OH)_2$	– 2.13
18	$NHSO_2NHSO_2NH_2$	– 2.11
19	$CHOHCH(CH_2OH)NHCOCH_2CN$	– 2.07
20	SO_2NHNH_2	– 2.04
21	$C{=}O(NHNH_2)$	– 1.90
22	$CHOHCH(CH_2OH)NHCOCH_3$	– 1.88
23	C=O(NHOH)	– 1.87
24	$N(COCH_3)SO_2CH_3$	– 1.84
25	$SO_2(NH_2)$	– 1.82
26	$NHSO_2NH_2$	– 1.73
27	$CHOHCH(CH_2OH)NHCOCH_2F$	– 1.70
28	$CH_2C{=}O(NH_2)$	– 1.68
29	SO_2CH_3	– 1.63
30	$P(O)(OH)_2$	– 1.59
31	$CH_2NHCOCH_2OH$	– 1.58
32	$S{=}O(CH_3)$	– 1.58
33	$CON(CH_3)_2$	– 1.51
34	$N(SO_2CH_3)_2$	– 1.51
35	$C{=}O(NH_2)$	– 1.49
36	$NHCONHC(=NH)NH_2$	– 1.48
37	$CHOHCH(CH_2OH)NHCOCHF_2$	– 1.43
38	$HgOC{=}O(CH_3)$	– 1.42
39	$NHCOCH_2OH$	– 1.42
40	$COCO_2H$	– 1.41
41	$NHC{=}S(NH_2)$	– 1.40
42	$OCH_2C{=}O$(N-MORPHOLINYL)	– 1.39
43	OCH_2CONH_2	– 1.37
44	$OCH_2CON(CH_3)_2$	– 1.36

Contd.

Table 2.3. Continued

No.	Substituent	π value
45	NH(OH)	– 1.34
46	$CH{=}NNHCONHNH_2$	– 1.32
47	$NHC{=}O(NH_2)$	– 1.30
48	$C{=}O(NHCH_3)$	– 1.27
49	$CHOHCH(CH_2OH)NHCOCH_2Cl$	– 1.26
50	NH_2	– 1.23
51	$C{=}O(NHNHCOCH_3)$	– 1.22
52	$(CH_2)_2C{=}O(NH_2)$	– 1.22
53	$CHOHCH(CH_2OH)NHCOCH_2Br$	– 1.19
54	$NHSO_2CH_3$	– 1.18
55	$P(O)(OCH_3)_2$	– 1.18
56	$NHC(=O)N(CH_3)_2$	– 1.15
57	$CHOHCH(CH_2OH)NHCOCH(CH_3)_2$	– 1.06
58	$OCONH_2$	– 1.05
59	1-TETRAZOLYL	– 1.04
60	CH_2NH_2	– 1.04
61	CH_2OH	– 1.03
62	$CHOHCH(CH_2OH)NHCOC_3H_7$	– 0.98
63	NHCHO	– 0.98
64	$NHC{=}O(CH_3)$	– 0.97
65	OCH_2CH_2OH	– 0.97
66	$SO_2OCH_2CH_3$	– 0.90
67	$NHNH_2$	– 0.88
68	OSO_2CH_3	– 0.88
69	$CH{=}N(O)C(CH_3)_3$	– 0.87
70	$CHOHCH(CH_2OH)NHCOCH(Cl)CH_3$	– 0.87
71	$CH{=}NNHCONH_2$	– 0.86
72	CHOH(2-PIPERIDINYL)	– 0.85
73	$NHC(=O)N(CH_3)(OCH_3)$	– 0.84
74	$CHOHCH(CH_2OH)NHCOCH_2I$	– 0.82
75	OCH_2CO_2H	– 0.79
76	CH_2OCH_3	– 0.78
77	$CHOHCH(CH_2OH)NHCOCF_3$	– 0.78
78	$SO_2N(CH_3)_2$	– 0.78
79	CH_2CH_2OH	– 0.77
80	$CH_2CH_2NH_2$	– 0.76
81	$COCH{=}NOH$	– 0.73
82	CH_2CO_2H	– 0.72
83	$CHOHCH(CH_2OH)NHCOCHCl_2$	– 0.71
84	$NHC{=}S(NHC_2H_5)$	– 0.71
85	CH_2COCH_3	– 0.69
86	OH	– 0.67
87	5-CHLORO-1-TETRAZOYL	– 0.65
88	CHO	– 0.65
89	$CS(NH_2)$	– 0.64

Contd.

Table 2.3. Continued

No.	Substituent	π value
90	$OC{=}O(CH_3)$	– 0.64
91	CH_2-(1-MORPHOLINYL)	– 0.61
92	$OP(O)(OCH_3)(NHCH_3)$	– 0.61
93	CH_2CN	– 0.57
94	CN	– 0.57
95	$OP(O)(OCH_3)_2$	– 0.57
96	$B(OH)_2$	– 0.55
97	$COCH_3$	– 0.55
98	$CHOHCH(CH_2OH)NHCO(CH_3)_3$	– 0.52
99	NHC=O(Et)	– 0.52
100	DEOXYPENTOFURANOSYL	– 0.50
101	$NHC{=}O(CH_2Cl)$	– 0.50
102	2-PYRROLIDINYL	– 0.48
103	$CHOHCH(CH_2OH)NHCOCHBr_2$	– 0.47
104	$NHCH_3$	– 0.47
105	$NHC{=}S(CH_3)$	– 0.42
106	3-PYRIDYLAMIDO	– 0.40
107	$CHOHCH_2NHCOCF_3$	– 0.39
108	CH_2NO_2	– 0.38
109	CH=NOH-*trans*	– 0.38
110	$CHOHCH(CH_2OH)NHCOCH(Ph)CN$	– 0.38
111	$OC{=}ON(CH_3)_2$	– 0.38
112	PENTOFURANOSYL	– 0.38
113	$CHOHCH(CH_2OH)NHCOCH_2C_6H_5$	– 0.33
114	$N(O){=}NN(CH_3)_2$	– 0.33
115	$C{=}O(NEt_2)$	– 0.32
116	CO_2H	– 0.32
117	$OCH_2C{=}O$(N-PIPERIDYL)	– 0.32
118	$CH_2C{=}O(OCH_3)$	– 0.30
119	$CH{=}NC_6H_5$	– 0.29
120	$CH_2CH_2CO_2H$	– 0.29
121	$N{=}CHC_6H_5$	– 0.29
122	$C{=}O(NHNHCH(CH_3)_2)$	– 0.28
123	NO_2	– 0.28
124	$CH{=}NNHC({=}S)NH_2$	– 0.27
125	CH_2NHCH_3	– 0.26
126	NHCN	– 0.26
127	2-IMIDAZOLYL	– 0.25
128	$OP(O)(OEt_2)$	– 0.24
129	CH=CHCHO	– 0.23
130	$CHOHCH(CH_2OH)NHCOC_6H_5$	– 0.22
131	$NHC{=}OCH(CH_3)_2$	– 0.18
132	$CH_2OC{=}O(CH_3)$	– 0.17
133	CH=CHCN	– 0.17
134	$CH_2N(CH_3)_2$	– 0.15

Contd.

Table 2.3. Continued

No.	Substituent	π value
135	CH_2SCN	– 0.14
136	$CHOHCH(CH_2OH)NHCOCHEt_2$	– 0.14
137	NO	– 0.12
138	CH_2CH_2NHEt	– 0.11
139	$S{=}O(C_6H_5)$	– 0.07
140	$CH{=}CHCOCH_3$	– 0.06
141	$CH_2CH_2NO_2$	– 0.05
142	OCH_2O^-	– 0.05
143	OCH_3	– 0.02
144	$C{=}O(OCH_3)$	– 0.01
145	$CH{=}CHCO_2H$	0.00
146	H	0.00
147	$C{=}O(CF_3)$	0.02
148	$OC{=}O(S^-)$	0.05
149	$CH{=}C(CN)_2$	0.05
150	$SO_2(F)$	0.05
151	COEt	0.06
152	NH-Et	0.08
153	$NHC{=}O(CF_3)$	0.08
154	$SC{=}O(CH_3)$	0.10
155	$CH_2NHCH_2CH_3$	0.10
156	$CH{=}CHNO_2$-*trans*	0.12
157	$CHOHCH(CH_2OH)NHCOCCl_3$	0.12
158	$N(CH_3)COCH_2OC_6H_5$	0.12
159	$OCH_2CON(CH_3)(C_6H_5)$	0.14
160	$C(OCH_3)_3$	0.14
161	$CH_2NHCH(CH_3)_2$	0.14
162	F	0.17
163	CH_2Cl	0.17
164	$CH_2CH_2N(CH_3)_2$	0.17
165	$NHC{=}O(OEt)$	0.18
166	$N(CH_3)_2$	0.22
167	$C{=}O(NHNHCH_2CH_2CONHCH_2Ph)$	0.25
168	$CH_2NHCH_2CH_2CH_3$	0.26
169	$(CH_2)_4NHCH_3$	0.27
170	$SO_2C_6H_5$	0.31
171	$OCHF_2$	0.32
172	2-PIPERIDINYL	0.32
173	$CHOHCH(CH_2OH)NHCOCBr_3$	0.36
174	$CH_2N(C_2H_5)_2$	0.38
175	OCH_2CH_3	0.39
176	SH	0.40
177	$C{\equiv}CH$	0.40
178	$CH{=}NOCH_3$	0.41
179	$N{=}CCl_2$	0.41

Contd.

Table 2.3. Continued

No.	Substituent	π value
180	SCN	0.43
181	$CH{=}NNHCOC_6H_5$	0.44
182	$P(CH_3)_2$	0.45
183	CH_3-(1-PYRROLIDINYL)	0.45
184	$NHSO_2C_6H_5$	0.45
185	4-PYRIDYL	0.46
186	$N{=}NN(CH_3)_2$	0.46
187	NNN	0.46
188	$CH{=}CHCH_2CH_2NHCH_3$-Cis	0.48
189	$C{=}O(NHC_6H_5)$	0.49
190	$CH_2N(CHO)(C_6H_5)$	0.49
191	$N(CHO)(CH_2C_6H_5)$	0.49
192	$NHCOC_6H_5$	0.49
193	2-PYRIDYL	0.50
194	C=O(OEt)	0.51
195	2-(1-CH_3-PYRROLIDINYL)	0.52
196	$CHOHC_6H_5$	0.54
197	$NHN{=}C(CN)_2$	0.54
198	$SO_2(CF_3)$	0.55
199	CH_3	0.56
200	$CH_2CH_2NEt_2$	0.58
201	$NHCOCH_2OC_6H_5$	0.60
202	$OCH_2CONHC_6H_5$	0.60
203	$(CH_2)_3N(CH_3)_2$	0.60
204	SCH_3	0.61
205	NH-C_4H_9	0.68
206	CH_2CH_2(1-PYRROLIDYL)	0.69
207	$CH_2NHC_4H_9$	0.69
208	$C{=}O(CH_2Ph)$	0.70
209	$P{=}O(C_6H_5)_2$	0.70
210	Cl	0.71
211	$SeCH_3$	0.74
212	CH_2Br	0.79
213	$CH_2N(C_3H_7)_2$	0.81
214	CH_2CH_2Cl	0.82
215	$CH_2N(C_4H_9)_2$	0.82
216	$CH{=}CH_2$	0.82
217	$(CH_2)_4$-$N(CH_3)_2$	0.84
218	1-PIPERIDINYL	0.85
219	Br	0.86
220	$CH{=}CHCO_2C_2H_5$	0.86
221	CF_3	0.88
222	CH=N-(*N*-PIPERIDINYL)	0.91
223	$OSO_2C_6H_5$	0.93
224	1-PYRRYL	0.95

Contd.

Table 2.3. Continued

No.	Substituent	π value
225	$CH=CHCOC_6H_5$	0.95
226	CH_2CH_2Br	0.96
227	$CH_2NHC_6H_5$	1.00
228	$NHCH_2C_6H_5$	1.00
229	CH_2CH_3	1.02
230	$CH=CHCH_2CH_2N(CH_3)_2$	1.03
231	OCF_3	1.04
232	$C=O(C_6H_5)$	1.05
233	$OCH_2CH_2CH_3$	1.05
234	S-Et	1.07
235	$CH_2CH=CH_2$	1.10
236	I	1.12
237	CYCLOPROPYL	1.14
238	NCS	1.15
239	$N(Et)_2$	1.18
240	$-CH_2CH_2CH_2-$	1.20
241	$CH=CHCH_3$-*trans*	1.22
242	SF_5	1.23
243	$CH_2N(NO)C_6H_5$	1.25
244	$COCOC_6H_5$	1.25
245	$N(NO)CH_2C_6H_5$	1.25
246	$C(OH)(CF_3)_2$	1.28
247	$(CH)_4(2,3)$	1.32
248	NHC_6H_5	1.37
249	$(CH_2)_4$	1.39
250	C_6H_4OH	1.44
251	SCF_3	1.44
252	$NH-C_4H_9$	1.45
253	C_6H_4OH	1.46
254	$COOC_6H_5$	1.46
255	$OC=O(C_6H_5)$	1.46
256	$OSO_2C_6H_4$-4′-(CH_3)	1.49
257	CH_2I	1.50
258	CBr_3	1.51
259	$CH(CH_3)_2$	1.53
260	C_3H_7	1.55
261	2-THIENYL	1.61
262	$C=O(OC_4H_9)$	1.62
263	$CH_2N(CH(CH_3))_2$	1.62
264	$SCCl_3$	1.65
265	CH_2OCH_3	1.66
266	$OCH_2C_6H_5$	1.66
267	$OCH_2CH_2OC_6H_5$	1.68
268	$N=NC_6H_5$	1.69
269	2-QUINOLINYL	1.77

Contd.

Table 2.3. Continued

No.	Substituent	π value
270	3-THIENYL	1.81
271	$C{=}O(OCH_2C_6H_5)$	1.84
272	CF_2CF_3	1.89
273	PHENYL	1.96
274	$C(CH_3)_3$	1.98
275	$CH_2Si(CH_3)_3$	2.00
276	$CH_2C_6H_5$	2.01
277	$CH(CH_3)(Et)$	2.04
278	OC_6H_5	2.08
279	$CH_2N(CH_3)C_6H_5$	2.09
280	$N(CH_3)CH_2C_6H_5$	2.09
281	2-BENZTHIAZOLYL	2.13
282	C_4H_9	2.13
283	3-INDOLYL	2.14
284	CYCLOPENTYL	2.14
285	SC_6H_5	2.32
286	FERROCENYL	2.46
287	$OP(O)(OC_6H_5)_2$	2.46
288	$Si(CH_3)_3$	2.59
289	$C{\equiv}CC_6H_5$	2.65
290	$CH_2CH_2C_6H_5$	2.66
291	$CH{=}CHC_6H_5$	2.68
292	2-(5-PHENYL)PYRIDYL	2.69
293	$C_6H_4(CH_3)$	2.69
294	CYCLOHEXYL	2.82
295	$(CH_2)_3C_6H_5$	3.16
296	1-ADAMANTYL	3.37
297	$N(C_6H_5)_2$	3.61
298	C_6H_4-4′-(C_6H_5)	4.09

given to high-performance liquid chromatography (HPLC) [59-64], where a k' value is determined from the retention time of the compound (t_r) and the retention time of the solvent (t_0) using the equation

$$k' = (t_r - t_0)/t \qquad (2.29)$$

The log k' values are then supposed to reproduce with high precision the log P values of n-octanol-water system. For a fairly large group of compounds the log P and log k' were shown to be highly correlated with each other as [60]

$$\log P = 1.025\ (\pm\ 0.06)\ \log k' + 0.797$$
$$n = 33,\ r = 0.987,\ s = 0.13 \qquad (2.30)$$

Though HPLC remains the method of choice for the determination of lipophilicity, recently a rapid method for it has been developed that uses gradient reversed phase/high pressure liquid chromatography (RP-HPLC) [65, 66]. In this method a chromatography hydrophobicity index (CHIN) is calculated, which was shown for a set of neutral molecules to be correlated with *C*log *P* (calculated log *P*) as [65]

$$C\log P = 0.057\ \text{CHIN} - 1.107$$
$$n = 52,\ r = 0.85,\ s = 0.85 \tag{2.31}$$

(c) Steric Parameters

Steric effects in drug receptor interactions play very crucial roles and efforts have been made to account for them quantitatively by a number of parameters. In steric effects, the size and shape of the drug molecules and the 3D structures of the binding sites of the receptor are very important, but so far no single parameter has been devised which can account for the effects of these factors together. However, steric effects and their descriptors have been extensively discussed [4-9, 67-73]. Some important ones are described here.

Taft Parameter

The first steric parameter to be used in QSAR studies has been the Taft steric parameter, E_s, defined as [69]

$$E_s = \log(k_X/k_H)_A \tag{2.32}$$

where k_X and k_H refer to the rates of acid hydrolysis of esters XCH_2COOR and HCH_2COOR, respectively (the subscript *A* stands for the acid medium). Hancock et al. [74] made a correction to this E_s to account for the hyperconjugation in the α-hydrogens of the acetate moiety and defined a corrected version of $E_s(E_s^c)$ as

$$E_s^c = E_s + 0.306\ (n - 3) \tag{2.33}$$

where *n* refers to the number of α-hydrogens and 0.306 is a constant derived from molecular orbital calculations [74]. However, because of the availability of the E_s and E_s^c for only a limited number of substituents, efforts were made to develop other steric parameters. van der Waals radii of symmetric substituents were also found to be good steric parameters as they were found to have good relationship with E_s values (Eq. 2.34) [75].

$$E_s = 3.484 - 1.839\ r_v(av)$$
$$n = 6,\ r = 0.996,\ s = 0.13 \tag{2.34}$$

Based on van der Waals radii, Charton defined a new parameter υ [76] as

$$\upsilon_X = r_{v,X} - r_{v,H} = r_{v,X} - 1.20 \tag{2.35}$$

where $r_{v,X}$ and $r_{v,H}$ are the minimum van der Waal radii of the substituent X and hydrogen, respectively. However, difficulties arise if one attempts to use it for nonsymmetrical substituents. This parameter was found to be highly correlated with E_s for a large number of substituents (Eq. 2.28) [49].

$$E_s = -2.2062\ (\pm\ 0.86)\ \upsilon - 0.194\ (\pm\ 0.10)$$
$$n = 104,\ r = 0.978,\ s = 0.25 \tag{2.36}$$

Verloop's STERIMOL Parameters

The steric parameter were enriched by the definition of STERIMOL parameters L, B_1, B_2, B_3 and B_4 by Verloop et al. [72, 73], where L refers to the length of the substituent along the axis of its substitution to the parent skeleton and B_1 to B_4 are the width parameters orthogonal to L with angles of 90° to each other (Fig. 2.7). They are arranged in such a manner that B_1 has the smallest value and B_4 the largest one.

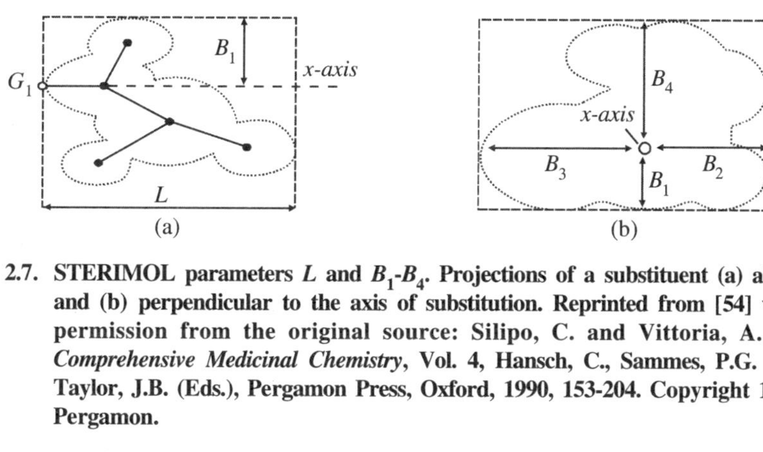

Fig. 2.7. STERIMOL parameters L and B_1-B_4. Projections of a substituent (a) along and (b) perpendicular to the axis of substitution. Reprinted from [54] with permission from the original source: Silipo, C. and Vittoria, A., In *Comprehensive Medicinal Chemistry*, Vol. 4, Hansch, C., Sammes, P.G. and Taylor, J.B. (Eds.), Pergamon Press, Oxford, 1990, 153-204. Copyright 1990 Pergamon.

These STERIMOL parameters were found to be useful in describing the intermolecular steric hindrance encountered in the interactions of the ligands with the biochemical receptors. However, their positive role in describing intermolecular interactions was also recognized. The other steric parameters discussed so far were largely developed to describe the intramolecular steric hindrance encountered in organic reactions in homogeneous solutions. Of the five STERIMOL parameters, B_1 was shown to have considerable collinearity with E_s ($r = 0.85$) [5]. For the calculation of these parameters, an algorithm was developed using standard bond angles, bond lengths, and reasonable conformations of substituents.

The use of all the five parameters, however, together with their squared terms sometimes might lead to false correlations. Because of this, Verloop reduced the four width parameters to only two: B_1 and B_5, referring only to the smallest and the largest widths, respectively [73] (Fig. 2.8). The angle between B_1 and B_5 was not fixed. Different possibilities can arise for

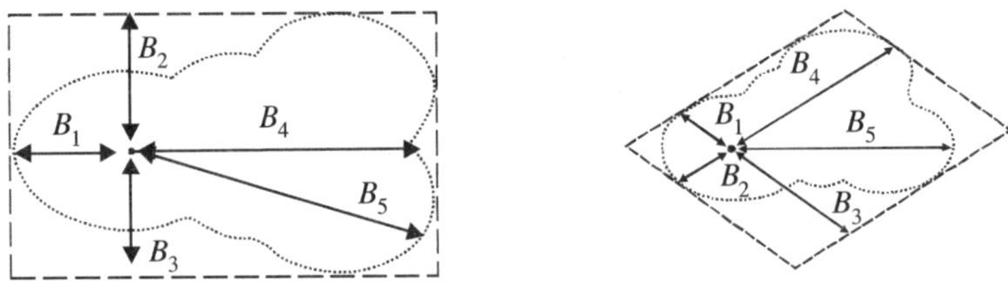

Fig. 2.8. Revised STERIMOL parameters L, B_1 and B_5 of OCH_3 group. B_1 is the minimum and B_5 the maximum width of the substituent. Reprinted from [54] with permission from the original source: Silipo, C. and Vittoria, A., In *Comprehensive Medicinal Chemistry*, Vol. 4, Hansch, C., Sammes, P.G. and Taylor, J.B. (Eds.), Pergamon Press, Oxford, 1990, 153-204. Copyright 1990 Pergamon.

the definition of B_5, depending on the selection of B_1. With unsymmetrical substituents, B_5 can be defined in a number of ways.

Molar Refractivity and Molar Volume

The molar refractivity (MR), which is related to the polarizability of the molecule α as shown by Eq. 2.37 and which, as a result, is most often treated as a polarizability parameter to describe the dispersion interaction between the ligands and the receptors, can also be used as a steric parameter since it is also related to the bulk of the molecule (the molar volume) as shown by Eq. 2.38, where n refers to the refractive index, MW is the molecular weight, and d is the density of the compound. In this equation (MW/d) defines the molar

$$\mathrm{MR} = \frac{4\pi N\alpha}{3} \quad (N \text{ being the Avagadro No.}) \tag{2.37}$$

$$\mathrm{MR} = [(n^2 - 1)/(n^2 + 2)]\ (\mathrm{MW}/d) \tag{2.38}$$

volume of the compound, which signifies the bulk of a molecule. If in QSAR equations MR surfaces with positive coefficient it describes the dispersion interaction and if it surfaces with negative coefficient it describes the steric effects. Also, studies with enzymes of known X-ray crystallographic structure have suggested that the bulk of substituent may assist in holding the ligand in place or cause a conformational change in receptor structure [77]. The molar refractivity can be calculated, using atomic contributions, in a way similar to that of log P [78].

However, as a bulk parameter the use of MR was preferred until only modern computational methods were not available for the calculation of the molar volume. Now a number of computational methods are available to calculate the molar volume, and the use of the molar volume in QSAR is now preferred to MR. Two different methods are usually used to calculate the volumes of the substituents or molecules [79, 80]. The volume calculated by Abraham and McGowan method [79] is referred to as *MG-Vol* and the one calculated as suggested by Pearlman [80] is referred to as *SA-Vol*. The values of these volumes and other steric parameters are listed in Table 2.4 for a large group of substituents [5]. For these substituents, the relationship among MR, MG-Vol, and SA-Vol are shown in the following correlation matrix.

Correlation matrix

	0.1 MR	MG-Vol	SA-Vol
0.1 MR	1.0	0.971	0.967
MG-Vol		1.0	0.997
SA-Vol			1.0

Table 2.4. Some important steric parameters. Reprinted with permission from [5]. Copyright 1995 American Chemical Society

No.	Substituent	E_s	MR[a]	B_1	B_5	L	MG-Vol	SA-Vol
1	H	0.00	0.10	1.00	1.00	2.06	0.022	1.48
2	F	– 0.46	0.10	1.35	1.35	2.65	0.040	7.05
3	CN	– 0.51	0.63	1.60	1.60	4.23	0.177	21.70
4	OH	– 0.55	0.28	1.35	1.93	2.74	0.081	10.42
5	OMe	– 0.55	0.79	1.35	3.07	3.98	0.221	27.24
6	NH_2	– 0.61	0.54	1.35	1.97	2.78	0.122	13.36
7	Cl	– 0.97	0.60	1.80	1.80	3.52	0.144	15.85
8	C_6H_5	– 1.01	2.54	1.71	3.11	6.28	0.630	72.20
9	NO_2	– 1.01	0.74	1.70	2.44	3.44	0.196	24.50
10	SH	– 1.07	0.89	1.70	2.33	3.47	0.185	20.29
11	SMe	– 1.07	1.38	1.70	3.26	4.30	0.326	37.50
12	CH(OH)Me	– 1.15	1.18	1.73	3.17	4.11	0.362	43.69
13	Br	– 1.16	0.89	1.95	1.95	3.82	0.197	23.51
14	CH_2OH	– 1.21	0.72	1.52	2.70	3.97	0.221	27.30
15	CH_3	– 1.24	0.57	1.52	2.04	2.87	0.163	18.78
16	Cy-C_4H_7	– 1.30	1.79	1.77	3.82	4.77	0.477	59.46
17	C_2H_5	– 1.31	1.03	1.52	3.17	4.11	0.304	35.35
18	I	– 1.40	1.39	2.15	2.15	4.23	0.280	31.31
19	CH_2OMe	– 1.43	1.20	1.52	3.40	4.78	0.362	44.40
20	CH_2F	– 1.48	0.54	1.52	2.61	3.30	0.180	22.62
21	CH_2Cl	– 1.48	1.05	1.52	3.46	3.89	0.285	32.78
22	$CH_2OC_2H_5$	– 1.61	1.67	1.52	4.45	6.01	0.503	61.11
23	CH_2Br	– 1.51	1.34	1.52	3.75	4.09	0.338	40.68
24	C_6H_{13}	– 1.54	2.89	1.52	5.96	8.22	0.867	101.91
25	$CH(OH)C_4H_9$	– 1.55	2.58	1.73	4.94	6.97	0.785	93.14
26	$(CH_2)_4COOH$	– 1.56	2.58	1.52	5.56	8.02	0.801	95.37
27	$CH_2OC_6H_5$	– 1.57	3.18	1.52	3.53	8.19	0.829	98.40
28	C_8H_{17}	– 1.57	3.81	1.52	7.39	10.27	1.149	135.20
29	$CH(OH)C_3H_7$	– 1.57	2.11	1.73	4.54	6.17	0.644	76.50
30	CH_2SMe	– 1.58	1.84	1.52	3.53	5.37	0.467	54.42

Contd.

Table 2.4. Continued

No.	Substituent	E_s	MR[a]	B_1	B_5	L	MG-Vol	SA-Vol
31	$CH_2CH_2CMe_3$	– 1.58	2.90	1.52	4.54	6.17	0.867	100.44
32	$CH(OH)C_2H_5$	– 1.58	1.65	1.73	3.49	4.92	0.503	59.86
33	$CH(OH)C_5H_{11}$	– 1.58	3.04	1.73	5.96	8.22	0.926	109.78
34	$(CH_2)_4OMe$	– 1.58	2.60	1.52	5.85	8.09	0.785	94.30
35	$CH_2CH_2CHMe_2$	– 1.59	2.43	1.52	4.54	6.17	0.726	84.59
36	C_3H_7	– 1.60	1.50	1.52	3.49	4.92	0.445	51.99
37	CH_2I	– 1.61	1.86	1.52	4.15	4.36	0.421	48.50
38	$CH_2C_6H_5$	– 1.61	3.00	1.52	6.02	4.62	0.771	89.34
39	$CH_2CH_2C_6H_5$	– 1.62	3.47	1.52	3.58	8.33	0.911	106.00
40	C_4H_9	– 1.63	1.96	1.52	4.54	6.17	0.585	68.63
41	$CH_2OC_3H_7$	– 1.63	2.14	1.52	4.87	6.82	0.644	77.75
42	$(CH_2)_3F$	– 1.64	1.48	1.52	4.07	5.35	0.462	55.86
43	C_5H_{11}	– 1.64	2.43	1.52	4.94	6.97	0.726	85.27
44	$(CH_2)_3COOH$	– 1.65	2.12	1.52	5.44	5.65	0.660	78.72
45	$CH_2OC_4H_9$	– 1.66	2.60	1.52	5.89	8.04	0.644	77.75
46	$(CH_2)_3OMe$	– 1.66	2.14	1.52	4.85	6.83	0.644	77.66
47	$(CH_2)_3CHMe_2$	– 1.67	2.89	1.52	5.59	6.97	0.867	101.24
48	$(CH_2)_3OC_2H_5$	– 1.69	2.60	1.52	5.87	8.06	0.785	94.36
49	$(CH_2)_3C_6H_5$	– 1.69	3.93	1.52	7.47	7.91	1.052	122.64
50	$CHMe_2$	– 1.71	1.50	1.90	3.17	4.11	0.445	51.33
51	$CH_2SC_2H_5$	– 1.71	2.41	1.52	4.60	6.65	0.608	71.06
52	$CH_2OCH_2CHMe_2$	– 1.71	2.60	1.52	5.50	6.82	0.785	94.18
53	$(CH_2)_3Cl$	– 1.72	1.98	1.52	4.91	5.94	0.567	66.05
54	$(CH_2)_3COOEt$	– 1.74	3.04	1.52	6.23	8.85	0.942	112.51
55	CH(Cl)Me	– 1.74	1.51	1.89	3.46	3.89	0.426	48.94
56	$(CH_2)_3CN$	– 1.74	1.94	1.52	5.57	6.04	0.599	71.57
57	Cy-C_5H_9	– 1.75	2.20	1.90	4.09	4.90	0.618	74.77
58	CH(OMe)Me	– 1.88	1.67	1.90	3.40	4.78	0.503	60.11
59	CHF_2	– 1.91	0.52	1.71	2.61	3.30	0.198	25.81
60	$CH(OC_2H_5)Me$	– 1.93	2.13	1.90	4.45	6.01	0.644	76.82
61	CH(Br)Me	– 1.93	1.80	1.91	3.75	4.09	0.479	56.51
62	C(OH)Me	– 1.95	1.64	2.40	3.17	4.11	0.503	59.63
63	CH_2COMe	– 1.99	1.51	1.52	4.39	4.54	0.460	54.16
64	C(CN)Me	– 2.00	1.94	2.77	4.12	4.11	0.599	69.99
65	CH_2CH_2OMe	– 2.01	1.67	1.52	4.49	5.55	0.503	61.01
66	Cy-C_6H_{11}	– 2.03	2.67	1.91	3.49	6.17	0.759	91.07
67	$CH_2SC_6H_5$	– 2.03	3.79	1.52	3.60	8.67	0.934	108.30
68	$CH(OH)CH_2OH$	– 2.05	1.35	1.73	3.38	4.79	0.421	52.17
69	CH_2CH_2COOEt	– 2.14	2.58	1.52	5.83	8.01	0.801	95.87
70	CH_2CH_2Cl	– 2.14	1.51	1.52	3.25	5.57	0.426	49.41
71	CH_2CH_2CN	– 2.14	1.48	1.52	3.17	6.28	0.458	54.93
72	$CH_2CH_2Me_2$	– 2.17	1.96	1.52	4.45	4.92	0.585	67.69
73	CH_2CN	– 2.18	1.01	1.52	4.12	3.99	0.317	38.27
74	CH_2CH_2COOH	– 2.21	1.65	1.52	3.31	5.97	0.519	62.08
75	CH_2-Cy-C_6H_{11}	– 2.22	3.13	1.52	5.42	6.09	0.900	107.16

Contd.

Table 2.4. Continued

No.	Substituent	E_s	MR[a]	B_1	B_5	L	MG-Vol	SA-Vol
76	CH_2CH_2Br	– 2.24	1.80	1.52	3.40	5.87	0.479	57.34
77	CH_2CH_2I	– 2.26	2.33	1.52	3.60	6.28	0.562	65.18
78	$CH_2CH(OH)Me$	– 2.31	1.65	1.52	3.78	4.92	0.503	60.37
79	CH(Me)Et	– 2.37	1.94	1.90	3.49	4.92	0.585	67.43
80	CF_3	– 2.40	0.50	1.99	2.61	3.30	0.216	29.30
81	$(CH_2)_3N(Me)_3^+$	– 2.59	-	1.52	5.49	6.88	0.989	-
82	CH(I)Me	– 2.60	2.32	1.91	4.15	4.36	0.562	115.85
83	CH_2NO_2	– 2.71	1.20	1.52	3.64	3.70	0.337	64.12
84	$CH(Me)SC_2H_5$	– 2.77	2.75	1.90	4.60	6.65	0.749	40.91
85	$C(Me)_3$	– 2.78	1.97	2.60	3.17	4.11	0.585	86.99
86	$CHCl_2$	– 2.78	1.53	1.88	3.46	3.89	0.408	67.20
87	$N(Me)_3^+$	– 2.84	-	2.57	3.11	4.02	0.566	46.40
88	$CH{=}CH_2$	– 2.84	1.10	1.60	3.09	4.29	0.261	65.83
89	CH=CHMe	– 2.87	1.56	1.60	3.13	4.29	0.402	29.27
90	SF_5	– 2.91	1.00	2.47	2.92	4.65	0.360	45.90
91	$CH_2C(Me)_3$	– 2.98	2.43	1.52	4.18	4.89	0.726	53.29
92	$CH(OH)Me_3$	– 2.98	1.64	2.40	3.17	4.11	0.503	83.27
93	$CH_2CH_2NH_3^+$	– 3.06	-	1.52	3.49	4.92	0.425	59.63
94	$CHMeCH_2C(Me)_3$	– 3.09	3.36	1.90	4.54	6.17	1.008	113.60
95	$CHBr_2$	– 3.10	1.68	1.92	3.75	4.09	0.513	61.76
96	$CH(Et)_2$	– 3.22	2.42	2.13	4.01	4.72	0.726	83.38
97	$CH_2CH_2N(Me)_3$	– 3.23	-	1.52	4.53	5.58	0.848	99.21
98	CCl_3	– 3.30	2.01	2.64	3.46	3.89	0.530	59.96
99	$CMe{=}CH_2$	– 3.32	1.56	1.73	3.11	4.29	0.402	45.56
100	$CH(C_3H_7)_2$	– 3.35	3.36	1.90	4.54	6.17	1.008	116.66
101	$Si(Me)_3$	– 3.36	2.50	2.76	3.48	4.09	0.690	81.26
102	$CH(SEt)_2$	– 3.55	4.01	1.90	5.81	6.65	1.053	122.68
103	CBr_3	– 3.67	2.88	2.86	3.75	4.09	0.688	82.59
104	$CH(CH_2CHMe_2)_2$	– 3.71	4.29	1.90	5.47	6.17	1.290	142.50
105	$C(Me)_2$-Cy-C_6H_{11}	– 3.73	4.08	2.60	5.83	6.17	1.181	137.42
106	$C(Me)_2CH_2C(Me)_3$	– 3.81	3.82	2.60	4.54	6.17	1.149	126.48
107	$CH_2N(Me)_3^+$	– 4.13	-	1.52	4.08	4.83	0.707	82.00
108	$CHMeC(Me)_3$	– 4.57	2.89	1.90	4.19	4.92	0.867	98.21
109	$C(Et)_3$	– 5.04	3.35	2.94	4.18	4.92	1.008	110.98
110	$C(Me)_2C(Me)_3$	– 5.14	3.36	2.60	4.45	4.92	1.008	113.02

[a]Scaled by 0.1

Compilation of different steric parameters are also given elsewhere [72, 73, 81, 82].

The bulk of the substituents or molecules can also be expressed by van der Waals volume (V_w) which is calculated as suggested by Moriguchi et al. [83]. Its applicability in QSAR has been nicely discussed by Gupta and Prabhakar [84].

Topological Indices

Topological indices are calculated from the 2D graph representation of the molecules [85-87]. They characterize the size, shape, and the degree of branching in molecules. An early example is the Wiener index [88] which simply represents the sum of the bond lengths D_{ij} of all bonds between the atoms (Eq. 2.39). In Eq. 2.39, n refers to the number of atoms present in a molecule and the factor 0.5 is just to avoid counting a bond twice over.

$$W = 0.5 \sum_{i=1}^{n} \sum_{j=1}^{n} D_{ij} \tag{2.39}$$

The best known and widely used topological indices are the molecular connectivity indices χ's first described by Randic [85] and subsequently developed by Kier and Hall [88]. They are calculated from the hydrogen-suppressed graph of the molecule and are of various orders. A simple first-order molecular connectivity index is defined as

$$^{1}\chi = \sum (\delta_i \, \delta_j)^{-1/2} \tag{2.40}$$

where δ is known as the degree of connectivity of an atom, which simply refers to the number of atoms (other than hydrogens) attached to a given atom i. For example, for an amino acid, cysteine ($HS\text{-}CH_2\text{-}CH(NH_2)COOH$), which will have the hydrogen-suppressed graph as

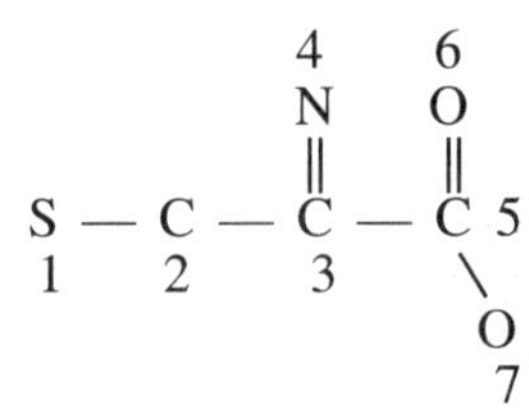

one will have the δ values as:

$\delta_1 = 1,\ \delta_2 = 2,\ \delta_3 = 3,\ \delta_4 = 1,\ \delta_5 = 3,\ \delta_6 = 1$ and $\delta_7 = 1$, and then

$$\begin{aligned} ^{1}\chi &= (\delta_1\delta_2)^{-1/2} + (\delta_2\delta_3)^{-1/2} + (\delta_3\delta_4)^{-1/2} + (\delta_3\delta_5)^{-1/2} + (\delta_5\delta_6)^{-1/2} + (\delta_5\delta_7)^{-1/2} \\ &= (1 \times 2)^{-1/2} + (2 \times 3)^{-1/2} + (3 \times 1)^{-1/2} + (3 \times 3)^{-1/2} + (3 \times 1)^{-1/2} \\ &\quad + (3 \times 1)^{-1/2} \\ &= 3.179 \end{aligned}$$

But this definition of χ completely ignored the unsaturation of the bonds. Therefore, Kier and Hall [89, 90] considered the valence of atoms to define δ (Eq. 2.41) and designated it as δ^v. In Eq. 2.41 Z_i^v is the number of valence electrons of atom i and h_i is the number of hydrogen atoms

$$\delta_i^v = Z_i^v - h_i \tag{2.41}$$

attached to it. But this definition of δ^v was applicable only upto the second row of atoms in the periodic table, i.e., upto only fluorine. For atoms beyond that the definition of δ^v was modified [90] to

$$\delta^v = (Z_i^v - h_i)/(Z_i - Z_i^v - 1) \quad (2.42)$$

where the additional term Z_i is the atomic number of atom i. Now a first-order valence molecular connectivity index ${}^1\chi^v$ takes the form

$${}^1\chi^v = \Sigma(\delta_i^v \, \delta_j^v)^{-1/2} \quad (2.43)$$

A zero-order connectivity index is also defined as

$${}^0\chi^v = \sum \left(\delta_i^v\right)^{-1/2} \quad (2.44)$$

where the summation extends over all the atoms.

High order χ indices involve summations over sequence of two, three, four, etc., bonds. But the most useful and capable of describing the ligand-receptor interactions has been only the first-order χ. Now, for the amino acid given above, the δ^v values would be

$$\delta_1^v = 0.55,\ \delta_2^v = 2,\ \delta_3^v = 4,\ \delta_4^v = 5,\ \delta_5^v = 4,\ \delta_6^v = 6,\ \delta_7^v = 5$$

and ${}^1\chi^v$ comes out to be 2.209.

Electrotopological State Indices

The electrotopological state index (E-state index) S_i of an atom i is a measure of availability of π and lone pair electrons on the atom and it is calculated as follows [91-95]:

To calculate S_i of an atom i, one first defines the intrinsic state I_i of that atom as

$$I_i = (\delta_i^v + 1)/\delta_i \quad (2.45)$$

where δ_i^v and δ_i are the valence and simple δ's, respectively, as already defined for connectivity indices. For higher quantum-level atoms (principal quantum number $N > 2$), the equation suggested is

$$I_i = [(2/N)^2 \, \delta_i^v + 1]/\delta_i \quad (2.46)$$

This equation can be treated as a general equation for the calculation of I_i since for $N = 2$, it reduces to Eq. 2.45.

This value of I_i, calculated using Eq. 2.45 or 2.46, however, does not take into account the effect of the field of other atoms present in a molecule. Therefore, a perturbation term ΔI_{ij} for I_i is defined as

$$\Delta I_{ij} = \sum_j (I_i - I_j)/n_{ij}^2 \quad (2.47)$$

where n_{ij} is the number of atoms in the path i and j including both atoms i to j. Then I_i plus the sum of all perturbations is taken to define the actual state of atom, which is termed as E-state index (S_i). Thus, S_i of an atom is expressed as

$$S_i = I_i + \sum_j \Delta I_{ij} \tag{2.48}$$

A sample calculation is illustrated below taking methyl acetate as an example [94].

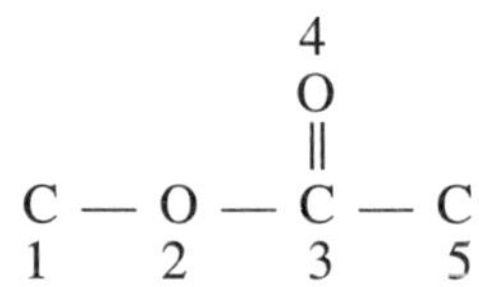

A hydrogen-suppressed graph of the molecule is drawn and atoms can be numbered in any order. For the order as shown here, the I-values are: $I_1 = 2$, $I_2 = 3.5$, $I_3 = 1.667$, $I_4 = 7.0$ and $I_5 = 2.0$ and consequently the values of ΔI_{ij} and $\sum_j \Delta I_{ij}$ are as shown in the following matrix.

Atom	ΔI_{ij}					$\sum_j \Delta I_{ij}$	S_i
	1	2	3	4	5		
1	0	– 0.375	0.037	– 0.313	0	– 0.651	1.35
2	0.375	0	0.458	– 0.389	0.16	0.611	4.11
3	– 0.037	– 0.458	0	– 1.333	– 0.83	– 1.911	– 0.25
4	0.313	0.389	1.333	0	0.556	2.591	9.59
5	0	– 0.167	0.083	– 0.556	0	– 6.40	1.36

The more electronegative atoms or groups have a richer content of lone pair electrons, giving rise to a higher calculated value of S. The higher the value of S, the greater the availability of π and lone pair electrons and their topological accessibility.

The term $(\delta^v - \delta)/N^2$ was referred to as the electronegativity of the atom by Kier and Hall [96]. A close correlation was found to exist between it and the Mulliken-Jaffe electronegativity of the atoms.

Here we have described some of the most widely used topological indices. Many other indices have also been formulated which can be found in software packages, e.g., Molconn-Z programme provides access to several hundred different descriptors [97].

However, the use of topological indices in QSAR studies has been criticized [81, 82, 98-100]. Notwithstanding the general recommendations on the selection of biologically meaningful parameters [101], the physicochemical meanings of the topological parameters are never clear. However, every new parameter and new approach is praised to be superior to the older ones and nobody bothers if some biological activities can fortuitously be explained by any combination of so many different parameters (chance correlations). The chance correlations may arise even from the uncritical combination of a large number of closely interrelated connectivity terms, including the normal and valence terms, higher order path and cluster ones, and their squares. Taylor [98] has been very critical of the use of molecular connectivity indices and writes that their use has had the unfortunate effect of diverting attention from the real work that needs doing. The use of topological parameters, in fact, throws no light on the mechanism of drug-receptor interactions.

References

[1] Randic, M., *J. Am. Chem. Soc.*, ***97*** (1975), 6609.

[2] Kier, L.B. and Hall, L.H., *Molecular Connectivity in Structure-Activity Analysis*, New York, Wiley (1986).

[3] Gupta, S.P., *Chem. Rev.*, ***87*** (1987), 1183.

[4] Hammett, L.P., *Chem. Rev.*, ***17*** (1935), 125.

[5] Hansch, C. and Leo, A., *Exploring QSAR: Fundamental and Applications in Chemistry and Biology*, American Chemical Society, Washington, D.C. (1995).

[6] Taft, R.W., Ehrenson, S., Lewis, I.C. and Glick, R.E., *J. Am. Chem. Soc.*, ***81*** (1959), 5352.

[7] Yukawa, Y., Tsuno, Y. and Sawada, M., *Bull. Chem. Soc. Japan*, ***45*** (1972), 1198.

[8] Sjöström, M. and Wold, S., *Chem. Script*, ***9*** (1976), 200.

[9] Topsom, R., *Prog. Phys. Org. Chem.*, ***12*** (1976), 1.

[10] Taft, R.W. and Lewis, I.C., *J. Am. Chem. Soc.*, ***80*** (1958), 2436; Taft, R.W. and Lewis, I.C., *J. Am. Chem. Soc.*, ***81*** (1959), 5343.

[11] Roberts, J.D. and Moreland, W.T., *J. Am. Chem. Soc.*, ***75*** (1953), 2163.

[12] Swain, C.G. and Lupton, E.C. Jr., *J. Am. Chem. Soc.*, ***90*** (1968), 4328.

[13] Hansch, C., Leo, A., Unger, S.H., Kim, K.H., Nikaitani, D. and Lien, E.J., *J. Med. Chem.*, ***16*** (1973), 1207.

[14] Holtz, H.D. and Stock, L.M., *J. Am. Chem. Soc.*, ***86*** (1964), 5188.

[15] Hansch, C., Leo, A. and Taft, R.W., *Chem. Rev.*, ***91*** (1991), 165.

[16] Ehrenson, S., Brownlee, R.T.C. and Taft, R.W., *Prog. Phys. Org. Chem.*, ***10*** (1973), 1.

[17] Taft, R.W., In *Steric Effects in Organic Chemistry*, M.S. Newman (Ed.), Wiley, New York (1956).

[18] Gupta, S.P., Singh, and Bindal, M.C., *Chem. Rev.*, ***83*** (1983), 633.

[19] Gupta, S.P., *Chem. Rev.*, ***87*** (1987), 1183.

[20] Gupta, S.P., *Chem. Rev.*, ***89*** (1989), 1765.

[21] Gupta, S.P., *Chem. Rev.*, ***91*** (1991), 1109.

[22] Gupta, S.P., *Chem. Rev.*, ***94*** (1994), 1507.

[23] Garg, R., Gupta, S.P., Gao, H., Babu, M.S., Hansch, C. and Debnath, A.K., *Chem. Rev.*, ***99*** (1999), 3525.

[24] Gupta, S.P., *Chem. Rev.*, ***107*** (2007), 3042.

[25] Gupta, S.P., *Quantum Biology*, New Age International (P) Ltd., New Delhi (1996).

[26] Karelson, M., Lobanov, U.S. and Katritzky, A.R., *Chem. Rev.*, ***96*** (1996), 1027.

[27] Streitwieser, A., *Molecular Orbital Theory for Organic Chemists*, John Wiley & Sons, New York (1961).

[28] Hoffman, R., *J. Chem. Phys.*, ***39*** (1963), 1937.

[29] Pople, J.A., Santry, D.P. and Segal, G.A., *J. Chem. Phys.*, ***43*** (1965), 5129.

[30] Pople, J.A. and Segal, J.A., *J. Chem. Phys.*, ***44*** (1966), 3289.

[31] Pople, J.A., Beveridge, D.L. and Dobosh, P.A., *J. Chem. Phys.*, ***47*** (1967), 2026.

[32] Bingham, R.C., Dewar, M.J.S. and Lo, D.H., *J. Am. Chem. Soc.*, ***97*** (1975), 1285.

[33] Dewar, M.J.S. and Thiel, W.J., *J. Am. Chem. Soc.*, ***99*** (1977), 4899.

[34] Dewar, M.J.S., Joebisch, E.G., Healy, E.F. and Stewart, J.J.P., *J. Am. Chem. Soc.*, ***107*** (1985), 3902.

[35] Stewart, J.J.P., *J. Comput. Chem.*, ***10*** (1989), 209.

[36] Gruber, C. and Buss, U., *Chemosphere*, ***19*** (1989), 1595.

[37] Sotomatsu, T., Murata, Y. and Fujita, T., *J. Comput. Chem.*, ***10*** (1989), 94.

[38] Gough, K.M., Belohorcova, K. and Kaiser, K.L.E., *Sci. Total Environ.*, ***142*** (1994), 179.

[39] De Benedetti, P.G., *J. Mol. Struct. (Theochem.)*, ***256*** (1992), 231.

[40] Fukui, K., Yonezawa, T. and Shingu, H., *J. Chem. Phys.*, ***20*** (1952), 722.

[41] Fukui, K., Yonezawa, T. and Nagata, C., *Bull. Chem. Soc. Jpn.*, ***27*** (1954), 423.

[42] Pullman, B., *Quantum Biochemistry*, Wiley-Interscience, New York (1963).

[43] Kier, L.B., *Molecular Orbital Theory in Drug Research*, Academic Press, New York, London (1971).

[44] Hansch, C., Maloney, P.P., Fujita, T. and Muir, R.M., *Nature (London)*, ***194*** (1962), 178.

[45] Hansch, C. and Fujita, T., *J. Am. Chem. Soc.*, ***86*** (1964), 1616.

[46] Fujita, T., Iwasa, J. and Hansch, C., *J. Am. Chem. Soc.*, ***86*** (1964), 5175.

[47] Collander, R., *Acta Chem. Scand.*, ***5*** (1951), 774; Collander, R., *Physiol. Plant*, ***7*** (1954), 420.

[48] Hansch, C., Muir, R.M., Fujita, T., Maloney, P.P., Geiger, F. and Streich, M., *J. Am. Chem. Soc.*, ***84*** (1963), 2817.

[49] Hansch, C. and Leo, A., *Substituent Constants for Correlation Analysis in Chemistry and Biology*, Wiley, New York (1979).

[50] Chou, J.T. and Jurs, P.C., *J. Chem. Inform. Comput. Sci.*, ***19*** (1979), 171: Pomona College Medicinal Chemistry Project, See Hansch, C., Björkroth, J.P. and Leo, A., *J. Pharm. Sci.*, ***76*** (1987), 663.

[51] Leo, A., *J. Chem. Rev.*, ***93*** (1993), 1281.

[52] Leo, A., Hansch, C. and Elkins, D., *Chem. Rev.*, ***71*** (1971), 525.

[53] Minick, D.J., Frenz, J.H., Patrick, M.A. and Brent, D.A., *J. Med. Chem.*, ***31*** (1988), 1923.

[54] Kubinyi, H., *QSAR: Hansch Analysis and Related Approaches*, VCH, Weiheim, New York (1993).

[55] Boyce, C.B.C. and Milborrow, B.V., *Nature (London)*, ***208*** (1965), 537.

[56] Tomlinson, E., *J. Chromatogr.*, ***113*** (1975), 1.

[57] Biagi, G.L., Recanatini, M., Barbaro, A.M., Guerra, M.C., Sapone, A., Borea, P.A. and Pietrogrande, M.C., In *QSAR: Rational Approaches to the Design of Bioactive Compounds, Pharmacochem. Libr.*, ***16*** Elsevier, Amsterdam (1991).

[58] Dross, K.P., Mannhold, R. and Rekker, R.F., *Quant. Struct.-Act. Relat.*, ***11*** (1992), 36.

[59] Mirrlees, M.S., Moulton, S.J., Murphy, C.T. and Taylor, P.J., *J. Med. Chem.*, ***19*** (1976), 615.

[60] Unger, S.H., Cook, J.R. and Hollenberg, J.S., *J. Pharm. Sci.*, ***67*** (1978), 1364.

[61] Unger, S.H. and Chiang, G.H., *J. Med. Chem.*, ***24*** (1981), 262.

[62] Lewis, S.J., Mirrlees, M.S. and Taylor, P.J., *Quant. Struct.-Act. Relat.*, ***2*** (1983), 100.

[63] Haky, J.E. and Young, A.M., *J. Liquid Chromatogor.*, ***7*** (1984), 6675.

[64] Smith, R.M. and Burr, C.M., *J. Chromatogr.*, ***475*** (1989), 75.

[65] Valko, K., Beran, C. and Reynolds, D., *Anal. Chem.*, ***69*** (1997), 2022.

[66] Valko, K., Du, C.M., Bevan, C., Reynolds, D.P. and Abraham, M.H., *Curr. Med. Chem.*, ***8*** (2001), 1137.

[67] Balaban, A.T., Chiriac, A., Motoc, I. and Simon, J., *Steric Fit in Quantitative Structure-Activity Relations*, *Lecture Notes in Chemistry 15*, Springer-Verlag, Berlin (1980).

[68] Blaney, J.M. and Hansch, C., In *Comprehensive Medicinal Chemistry, Vol. 4: Quantitative Drug Design*, Hansch, C., Sammes, P.G. and Taylor, J.B. (Eds.), Ramsden, C.A. (Series Ed.), Pergamon Press, Oxford (1990), 459.

[69] Taft, R.W. Jr., In *Steric Effects in Organic Chemistry*, Newman, M.S. (Ed.), Wiley, New York (1956), 556.

[70] Unger, S.H. and Hansch, C., *Prog. Phys. Org. Chem.*, ***12*** (1976), 91.

[71] Fujita, T., *Pure Appl. Chem.*, ***50*** (1978), 987.

[72] Verloop, A., Hoogenstraaten, W. and Tipker, J., In *Drug Design*, Vol. VII, Ariën, E.J. (Ed.), Academic Press, New York (1976), 165.

[73] Verloop, A., *The STERIMOL Approach to Drug Design*, Marcel Dekker, New York (1987).

[74] Hancock, C.K., Meyers, E.A. and Yager, B.J., *J. Am. Chem. Soc.*, ***83*** (1961), 4211.

[75] Kutter, E. and Hansch, C., *J. Med. Chem.*, ***12*** (1969), 647.

[76] Charton, M., In *Steric Effects in Drug Design*, Charton, M. and Motoc, I. (Eds.), Springer, Berlin (1983), 57.

[77] Hansch, C. and Klein, T., *Acc. Chem. Res.*, ***19*** (1986), 392.

[78] Leo, A. and Weininger, A., CMR 3 Reference Manual Available at *www.daylight.com/dayhtml/doc/cmr/cmrref.html*

[79] Abraham, M. and McGowan, J., *Chromatographia*, ***23*** (1987), 243.

[80] Pearlman, R., SAVOL, University of Texas, Austin, Texas, The Software Package is Distributed by Tripos.

[81] Van de Waterbeemed, H. and Testa, B., *Adv. Drug Res.*, ***16*** (1987), 85.

[82] Silipo, C. and Vittoria, A., In *Comprehensive Medicinal Chemistry, Vol. 4: Quantitative Drug Design*, Hansch, C., Sammes, P.G. and Taylor, J.B. (Eds.), Ramsden, C.A. (Series Ed.), Pergamon Press, Oxford (1990), 153.

[83] Moriguchi, I., Kanada, Y. and Komatsu, K., *Chem. Pharm. Bull.*, Tokyo, ***24*** (1976), 1799.

[84] Gupta, S.P. and Prabhakar, Y.S., *J. Scient. Indus. Res.*, ***44*** (1985), 189.

[85] Randic, M., *J. Am. Chem. Soc.*, ***97*** (1975), 6609.

[86] Randic, M., *J. Mol. Graph. Model.*, ***20*** (2001), 19.

[87] Lowell, H., Hall, L.H. and Kier, L.B., *J. Mol. Graph. Model.*, ***20*** (2001), 4.

[88] Kier, L.B. and Hall, L.H., *Molecular Connectivity in Chemistry and Drug Research*, Academic Press, New York (1976).

[89] Kier, L.B. and Hall, L.H., *J. Pharm. Sci.*, ***65*** (1976), 1806.

[90] Kier, L.B. and Hall, L.H., *Molecular Connectivity in Structure-Activity Analysis*, Wiley, New York (1986).

[91] Kier, L.B. and Hall, L.H., *Pharm. Res.*, ***1*** (1990), 801.

[92] Hall, L.H. and Kier, L.B., *J. Chem. Inf. Comput. Sci.*, ***31*** (1991), 76.

[93] Hall, L.H. and Kier, L.B., *Quant. Struct.-Act. Relat.*, ***10*** (1991), 43.

[94] Kier, L.B. and Hall, L.H., In *QSAR in Design of Bioactive Compounds*, Kuchar, M. (Ed.), *J.R. Prous Sci.*, Barcelona (1992), 23.

[95] Kier, L.B. and Hall, L.H., *Molecular Structure Description: The Electrotopological State*, Academic Press, San Diego (1999).

[96] Kier, L.B. and Hall, L.H., *J. Pharm. Sci.*, ***70*** (1981), 583.

[97] Mollconn-Z. edusoft, LC, PO Box 1811, Ashland, VA 23005, USA. Also see *www.eslc.vabiotech.com*

[98] Taylor, P.J., In *Comprehensive Medicinal Chemistry, Vol. 4: Quantitative Drug Design*, Hansch, C., Sammes, P.G. and Taylor, J.B. (Eds.), Ramsden, C.A. (Series Ed.), Pergamon Press, Oxford (1990), 241.

[99] Kubinyi, H., *Fortschr. Arzeimittelforch.* (*Prog. Drug Res.*), ***23*** (1979), 97.

[100] Lopez de Compadre, R.L., Compadre, C.M., Castillo, R., Dunn III, W.J., *Eur. J. Med. Chem.*, ***18*** (1983), 569.

[101] Unger, S.H. and Hansch, H., *J. Med. Chem.*, ***16*** (1973), 745.

3

Drug-Receptor Interactions

The ultimate effect of a drug is elicited when it interacts with a receptor. According to A.S.U. Burgen "Contemporary ideas of drug action and drug specificity are all based on the assumption that the initial process in drug action is the formation of a reversible complex between the drug and a cell component generally known as the drug receptor". It is generally accepted that a receptor is an elastic three-dimensional entity, consisting perhaps in most cases of protein constituent amino acids, whose stereochemical structure is often complementary to that of the drug and which sometimes, after undergoing conformational change, is able to interact with it, usually in its preferred conformation, in order to form a complex held together by various binding forces [1].

3.1 Types of Receptors

The integral proteins of the cell membranes that are embedded in the phospholipid bilayer of the membranes act as non-catalytic receptors. They typically function in the membrane environment; consequently their properties and mechanisms of action depend on the phospholipid milieu. Enzymes form a special class of receptors that have catalytic properties. Another class of receptors is DNA (deoxyribonucleic acid), the polynucleotide that carries the genetic information in cells.

The receptors may have different active sites with which a drug molecule can interact. The efficacy of a drug would depend on with how many sites of the receptors a drug molecule can interact.

For *noncatalytic receptors*, Ehrlich [2] had suggested a *side chain theory* according to which cells have side chains attached to them that contain specific groups capable of combining with a particular group of toxins. Ehrlich termed these side chains as receptors. Another facet of this hypothesis was that when toxins combined with the side chains, excess side chains were produced and released into the blood stream. In today's terminology, these excess side chains are called *antibodies*, which combine with toxins stoichiometrically.

Langley's studies on antagonistic effects of some alkaloid poisons on nicotine stimulation of skeletal muscle [3, 4] had led him to suggest that there was a receptive substance that received the stimulus and, by transmitting it, caused muscle contraction. Thus, a receptor was assumed to possess two fundamental characteristics: a *recognition capacity* for specific ligands and an *amplification component*, the ability of the ligand-receptor complex to initiate a biological response. This definition of receptor is completely fulfilled by ion channels: they selectively bind ions and mediate a response, namely, ion transport.

An ion channel is a transmembrane *pore* that is composed of three elements, viz. a *pore* responsible for the transit of the ion, one or more *gates* that open and close in response to stimuli, and *sensors* that receive the stimuli. A channel has three states: closed, open and activated, which are regulated by the conformational changes in the channel. The conformational mobility is an integral component of the function of the ion channels.

Enzymes (E) act as *catalytic receptors*. They are nothing but the proteins that catalyze the chemical reactions in biological systems. They interact with substrates (S) to form enzyme-substrate complexes (E-S), which then break into the enzymes and the products as expressed by the reaction

$$\mathrm{E} + \mathrm{S} \rightleftharpoons \mathrm{E} - \mathrm{S} \xrightarrow[k_{-1}]{k_1} \mathrm{E} + \mathrm{P} \tag{3.1}$$

A substrate can bind to only a small part of the enzyme known as *active site*. Enzymes are usually very large in size. The remaining portion of the enzymes outside the *active site* functions to hold the active site in the proper geometry for catalysis. Another function of the enzyme molecule outside the active site may be to channel the substrate into the active site. A large size of the enzyme is necessitated in order to have the atoms closely packed within the molecule so that the large binding energy may be involved when the substrate binds with the enzyme [5].

The most important feature of the enzyme-catalyzed reactions is the specificity – the specificity of the binding and the specificity of the reaction. The binding specificity refers to essentially the binding of only one substrate molecule with an enzyme to form an E-S complex, which then leads to the formation of the product. The reaction specificity refers to the reaction of other constituents of active site with a specific portion of the substrate, though there can be many more such identical portions at the substrate.

Many drugs function by inhibiting the activity of the enzymes. Such drugs, called enzyme inhibitors, can be of the following types.

(a) Competitive Inhibitors

These inhibitors compete with the substrate for the same site of the enzyme with which the substrate combines and binds and, thus, prevent the substrate from binding with the enzyme.

(b) Uncompetitive Inhibitors

These inhibitors do not compete with the substrate but combine with the enzyme-substrate complex, interacting with the enzyme at a site different from the one with which the substrate is combined. This combination of the inhibitors with the enzyme-substrate complex does not permit the complex to dissociate into the product. These types of inhibitors are also called *anticompetitive inhibitors.*

(c) Noncompetitive Inhibitors

These inhibitors combine with the enzyme and the enzyme-substrate complex with almost equal ease.

(d) Allosteric Inhibitors

It is assumed that certain enzymes that are usually oligomers, built up by subunits or protomers, contain at least two noninterpenetrating and stereo specifically different receptor sites – the *active site* and *allosteric site*. The first one binds to the substrate, triggering the biological activity. The second one can bind with substances having no structural similarity with the substrate, followed by a conformational change in the enzyme. This conformational change in the enzyme, which leads to a decrease in the affinity of the active site for the substrate and which is reversible, is called *allosteric transition*, and the enzyme capable of undergoing such transition is called *allosteric enzyme*. The ligands responsible for such a change and the modification in the properties of the active site are called *allosteric inhibitors* and the whole phenomenon is called *allosteric inhibition*. The site at which the allosteric inhibitors bind is called *allosteric site*. The name allosteric comes from the ability of the enzyme to change shape when exposed to effectors.

(e) Transition State Analog Inhibitors

It is well known that an enzyme accelerates the rate of biochemical reaction by stabilizing the transition state, leading to lowering of free energy of activation. At the transition state, the strongest interactions occur between the substrate and the active site of the enzyme, and this happens because of the change in the confirmation of the enzyme molecule. In some cases, however, there occurs straining or distortion of the substrate molecule towards the transition state. This is known as *catalysis-by-strain*. Some enzyme inhibitors owe their effectiveness to a resemblance to the strained structure of the substrates and this led to the postulate that the inhibitor molecules resembling the transition state species would be much more tightly bound to the enzyme than the substrate [6]. Such inhibitors are called *transition state analog inhibitors.*

All the aforementioned types of inhibitors are reversible inhibitors, where the enzyme-inhibitor complex (E-I) formation reaction is reversible, i.e.

$$\mathrm{E} + \mathrm{I} \underset{k_{-1}}{\overset{k}{\rightleftharpoons}} \mathrm{E} - \mathrm{I} \tag{3.2}$$

A reversible inhibitor is effective as long as a suitable concentration of the inhibitor is present to drive the equilibrium in reaction (3.2) to the right. Thus, a reversible inhibitor drug is effective only till the drug concentration is maintained at a high enough level to sustain the enzyme-inhibitor complex and that is why, because of the drug metabolism and excretion, repetitive administration of the drug is required.

There are also *irreversible inhibitors* where the enzyme substrate complex formed cannot dissociate. These inhibitors are also known as *active site-directed irreversible inhibitors* or *enzyme activators*. These inhibitors usually form covalent bonds with the active site of the enzymes and in their case it is not necessary to sustain their concentration in order to retain the enzyme-inhibitor interaction.

Other types of receptors that play important role in drug actions are *DNAs* – the polynucleotides that carry the genetic information in cells. The DNAs of the normal cells are very vital for human life but those in the abnormal cells can be dangerous. Since there are little differences between the normal and abnormal cell DNAs, a DNA-interactive drug that can be given to stop the growth of abnormal cells may be toxic to normal cells. Therefore, these drugs are used only for life threatening diseases such as cancers or virus infections.

The DNA-interactive drugs interact with DNAs either by *intercalation*, where they insert between the base pairs of the double helix of DNA, leading to the unwinding of the helix, or by *alkylation*, where they react covalently with DNA bases, or by *DNA strand breaking*, in which they generate reactive radicals that produce cleavage of the polypeptide strands [7].

3.2 Forces Involved in Drug-Receptor Interactions

In general, the bonds formed between a drug molecule and a receptor involve the noncovalent and nonionic interactions. The covalent bonds have energy values in the range of about 170-600 kJ mol^{-1}. As they are irreversible, they are not important for most therapeutically relevant drugs that form reversible drug-receptor complex. Only alkylating agents (some anticancer drugs) or active site-directed drugs (enzyme activators) can form the covalent bonds.

Ionic bonding (NaCl type) is also rare in drug-receptor interactions, but an electrostatic interaction, where oppositely charged portions of drug and receptor can be attracted to each other, is common. In protein receptor, at physiological pH (~ 7.4), basic groups such as amino acid side chains of arginine, lysine, and to some extent histidine are protonated and, thus, provide a cationic environment, and likewise acidic groups, such as carboxylic side chains of aspartic acid and glutamic acid, are deprotonated to produce anionic groups. These cationic and anionic moieties of proteins then can attract the anionic and cationic portions, respectively, of any drug molecule interacting with the proteins. This kind of interaction can be indicated in the QSAR study by the presence of any charge descriptor.

The most common interaction between the drugs and receptors are *van der Waals interactions* (which include ion-dipole, dipole-dipole, dipole-induced dipole, and induced dipole-induced dipole (dispersion) interactions), hydrogen bonding, and hydrophobic interaction.

In an *ion-dipole* interaction, a dipole (a molecule that has one end positively charged and the other end negatively charged) can interact with both a positive ion and a negative ion – its negative end will interact with positive ion and the positive end with a negative ion. A molecule having a negative site or positive site can always have, if properly oriented, such an interaction with a dipolar moiety, if present, of the receptor. It would be true the other way also, i.e., if the drug molecule is a polar molecule, it can interact with any positive or negative site present in the receptor. In QSAR, this type of interaction can be described by the charge on the atoms or the dipole moment of the drug molecules.

In *dipole-dipole* interaction a dipole can interact with another dipole, if the charges in the two dipoles are properly aligned. Since the charge of a dipole is less than that of an ion, a dipole-dipole interaction is weaker than an ion-dipole interaction. Figure 3.1 [8], in which an acetylcholine molecule has been shown to interact with a receptor, demonstrates both ion-dipole and dipole-dipole types of interaction.

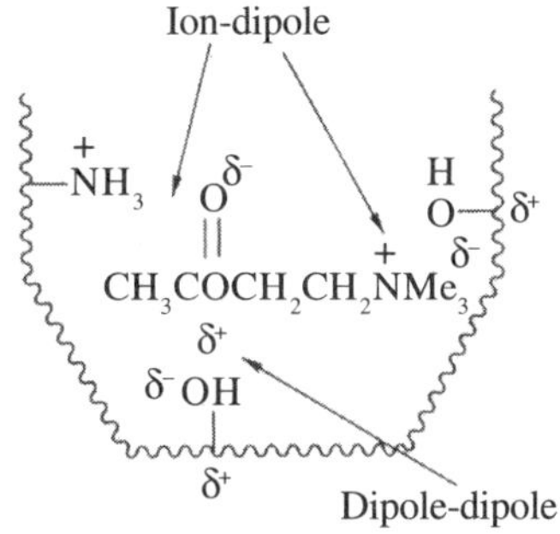

Fig. 3.1. Ion-dipole and dipole-dipole interactions exemplified by acetylcholine's interaction with its receptor. The wavy line represents the surface of the receptor. Reprinted with permission from Silverman [8]. Copyright 1992 Academic Press.

If there are two molecules in which one is polar and the other is non-polar and they are kept close to each other, the polar molecule may either attract the electrons of the non-polar molecules towards itself or repel them away from itself depending on whether its positive end or its negative end is facing towards the non-polar molecule. This attraction or repulsion of the electron induces the polarity in the non-polar molecule and the molecule is said to be an *induced dipole*. The interaction between this induced dipole and the permanent dipole is called *dipole-induced dipole interaction*. It is a very weak interaction but plays important role in drug-receptor interaction.

If both the interacting molecules are non-polar, then they undergo the *induced dipole-induced dipole interaction*, also called as *dispersion* or *London-van der Waals interaction*. In this type of interaction, atoms of a non-polar molecule may acquire temporarily a nonsymmetrical distribution of electrons, resulting into the generation of a temporary dipole. This induced polarity of a molecule may then induce the polarity in the other molecule in its vicinity and then both induced dipoles may undergo the interaction to be called *induced dipole-induced dipole interaction*. In drug receptor interaction, this kind of interaction is very common, but it is a very weak interaction and produces significant effect only when there is a close surface contact between the atoms of drug molecule and those of receptor. When there is molecular complementarity between the drug molecules and the receptor sites, numerous atomic interactions take place (each contributing about – 0.5 kcal mol^{-1} to the free energy change, ΔG), which can add upto a significant overall drug-receptor binding component. In QSAR, this interaction can be described by MR or volume-parameters.

The affinity of a drug to its binding site at the receptor is determined by the free energy change (ΔG) upon the binding. The spontaneous interaction between a drug and the receptor occurs with a decrease in the free energy, that is, ΔG is negative. The ΔG is related to the enthalpy change (ΔH) and the entropy change (ΔS) in the process as

$$\Delta G = \Delta H - T\Delta S \tag{3.3}$$

Another kind of important interaction is the *hydrogen bonding*. This occurs between two such molecules (or within a molecule) where hydrogen atom is bonded to a highly electronegative atom, such as N, O, F or S. Take for example –OH group. In this, the highly electronegative atom oxygen greatly attracts the bond pair of the electrons towards itself, acquiring a partial negative charge and leaving hydrogen with a partial positive charge. If there is another such group present in the same molecule, say $-NH_2$ (or OH itself), then in NH_2, nitrogen will have a partial negative charge and both the hydrogens will have a partial positive charge. If these two groups are very near to each other, as in ortho-hydroxyl amine (**1**), the hydrogen of $-NH_2$ can be attracted towards the oxygen of the –OH group forming an N—H---O bond. This is known as *hydrogen bonding*. If it occurs in the same molecule as in **1**, it is called *intramolecular hydrogen bonding* and if it occurs between two molecules (same or different), it is called *intermolecular hydrogen bonding* as in **2**.

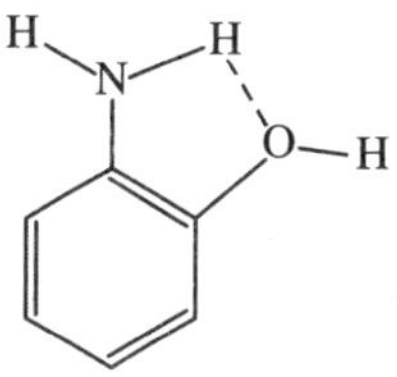

1

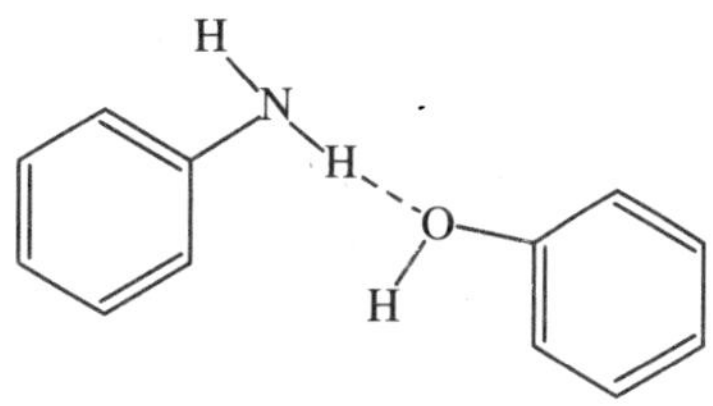

2

The best example of intramolecular hydrogen bonding is the helical structure of proteins and the best example of the intermolecular hydrogen bonding is the double-stranded DNA molecule. Hydrogen bonds are a type of dipole-dipole interaction occurring between a positively charged end ($H^{\delta+}$) of one group (X-H) and the negatively charge end (electronegative atom) of another group (Y-H). Many drug-receptor interactions involve this hydrogen bonding and in QSAR it can be described by introducing the hydrogen bond parameters. For this purpose we define hydrogen-bond donor (D_H) group and hydrogen-bond acceptor (A_H) group. In **1**, $-NH_2$ acts as a D_H group because it is donating the H-atom for hydrogen bonding and –OH acts as an A_H group because it is accepting the hydrogen. However, $-NH_2$ can also act as an A_H group and likewise –OH can also act as a D_H group as well, but there are certain groups which can act only as a D_H or an A_H group. For example, group like SH will act only as donor and groups like OCH_3, NO, CN, CO_2^-, 1-pyrryl, etc. will act only as acceptor. A value of 1 can be assigned to D_H as well as to A_H to account for hydrogen bonding in drug-receptor interaction [9]. Dearden and Ghafourian [10] have, however, reviewed many other attempts to parameterize the hydrogen bondings, but their use is limited.

Charge Transfer Interaction

It involves the transfer of some charge from an electron donor molecule or group to an electron acceptor molecule or group. This phenomenon leads to the formation of charge-transfer complex, that tantamounts to a molecular dipole-dipole interaction. The charge (electron) donation usually occurs from the molecules or groups that have π-electrons, such as alkenes, alkynes, and aromatic moieties or that contain moieties having nonbonded pairs of electrons, such as oxygen, nitrogen, or sulfur. This electron donation can be accepted by the groups that contain electron-deficient π-orbitals, such as alkenes, alkynes, and aromatic moieties having electron-withdrawing substituents, or weakly acidic protons. The potential energy of charge-transfer interaction is related to the difference between the ionization-potential of the donor and the electron affinity of the acceptor. In QSAR, this is accounted for by the electronic parameters such as energy of highest occupied molecular orbital (E_{HOMO}), energy of lowest unoccupied molecular orbital (E_{LUMO}), charge density (q), frontier electron density indices (f^E and f^N) and superdelocalizability indices (S^E and S^N).

Hydrophobic Interaction

It is the most popular drug-receptor interaction. Majority of drug effects have the partial or total dependence on the hydrophobic parameter log P. This interaction takes place between two nonpolar molecules or groups when present in an aqueous environment. If the nonpolar molecules are added to an aqueous medium, the water molecules in their immediate vicinity no longer move randomly, rather become more ordered. In fact, these nonpolar molecules form clathrates with water. But the second law of thermodynamics states that systems tend to maximize their entropy or degree of disorder. To follow this, the nonpolar molecules coalesce, freeing the maximum possible number of water molecules in their original disordered state. The thermodynamics of this process can be explained as follows.

Suppose two nonpolar molecules R_1 and R_2 are dissolved in water. These molecules will from clathrates as

$$R_1 + R_2 + 2n\ H_2O \longrightarrow R_1(H_2O)_n + R_2(H_2O)_n$$

Since the formation of clathrate is usually exothermic, the enthalpy change (ΔH) for this process can be negative. Further, since the water molecules have come to an ordered state, the entropy change (ΔS) will also be negative. But for the stability of clathrates, what is essential is that the free energy change ΔG of the reaction, which is related to ΔH and ΔS as

$$\Delta G = \Delta H - T\Delta S$$

be negative. Unfortunately, the decrease in entropy in the formation of clathrates is so significant that even at the room temperature the factor $T\Delta S$ becomes more negative than ΔH, giving ΔG a positive value. Therefore, clathrates try to dislodge the water molecules and undergo the following reaction.

$$R_1(H_2O)_n + R_2(H_2O)_n \longrightarrow R_1–R_2 + 2nH_2O$$

This reaction is endothermic, but the entropy change in it is so highly positive that the ΔG becomes negative and the reaction becomes spontaneous. Thus, R_1 and R_2 groups come closer to each other and are said to have undergone the hydrophobic interaction.

Hydrophobic interactions are the most important single factor providing the driving force for noncovalent interactions in aqueous medium, especially in the case of large hydrophobic areas. They are merely entropic interactions.

3.3 Drug-Receptor Theories

While according to Emil Fischer's lock-and-key theory, the fundamental requirement of a drug to effectively interact with the receptor is that its structure should be structurally complementary to the active site in the receptor, so that it fits in the latter exactly in the same manner as a key fits into a lock, theories have been proposed to explain the variation in the intensity of the pharmacological effect of a drug. Gaddum [11] and Clark [12] proposed the *occupancy theory* which states that the intensity of the pharmacological effect of a drug is directly proportional to the number of receptors it occupies. The response ceases when the drug-receptor complex dissociates. However, since not all agonists were observed to produce the maximal response, this theory does not rationalize the partial agonists.

To account for the partial agonists, a term coined by Stephenson [13], Stephenson [13] and Ariëns [14] defined the terms *affinity* and *intrinsic activity* to refer to the two stages of drug-receptor interactions proposed by Langley [3, 4] and discussed earlier. The *affinity* refers to the first stage where the drugs make a complex with the receptor and the *intrinsic activity* refers to the second stage when the biological effect is initiated. The term *intrinsic activity* was coined by Ariëns, but Stephenson called it *efficacy. Affinity* is then taken as a measure of the capacity of a drug to bind to the receptor and the *intrinsic activity* or *efficacy* (α) as a measure of the ability of the drug-receptor complex to initiate the response. Agonists bind tightly to a receptor (high affinity) but exhibit no activity (no efficacy). Potent agonists may have less affinity for their receptors than partial agonists and antagonists. The modified occupancy theory accounts for the existence of partial agonists and antagonists, but is unable to explain as to why two drugs that can occupy the same receptor can act differently, namely one as an agonist and the other as an antagonist.

As an alternative to the occupancy theory, a *rate theory* was proposed [15], according to which the activation of receptors is proportional to the total number of encounters of the drug with its receptor per unit time, meaning thereby that the pharmacological activity of a drug is a function of its rate of association with the receptor, and not the number of occupied receptors. For agonists, the rates of both association and dissociation would be fast (the latter faster than the former, but for antagonists the former would be fast and the latter would be slow). Partial agonists would have intermediate rates for both. At equilibrium the occupancy and rate theories are mathematically equivalent and like occupancy theory, the rate theory also does not explain as to why two drugs that can occupy the same receptor can act differently.

The most important theory for drug-receptor interaction was, however, proposed by Koshland [16]. Though it was originally proposed for substrate-enzyme interaction, it could apply to drug-receptor interactions as well. According to this theory, a drug molecule can induce a conformational change in the receptor, or itself can undergo a conformational change as the need may be. The receptor was suggested to be elastic, so that it could return to its original conformation after the drug was released. The conformational change in the receptor could be responsible for the initiation of the biological response. This theory was known as *induced-fit theory.*

According to *induced-fit theory*, an agonist would induce a conformational change and elicit a response, but an antagonist would bind without a conformational change. This theory corroborates the *rate theory.* A conformational change induced in the receptor by an agonist may be such that it binds the agonist less tightly and from which the agonist may dissociate more easily. If no conformational change is induced in the receptor by a drug, the drug-receptor complex will be stable and an antagonist will result. A partial agonist may cause a partial conformational change.

There are some other theories also for the drug-receptor interactions, such as macromolecular perturbation theory and activation-aggregation theory [8], but they are not as important as those mentioned above.

References

[1] Korolkovas, A., *Essentials of Molecular Pharmacology*, Wiley Interscience, USA (1970).

[2] Ehrlich, P., *Klin. Jahr.*, ***6*** (1897), 299.

[3] Langley, J.N., *J. Physiol. (London)*, ***33*** (1905), 374.

[4] Langley, J.N., *J. Physiol. (London)*, ***B78*** (1906), 170.

[5] Richards, F.M., *Annu. Rev. Biophys. Bioeng.*, ***6*** (1977), 151.

[6] Bernhard, S.A. and Orgel, L.E., *Science*, ***130*** (1959), 625.

[7] Gupta, S.P., *Chem. Rev.*, ***94*** (1994), 1507.

[8] Silverman, R.B., *The Organic Chemistry of Drug Design*, Academic Press, San Diego (1992), 57.

[9] Hansch, C. and Leo, A., *Substituent Constants for Correlation Analysis in Chemistry and Biology*, Wiley, New York (1979).

[10] Dearden, J.C. and Ghafourian, T., *J. Chem. Inf. Comput. Sci.*, ***39*** (1991), 231.

[11] Gaddum, J.H., *J. Physiol. (London)*, ***61*** (1926), 141.

[12] Clark, A.J., *J. Physiol. (London)*, ***61*** (1926), 530.

[13] Stephenson, R.P., *Br. J. Pharmacol. Chemother.*, ***11*** (1956), 379.

[14] Ariëns, E.J., *Arch. Intern. Pharmacodyn. Ther.*, ***99*** (1954), 32; van Rossum, J.M. and Ariëns, E.J., *Arch. Int. Pharmacodyn. Ther.*, ***136*** (1962), 385.

[15] Paton, W.D.M., *Proc. Royal Soc. London, Ser. B*, ***154*** (1961), 21.

[16] Koshland, D.E., Jr., *Proc. Nat. Acad. Sci. USA*, ***44*** (1958), 981; Koshland, D.E., Jr., *Biochem. Pharmacol.*, ***8*** (1961), 57; Koshland, D.E., Jr. and Neet, K.E., *Annu. Rev. Biochem.*, ***37*** (1968), 359.

4

Models for QSAR Analysis

Various mathematical models have been used to analyze the biological activities of drugs in relation to their structures and physicochemical properties. To name a few, we have Multiple Linear Regression Analysis, Free-Wilson Analysis, Discriminant Analysis, Principal Component Analysis, Factor Analysis, Partial Least Square Analysis, Adaptive Least Square Analysis, Pattern Recognition, Distance Geometry Approach, Cluster Analysis, Fibbinicci Search, Minimal Steric Difference, Minimal Topological Difference, Hypothetical Active Site Lattice, and Neural Network. These methods are basically for 2D QSAR analysis. For 3D QSAR, entirely different methodologies are adopted which altogether form a different chapter (Chapter 5).

4.1 Multiple Linear Regression Analysis

Of all the mathematical models named above, the most widely used model has been the Multiple Linear Regression (MLR) analysis. The regression analysis is a powerful tool for establishing a correlation between a dependent variable Y (say biological activity) and one or more independent variables, say X_1, X_2, X_3, etc. Now getting a correlation is based on the following assumptions and operations.

Suppose we relate Y with k independent variables $X_1, X_2, X_3, \ldots, X_k$ as

$$Y = b_0 + b_1 X_1 + b_2 X_2 + b_3 X_3 + \ldots + b_k X_k \qquad (4.1)$$

Then suppose there are n compounds with different Y-values, $Y_1, Y_2, Y_3, \ldots, Y_n$ and that for each compound there are different values of each independent variable $X_1, X_2, X_3, \ldots, X_k$ as explained in Table 4.1 in which a value X_{ij} refers to a value of jth variable for i^{th} compound. Now using Eq. 4.1 we can estimate the value of Y of an ith compound substituting the values of each dependent variable for it, i.e.

$$Y_i = b_0 + b_1 X_{i1} + b_2 X_{i2} + b_3 X_{i3} + \ldots + b_k X_{ik} \qquad (4.2)$$

Table 4.1. A model table with values of dependent and independent variables

Compound No.	X_1	X_2	X_3	...	X_k	Y
1	X_{11}	X_{12}	X_{13}	...	X_{1k}	Y_1
2	X_{21}	X_{22}	X_{23}	...	X_{2k}	Y_2
3	X_{31}	X_{32}	X_{33}	...	X_{3k}	Y_3
.	.	.	.	...	.	.
.	.	.	.	...	.	.
.	.	.	.	...	.	.
n	X_{n1}	X_{n2}	X_{n3}	...	X_{nk}	Y_k
Average	$\overline{X}_1$	$\overline{X}_2$	$\overline{X}_3$		$\overline{X}_k$	$\overline{Y}$

But this estimated value (we can denote it by $Y_{i,\text{cald}}$) may not be the exact observed value as given in Table 4.1 for this compound. Suppose the observed value (we can denote it by $Y_{i,\text{obs}}$) differs from $Y_{i,\text{cald}}$ by an amount ε_i, then

$$Y_{i,\text{obs}} = b_0 + b_1 X_{i1} + b_2 X_{i2} + b_3 X_{i3} + ... + b_k X_{ik} + \varepsilon_i \tag{4.3}$$

Our regression equation (Eq. 4.2), therefore, should be such that the difference between $Y_{i,\text{obs}}$ and $Y_{i,\text{cald}}$ should be as low as possible, i.e, ε_i should be minimum. Since ε_i can be both negative and positive, its square term is considered for minimization, which is given by

$$\begin{aligned}\varepsilon_i^2 &= (Y_{i,\text{obs}} - Y_{i,\text{cald}})^2 \\ &= (Y_{i,\text{obs}} - b_0 - b_1 X_{i1} - b_2 X_{i2} - b_3 X_{i3} - .... - b_k X_{ik})^2\end{aligned} \tag{4.4}$$

The minimization is actually done over the sum of ε_i^2, which can be given as

$$\sum_{i=1}^{n} \varepsilon_i^2 = \sum_{i=1}^{n}\left(Y_{i,\text{obs}} - b_0 - b_1 X_{i1} - b_2 X_{i2} - b_3 X_{i3} - .... - b_k X_{ik}\right)^2 \tag{4.5}$$

This sum of squares, which is the sum of the squares of the deviations of the observed values from the calculated ones, is known as unexplained variance (SS_Q). Thus, Eq. 4.5 will be written as

$$SS_Q = \sum_{i=1}^{n}\left(Y_{i,\text{obs}} - b_0 - b_1 X_{i1} - b_2 X_{i2} - b_3 X_{i3} - .... - b_k X_{ik}\right)^2 \tag{4.6}$$

Now this SS_Q is minimized by taking its partial derivative with respect to each adjustable parameter b_1 to b_k and putting each one equal to zero. This gives the so-called *reduced normal equations* as

$$b_1 a_{11} + b_2 a_{12} + ... + b_k a_{1k} = a_{1y}$$
$$b_1 a_{21} + b_2 a_{22} + ... + b_k a_{2k} = a_{2y}$$

$$b_1\, a_{31} + b_2\, a_{32} + ... + b_k\, a_{3k} = a_{3y}$$

$$\begin{matrix} . & . & .... \\ . & . & .... \end{matrix}$$

$$b_1\, a_{k1} + b_2\, a_{k2} + ... + b_k a_{kk} = a_{ky} \tag{4.7}$$

where $$a_{ii'} = \sum_{j=1}^{n} \left(X_{ji} - \bar{X}_i\right)\left(X_{ji'} - \bar{X}_{i'}\right) \quad (i,\ i' = 1 \rightarrow k)$$

$$a_{iy} = \sum_{j=1}^{n} \left(X_{ji} - \bar{X}_i\right)\left(Y_i - \bar{Y}\right) \tag{4.8}$$

The number of these reduced normal equations is always equal to the number of independent variables k and solving them we can find the values of b_1 to b_k. The b_0 (called the intercept of the regression) is given by

$$b_0 = \bar{Y} - \sum_{j=1}^{k} b_i\, \bar{X}_i \tag{4.9}$$

The best fitted regression equation for the sample data is then given by

$$Y = b_0 + b_1\, X_1 + b_2\, X_2 + ... + b_k X_k$$

or $$Y - \bar{Y} = b_1\left(X_1 - \bar{X}_1\right) + b_2\left(X_2 - \bar{X}_2\right) + ... + b_k\left(X_k - \bar{X}_k\right) \tag{4.10}$$

For solving these reduced normal equations, the simplest way is to take the matrix **A** given as

$$\mathbf{A} = \begin{bmatrix} a_{11} & a_{12} & a_{13} & . & . & . & . & a_{1k} \\ a_{21} & a_{22} & a_{23} & . & . & . & . & a_{2k} \\ a_{31} & a_{32} & a_{33} & . & . & . & . & a_{3k} \\ . & . & . & . & . & . & . & . \\ a_{k1} & a_{k2} & a_{k3} & . & . & . & . & a_{kk} \end{bmatrix} \tag{4.11}$$

and then find its inverse. Suppose its inverse is a matrix **C** as

$$\mathbf{A}^{-1} = \mathbf{C} \equiv \begin{bmatrix} c_{11} & c_{12} & c_{13} & . & . & . & . & c_{1k} \\ c_{21} & c_{22} & c_{23} & . & . & . & . & c_{2k} \\ c_{31} & c_{32} & c_{33} & . & . & . & . & c_{3k} \\ . & . & . & . & . & . & . & . \\ c_{k1} & c_{k2} & c_{k3} & . & . & . & . & c_{kk} \end{bmatrix} \tag{4.12}$$

then the values of b_i can be found as

$$b_i = c_{i1}\, a_{1y} + c_{i2}\, a_{2y} + c_{i3}\, a_{3y} + ... + c_{ik}\, a_{ky} \tag{4.13}$$

Once the regression equation (Eq. 4.10) is obtained, various statistical parameters are calculated to judge its significance. The most important parameters are *standard deviation s*, *correlation coefficient r* (for $k > 1$ it is called *multiple correlation coefficient*, which many authors prefer to express as R), *standard error of coefficients* SE_i or *95% confidence interval* for coefficients CI_i (both of these are written along with the coefficients b_i within the parentheses; while the values of SE_i are written without any plus or minus sign, the values of CI_i are written with ± sign), *t-test*, and *F-ratio*. These various statistical parameters are evaluated as follows:

$$\textit{Standard deviation}\quad s = \left[\sum_{i=1}^{n}\left(Y_{i,\mathrm{obs}} - Y_{i,\mathrm{cald}}\right)^2 \Big/ (n-k-1)\right]^{1/2} \tag{4.14}$$

$$\textit{Correlation coefficient}\quad r = \left(\frac{b_1\, a_{1y} + b_2\, a_{2y} + \ldots\ldots + b_k\, a_{ky}}{a_{yy}}\right)^{1/2} \tag{4.15}$$

$$a_{yy} = \sum_{i=1}^{n}\left(Y_i - \bar{Y}\right)^2$$

Standard error of a coefficient, $SE_i = s\,(c_{ii})^{1/2}$ $(i = 1 \text{ to } k)$ (4.16)

95% confidence interval of a coefficient, $CI_i = (SE_k) \times t_{n-k-1}\,(0.05)$ (4.17)

where $t_{n-k-1}(0.05)$ is the percentage point of the *t-distribution* for $(n - k - 1)$ degrees of freedom at 5% level. Some t-distribution values are given in Appendix I [1] and a model MLR analysis is given in Appendix II.

t-Test: The value of t for a given coefficient b_i is calculated as

$$t = \frac{|b_i|}{SE_i} \tag{4.18}$$

For b_i to be significant at a given level, its t-value should be greater than t-value at that level.

$$\textit{F-ratio}\quad F = \frac{r^2}{1-r^2}\,\frac{n-k-1}{k} \tag{4.19}$$

All the parameters defined above are a measure of the significance of the correlation obtained. The correlation coefficient r is a measure of quality of fit of the model. For a perfect correlation where the difference between Y_{cald} and Y_{obs} may be zero (standard deviation $s = 0$), r would be equal to 1, but this is an ideal situation. In reality r is less than 1, but for an appreciably good quality of model, r should be greater than 0.9. The higher is the value of r, the lower would be the value of s. Ideally, s should approach to zero, but in experimental situation, just like r, it is not so. However, the value of s should be as small as possible but it cannot be lower than the value of the standard deviation of the experimental data. The magnitude of s may be attributed to some experimental error in the data as well as imperfections in the biological model. A larger data set and a small number of variables generally lead to low value of s.

To rely on the high value of r and the low value of s of a regression model, we should also consider the F-value. The calculated value of F is compared with the corresponding standard statistical value given in the literature [1] (some values are represented in Appendix III). If the computed value is greater than the corresponding tabulated one, the regression model is said to be significant at a particular confidence level. Higher values of F impose greater confidence in the model. The standard statistical table provides values of F as a function of $(n - k - 1)$ and k.

The standard errors or 95% confidence intervals of the coefficients b_i's indicate the significance of the coefficients. The smaller their values than those of corresponding b_i's, the more significant are the b_i's.

4.1.1 Cross-Validation

Cross-validation is a statistical analysis that allows us to check the predictive ability of a regression model. It involves the removal of some of the data points from the data set, the derivation of a QSAR model using the remaining data points, and then the application of this model to predict the values of the removed data points. These predicted values then can be compared with observed ones. This operation can be repeated several times, removing the same number of different data points every time.

The simplest form of cross-validation is the leave-one-out (LOO) jackknife procedure, where a single data point is removed every time and a new QSAR is obtained with $(n - 1)$ data points. This process is repeated till each data point has been removed one-by-one and every time a new QSAR model has been derived. Thus, n new QSAR equations are obtained from which a cross-validated R^2 (written as r^2_{cv}, Q^2 or q^2) is calculated using the equation

$$Q^2 = 1 - \frac{\text{PRESS}}{\sum_{i=1}^{n}\left(Y_{i,\text{obs}} - \bar{Y}\right)^2} \tag{4.20}$$

where PRESS (Predictive Residual Sum of Squares) is defined as

$$\text{PRESS} = \sum_{i=1}^{n}\left(Y_{i,\text{obs}} - Y_{i,\text{pred}}\right)^2 \tag{4.21}$$

The value of $\overline{Y}$ in Eq. 4.20 strictly refers to the mean of the Y-values for the appropriate cross-validation group, rather than the mean for the entire data set, but the latter is often used for convenience.

If the value of Q^2 thus calculated is greater than 0.6, it indicates a good predictive ability of the model. The value of Q^2 is normally lower than the simple R^2 (square of regression coefficient) value of the model, but it is a true guide to the predictive ability. Thus, while R^2 measures goodness-of-fit, Q^2 measures goodness-of-prediction. Another parameter that is calculated to measure the goodness-of-fit is S_{PRESS}, which is defined as

$$S_{\text{PRESS}} = \left(\frac{\text{PRESS}}{n - k - 1} \right)^{1/2} \tag{4.22}$$

The lower the value of S_{PRESS} (< 0.4), the better the predictive ability of the model.

The simple leave-one-out method can be replaced by a more robust approach, in which the whole data set can be divided into four or five groups, each of which can be left out in turn to generate the Q^2 value. By repeating this procedure a large number of times (say 100 or more), selecting groups at random each time, a mean Q^2 can be derived. For a well behaved function there should not be much difference between R^2 and Q^2 values, nor should there be any large variation in the values of Q^2 obtained in each repetition.

4.1.2 Designing and Validating a Multiple Linear Regression Model

In order to provide a useful and predictive QSAR model, the following guidelines should be followed:

1. A general rule of thumb is that the number of data points for the dependent variable should be at least five times the number of independent variables used or to be used.
2. There should be a good spread in data set and so should be in the values of the descriptors.
3. Minimum number of compounds (outliers) should be excluded from the regression. Outliers, i.e., the compounds that cannot be explained by the model, constitute a serious problem in obtaining a good model. Most often they are omitted from the data set without assigning any reason, which is not a good practice. A careful inspection of the structure of outliers might provide a much deeper insight into the mechanism of drug-receptor interaction.
4. No two such descriptors should be used together which are mutually correlated. Of the two, the one which has better correlation with the data set should be selected. If there are number of variables mutually

correlated to each other, then the *principal component analysis* technique should be used, which derives a new set of variables that have, by definition, no correlation with each other. This technique is described later.

5. A forward- or a backward-stepping regression should be performed to decide which of the selected variables should be finally retained in the model. The forward-stepping regression just starts with one variable that is supposed to be the most crucial and then adds one-by-one other variables with a simultaneous check on their significance. The significance of a parameter is checked by the effect of its inclusion on the values of r, s and F and from its t-test or the value of 95% confidence interval of its regression coefficient. If a descriptor is not found to be significant from these yardsticks, it is ignored and the next descriptor is added. In the backward-stepping regression, first all the variables are included and then starting with the least significant one all those variables that appear to be statistically insignificant are removed. This procedure is found to be more convenient, because it tells in the starting itself which variables may not be useful.

For the validity of a QSAR model, all important criteria have already been discussed. In summary, we can say that a QSAR model can be accepted if the correlation coefficient r is around or larger than 0.9 for *in vitro* data and 0.8 for whole animal data, the standard deviation s is not much larger than the standard deviation of the biological data (normally around 0.3, which closely corresponds to the mean error of most biological data; this value may be considerably smaller for *in vitro* data), the t-values for all regression coefficients at a described level are larger than the corresponding tabulated values at that level or the 95% confidence interval for each regression coefficient is significantly less than the regression coefficient, and the F-value of the model is quite high as compared to its tabulated value at 95% level. Above all, a cross-validation check should be performed.

This multiple regression analysis, where biological data are correlated with different descriptors, is now called *Hansch Analysis*, and according to Hansch, a QSAR thus obtained neither provides the solution to all our problems, nor can it only be considered as an academic game; "*the great advantage of the QSAR-paradigm lies not in the extrapolations which can be made from known QSAR to fantastically potent new drugs, but in the less spectacular slow development of science in medicinal chemistry*" [2].

In most cases, QSAR do not directly contribute to the development of new drugs. However, they do increase our ability and performance in drug design and in the optimization of lead structures by providing more and more evidence of the importance of lipophilicity, dissociation, polarizability, electronic and hydrogen-bonding interactions and steric fit in drug action

[3]. In fact, as Kubinyi states [3], prediction is not the main goal of a QSAR analysis, rather QSARs provide certain other information which are much more often very important for the optimization of a lead structure, e.g., the general conclusion on the selectivity, optimum lipophilicity to pass blood-brain barrier, minimization of CNS effects, and the reduction of the toxic effects. The QSAR is also an important tool to decide when to initiate and when to stop a synthetic program [4, 5].

Kubinyi writes [3] "we have the ability to intuitively extract high level information from facts at different levels without being programmed like a computer". The QSARs cannot and will never substitute the creativity and intuition of an experienced medicinal chemist or biologist. But our logical reasoning is limited to one or two, at most three, dimension. QSAR aims at giving an objective interpretation of multidimensional results in medicinal chemistry and at deriving new hypothesis to an extent which is far beyond the intellectual capacity of the human mind. In drug design, theoretical chemistry, physical organic chemistry, QSAR studies, protein crystallography, and molecular modeling work hand in hand. They cannot predict drugs, but they lead to deeper insights, they generate new ideas, and they rationalize and shorten the way from lead structure to an active analog with the desired biological activity, selectivity, and pharmacokinetic properties – the new remedy for a certain disease.

Following are few examples of regression models to see what information we can extract from them.

Antibacterial Aminoacridines

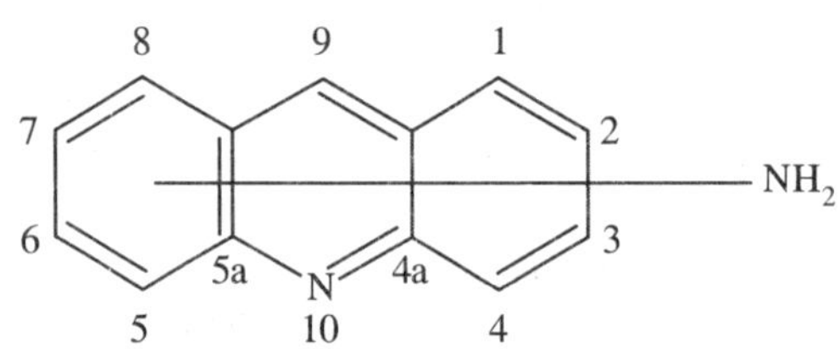

(1)

This is the simplest and the best example to explain the importance of QSAR to the beginners. For a set of 20 aminoacridines (**1**), their antibacterial activity was shown to be significantly correlated with the electronic density at the nitrogen (Eq. 4.23) [6]. Equation 4.23 is a simple linear equation

$$\log(1/C) = 21.48\, q_N - 22.478$$
$$n = 20,\ r = 0.896,\ s = 0.31,\ F_{1,18} = 73.30\ (8.28) \qquad (4.23)$$

which exhibits that the antibacterial activity of the compound will increase as the electronic density at the nitrogen will increase, which can be changed by changing the substituents and their positions in the molecule. Now the question is how the electronic density at the nitrogen affects the antibacterial activity. An answer to this question will constitute the mechanism of antibacterial action of aminoacridines. We may think that the nitrogen may either participate in some electrostatic interaction with a cationic site of the receptor or form a charge-transfer complex with the receptor. But, fortunately the mechanism of antibacterial activity is known and this correlation simply corroborates it.

The antibacterial activity of the acridines (B) has been found to be proportional to the fraction ionized as cations (BH^+) [7-9]. These cations can be formed by the attachment of protons to the nitrogen (N-10) of the acridine molecules. These cations are then supposed to compete with the hydrogen ions for a vitally important anionic group (A^-) on the bacterium [10]. The vital activity of this anionic group is supposed to be reduced by the formation of a feebly dissociated complex ABH with the cation BH^+. The more feebly the complex is dissociated into A^- and BH^+ ions, the greater would be the reduction in the vital activity of the anion. The dissociation of the complex is suppressed only when the cation BH^+ is present in excess and this will depend on the ability of the nitrogen to pick up the H^+. Obviously, this would be the function of the electronic density of the nitrogen, and thus ultimately the antibacterial activity is found to be correlated to q_N.

It is not only essential that cations should be formed, but it is also essential that once formed they should remain stable. These cations exhibit the resonance phenomenon as

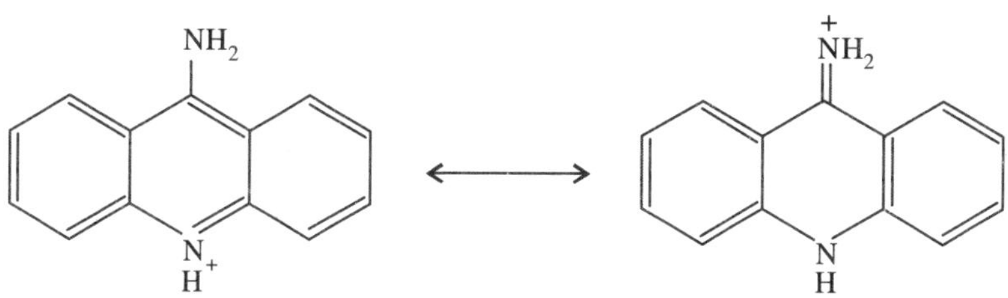

Therefore, their stability can be measured by the resonance energy or the difference in their π-bond energies $\Delta E_{\pi b}$, which can be calculated by simple HMO method. The activity was then found to be as significantly correlated with this $\Delta E_{\pi b}$ (Eq. 4.24) as with q_N.

$$\log(1/C) = 20.52\ \Delta E_{\pi b} - 48.08$$
$$n = 20,\ r = 0.897,\ s = 0.31,\ F_{1,18} = 74.74\ (8.28) \qquad (4.24)$$

In both Eqs. 4.23 and 4.24, the values given in the parentheses for F are the F-values at 99% level. The correlation of activity with q_N and $\Delta E_{\pi b}$ with equal significance is due to the existence of very high correlation between the two variables (Eq. 4.25). Both the parameters, therefore, cannot be used together in the same equation.

$$\Delta E_{\pi b} = 1.057 q_N + 1.235$$
$$n = 20,\ r = 0.998,\ s = 0.001,\ F_{1,18} = 6299\ (8.28) \qquad (4.25)$$

Cholecystokinin Antagonists

In order to understand the mechanism of interaction of cholecystokinin (CCK), a gastrointestinal peptide hormone closely related chemically to gastrin, a study was conducted on the interaction of some of its nonpeptidal antagonists. Receptors of CCK are found in both peripheral and central nervous systems. Those present in peripheral systems are termed as CCK-A receptors and those present in central nervous system as CCK-B. For a series of benzodiazepine derivatives (**2**), the binding activity of the

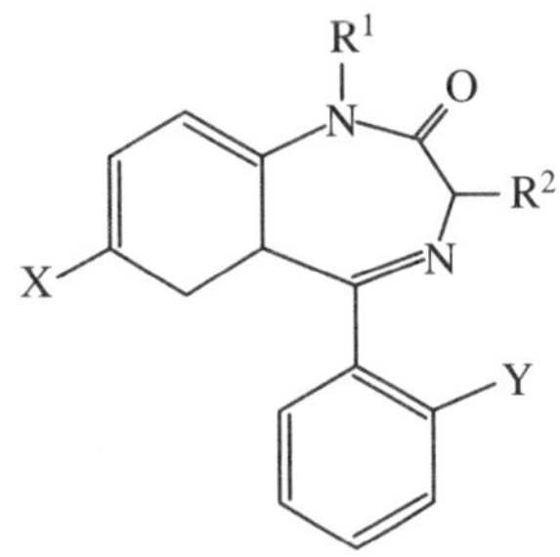

(2)

compounds with CCK-A was found to be correlated [11, 12] with log P and some indicator parameters as

$$\log(1/\mathrm{IC}_{50})_{\mathrm{CCK\text{-}A}} = 3.229\ (\pm\ 1.669)\ C\log P - 0.429\ (\pm\ 0.235)\ (C\log P)^2 + 0.723\ (\pm\ 0.491)\ I_{R1} + 1.268\ (\pm\ 0.552)\ I_{R2} - 1.121\ (\pm\ 0.817)\ I_X - 0.909\ (\pm\ 0.541)\ I_R + 0.932$$
$$n = 29,\ r = 0.926,\ s = 0.59,\ F_{6,22} = 22.16\ (3.76),\ (C\log P)_o = 3.76 \qquad (4.26)$$

In this equation, the figures written with ± sign within parentheses following the regression coefficients are the 95% confidence intervals. The Clog P stands for the calculated log P and (Clog $P)_o$ refers to the optimum value of Clog P. This is obtained by partially differentiating the activity term with respect to Clog P and then putting the derivative equal to zero. The terms I_{R1}, I_{R2}, I_X and I_R are the indicator variables, where the first three have been used with a value of 1 each for the substituents $R^1 = CH_3$, R^2 = an NHCO-containing group and X = Cl, respectively. For other substituents they are zero. The fourth indicator variable I_R was for the stereospecificity of R^2-substituent and had a value of 1 for R-configuration. Based on the role of these parameters and Clog P in Eq. 4.26, a model of interaction of benzodiazepine series with CCK-A was proposed as shown in Fig. 4.1. This model explains the positive effect of R^1-group (CH_3, the smallest in the series) due to its involvement with a small hydrophobic site and that of NHCO-containing group due to the involvement of NHCO moiety in double hydrogen bondings. The remaining part of this group, which was an aromatic moiety, could be assumed to have some polar interaction. The negative role of X-substituent (Cl) is explained due to its inability to have any interaction with a large hydrophobic site. The value of $(C\log P)_0 = 3.76$ indicates that molecules having reasonably high lipophilicity would be accommodated.

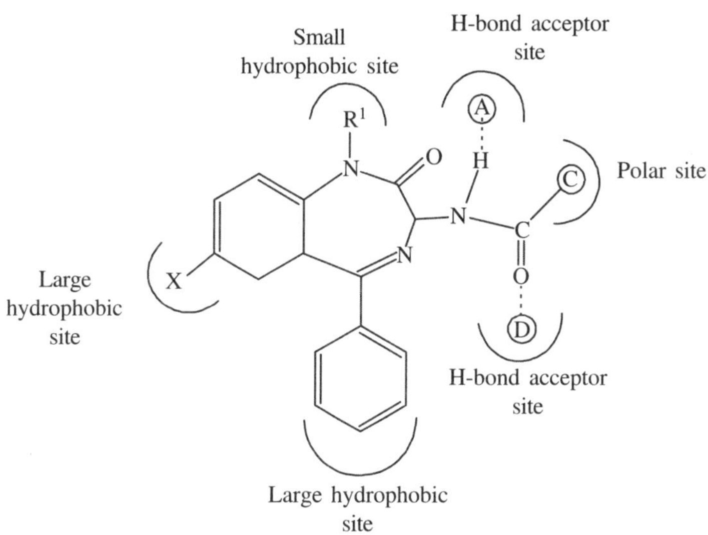

Fig. 4.1. A model of interaction of a benzodiazepine derivative with CCK-A receptor. Only the active sites of the receptors are shown. Reprinted with permission from [11]. Copyright 1990 Elsevier Science Ltd.

Inhibition of Dihydrofolate Reductase

For the dihydrofolate reductase inhibition activity of a very large series of dihydrotriazines (**3**), Fukunaga et al. [13] had derived a correlation as given by Eq. 4.27.

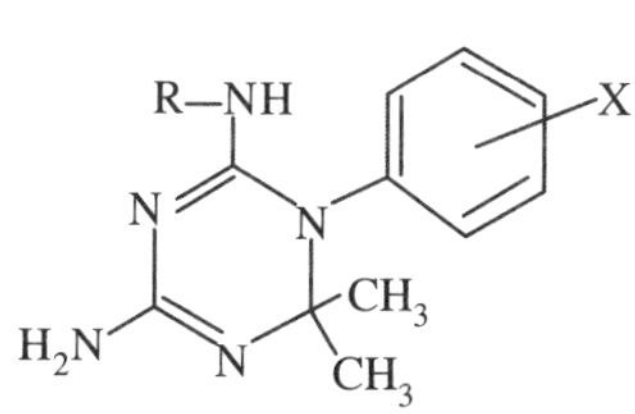

(3)

$$\log(1/C) = 0.680\ (\pm\ 0.12)\ \pi_3 - 0.118\ (\pm\ 0.03)\ \pi_3^2 + 0.230\ (\pm\ 0.07)\ MR_4 - 0.0243\ (\pm\ 0.009)\ MR_4^{\ 2} + 0.238\ (\pm\ 0.12)\ I_1 - 2.530\ (\pm\ 0.27)\ I_2 - 1.991\ (\pm\ 0.29)\ I_3 + 0.877\ (\pm\ 0.23)\ I_4 + 0.686\ (\pm\ 0.14)\ I_5 + 0.704\ (\pm\ 0.16)\ I_6 + 6.489\ (\pm\ 0.16)$$
$$n = 244,\ r = 0.923,\ s = 0.377,\ (\pi_3)_o = 2.9,\ (MR_4)_o = 4.7 \quad (4.27)$$

In this equation π_3 and MR_4 refer to hydrophobic and molar refractivity parameters for 3- and 4-substituents of the phenyl ring, respectively, and the indicator parameters were defined as follows:

I_1 = 1 for data points based on enzyme from Walker Tumor
= 0 for data points based on enzyme from *L* 1210 leukemia
I_2 = 1 for a substituent other than NH_2 at position 2 of the triazine ring
I_3 = 1 for rigid structure (C_6H_5 or $CONHC_6H_5$) attached at 3- or 4-position of phenyl ring
I_4 = 1 for congeners containing active leaving group like SO_2OAr
I_5 = 1 for a flexible bridge group like $(OCH_2)_n$ between heterocyclic and phenyl rings
I_6 = 1 for an amide bridge

Equation 4.27 thus led Fukunaga et al. [13] to propose an interaction model as shown in Fig. 4.2.

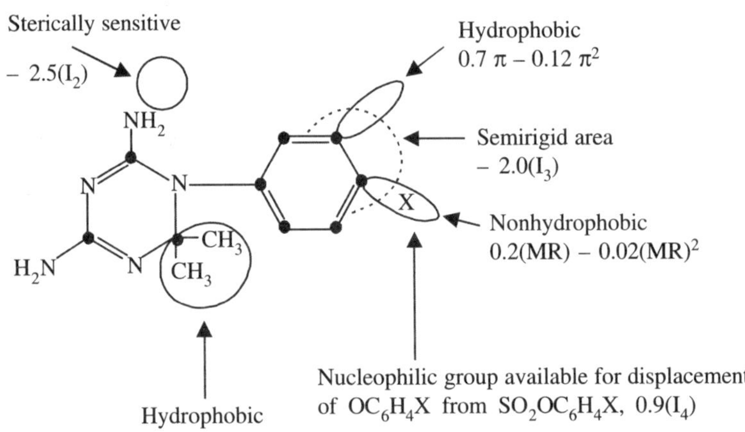

Fig. 4.2. A schematic representation of dihydrofolate reductase inhibition based on Eq. 4.27. Reprinted with permission from [13]. Copyright 1976 American Chemical Society.

4.2 Free-Wilson Analysis

This is an additive model by which we can find the contribution of each different substituent present at different positions of a common parent structure of a given series of drug molecules or of different structural features present in the series [14]. It also involves multiple regression analysis where each substituent acts as independent variable, with a value of 1 and 0; 1 for its presence and 0 for its absence at a given position. For each substituent an indicator parameter can also be used. Thus, if there are n substituents x_1, x_2, x_3, x_4,..., x_n, we can find the equation

$$Y = a + b_1 x_1 + b_2 x_2 + b_3 x_3 + ... + b_n x_n$$

or

$$y = a + b_1 I_1 + b_2 I_2 + b_3 I_3 + ... + b_n I_n \qquad (4.28)$$

Here the resulting regression coefficients b_i's of the variables will be the activity contributions of the corresponding substituents or structural features relative to H. Constant a refers to the activity associated with unsubstituted parent structure. As an example, Table 4.2 lists a series of antiadrenergic *meta*- and *para*-substituted N,N-dimethyl α-bromo-phenethylamines and

Table 4.2. Free-Wilson analysis of antiadrenergic activities of *meta*- and *para*-substituted N,N-dimethyl-α-bromo-phenethylamines [15]

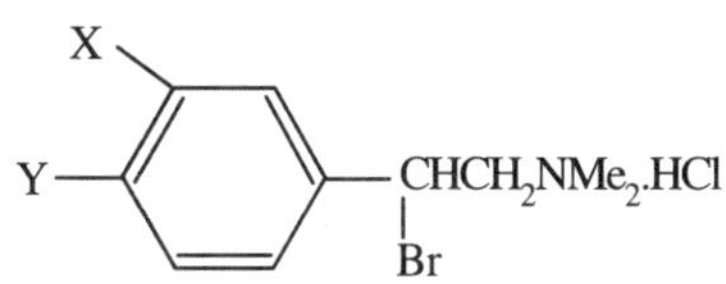

Meta	Para	*Meta*-substituents					*Para*-substituents					log(1/*C*)	log(1/*C*)
(X)	(Y)	F	Cl	Br	I	Me	F	Cl	Br	I	Me	(obs)	(calcd)
H	H											7.46	7.82
H	F						1					8.16	8.16
H	Cl							1				8.68	8.59
H	Br								1			8.89	8.84
H	I									1		9.25	9.25
H	Me										1	9.30	9.08
F	H	1										7.52	7.52
Cl	H		1									8.16	8.03
Br	H			1								8.30	8.26
I	H				1							8.40	8.40
Me	H					1						8.46	8.28
Cl	F		1				1					8.19	8.37
Br	F			1			1					8.57	8.60
Me	F					1	1					8.82	8.62
Cl	Cl		1					1				8.89	8.80
Br	Cl			1				1				8.92	9.02
Me	Cl					1		1				8.96	9.04
Cl	Br		1						1			9.00	9.05
Br	Br			1					1			9.35	9.28
Me	Br					1			1			9.22	9.30
Me	Me					1					1	9.30	9.53
Br	Me			1							1	9.52	9.51

explains how the values of different substituents can be assigned for Free-Wilson analysis [15]. The regression analysis of the data of Table 4.2 had revealed the following equation [15]:

$$\begin{aligned}\log(1/C) = {} & 7.821\ (\pm\ 0.27) - 0.301\ (\pm\ 0.50)\ [m\text{-F}] \\ & + 0.207\ (\pm\ 0.29)\ [m\text{-Cl}] + 0.434\ (\pm\ 0.27)\ [m\text{-Br}] \\ & + 0.579\ (\pm\ 0.50)\ [m\text{-I}] + 0.454\ (\pm\ 0.27)\ [m\text{-Me}] \\ & + 0.340\ (\pm\ 0.30)\ [p\text{-F}] + 0.768\ (\pm\ 0.30)\ [p\text{-Cl}] \\ & + 1.020\ (\pm\ 0.30)\ [p\text{-Br}] + 1.429\ (\pm\ 0.50)\ [p\text{-I}] \\ & + 1.256\ (\pm\ 0.33)\ [p\text{-Me}]\end{aligned}$$

$$n = 22,\ r = 0.969,\ s = 0.194,\ F = 16.99 \tag{4.29}$$

Equation 4.29 indicates the highest activity associated with I at both *meta* and *para* positions. Therefore, the most active compound in the series may be *m*, *p*-diiodo derivative with $\log(1/C) = 9.83$. With five substituents at *meta* position and same at *para* position, we can prepare 10 monosubstituted derivatives and 25 (5 × 5) disubstituted derivatives with a total of 35 compounds. Out of these 35 compounds, the compound that can have the highest activity is predicted by the Free-Wilson analysis. This is one of the important information that can be derived from this approach.

The confidence intervals in Eq. 4.29 do not have the same meaning as they have in Hansch analysis. While in Hansch analysis, they are a measure of the significance of the corresponding variables, here they only indicate whether the contributions of the substituents are significantly different or not from that of the reference substituent (*H*, for which contribution is taken equal to zero). Therefore, the terms appearing as "nonsignificant" are usually not eliminated in Free-Wilson analysis.

This kind of analysis, however, is not the actual Free-Wilson model. This is a modified version developed by Fujita and Ban [16]. Nowadays only this modified version is used and still with the name of Free-Wilson model, though one may also call it *Fujita-Ban* model

A key advantage of the Free-Wilson approach is that it does not require any physicochemical parameters, only the activity is needed. However, it is based on certain assumptions, such as: (1) each substituent in the series makes a constant contribution, (2) substituent contributions are additive, and (3) there are no interactions between the substituents nor between the substituents and the parent structure, which may not be valid for certain series of compounds or their activity.

The Free-Wilson model is easy to apply, but it has certain limitations such as:

(a) It can be applied to only linear additive SAR analysis and no nonlinear relationships can be obtained.
(b) It cannot predict activities for the molecules that may contain substituents other than listed in the data set.

(c) It cannot be applied where the structural variation is limited to only one position, otherwise meaningless group contributions would result, one for each compound.
(d) It can be meaningfully applied only when the number of substituents is fairly small as compared to the number of data points.

The Free-Wilson approach can be combined with Hansch approach. Equations 4.26 and 4.27 are in fact the results of the mixed approach.

4.3 Kubinyi's Bilinear Model

Biological activities have usually nonlinearship with lipophilicity which is described in Hansch analysis by adding the square term of log P in the regression. Thus, the relationship is expressed as

$$\log(1/C) = a \log P + b (\log P)^2 + c \tag{4.30}$$

which describes a parabolic correlation. Though this model of relationship is very simple and has general applicability over a wide range of lipophilicity, but if the biological activities are measured over a wide range of lipophilicity, the observed lipophilicity-activity relationship has linear ascending and descending sides, while the sides of theoretical parabola are more or less curved [17, 18].

A bilinear model was then developed by Kubinyi [17] which is of the form

$$\log(1/C) = a \log P - b \log(\beta P + 1) + c \tag{4.31}$$

This bilinear model was, in fact, a developed form of McFarland bilinear model [19]. McFarland model was based on the probability of the movement of drugs through membrane system. For a compound at an aqueous-lipid boundary, the probability that it will partition into a lipid phase $p_{0,1}$ would be proportional to k_1 (the rate constant for the transport from the aqueous phase to the lipid phase) and the probability of the reverse process $p_{1,0}$ would be proportional to k_2 (the rate constant for the reverse process), i.e.

$$p_{0,1} = \frac{k_1}{k_1 + k_2} \quad \text{and} \quad p_{1,0} = \frac{k_2}{k_1 + k_2} \tag{4.32}$$

Dividing both numerator and denominator of this equation by k_2 and substituting P for k_1/k_2, we can have

$$p_{0,1} = \frac{P}{P+1} \quad \text{and} \quad p_{1,0} = \frac{1}{P+1} \tag{4.33}$$

from which it follows that for a multi-component system, the probability of a drug molecule reaching the last compartment in a given time will be

$$p_{0,n} = (p_{0,1})\ (p_{1,2})\ \ldots\ldots\ (p_{n-1,n}) = \frac{P^{n/2}}{(P+1)^n} \tag{4.34}$$

Now, since the concentration of the drug in the receptor phase (last compartment) C_r would be proportional to $p_{0,n}$, we can write

$$C_r = \text{Constant} \times \frac{P^{n/2}}{(P+1)^n} \tag{4.35}$$

which will lead to

$$\log C_r = a \log P - 2a \log(P + 1) + c \tag{4.36}$$

With certain other considerations, Kubinyi modified this equation to take the form of Eq. 4.31 [17]. The terms *a, b* and *c* of this bilinear model, which are linear terms, are determined in the usual way by applying the multiple regression analysis, but the term β, which is a nonlinear term, is determined by an iterative procedure, using either a stepwise method or the Taylor theorem. A brief description of the former is given here; for the latter the readers may refer to Kubinyi and Kehrhahn [20].

In the stepwise procedure, the iteration starts with an arbitrary value of β, taken in terms of log β, since β is very small value of β should be such that − log β falls in the range of values of log P_0 (1.5-5.0 for most biological activities)), as Eq. 4.31 gives

$$P_0\ (\text{optimum } P) = \frac{a}{\beta(b-a)}\ (\text{only valid for } b > a)$$

which leads to

$$\log P_0 \approx -\log \beta$$

Then, for this value of β, each log P value given for a series of compounds is converted to log(βP + 1) value. Now, log P and log(βP + 1) are used as two independent variables in regression analysis to obtain the correlation of the type of Eq. 4.31. The resulting *r*, *s* and *F* values (*F* being the most sensitive parameter) are taken as a measure of the fit. This procedure is repeated taking a slightly higher value of β and a new regression model with new set of *r*, *s* and *F* values is obtained. The new *F*-value is compared with the preceding *F*-value. If it is larger than the preceding *F*-value, the procedure is again repeated with a new higher value of β. This repetition is performed till we get the optimum value of log β, leading to the highest value of F and that differs only slightly from the preceding one. Then the regression equation obtained with this value of β becomes the final correlation. Tables 4.3 and 4.4 are cited as examples of this type of

Table 4.3. Hemolytic activity of N-alkylpiperdines [20]

Alkyl group	log P	$\log(1/C_{obs})$	Bilinear Model[a]		Parabolic Model[b]	
			$\log(1/C_{cald})$	d	$\log(1/C_{cald})$	d
Heptyl	0.27	1.61	1.56	0.05	1.41	0.20
Octyl	0.77	1.97	2.04	– 0.07	2.07	– 0.10
Nonyl	1.27	2.55	2.52	0.03	2.65	– 0.10
Decyl	1.77	3.02	3.00	0.02	3.14	– 0.12
Undecyl	2.27	3.40	3.46	– 0.06	3.54	– 0.14
Dodecyl	2.77	3.92	3.88	0.04	3.85	0.07
Tridecyl	3.27	4.18	4.20	– 0.02	4.07	0.11
Tetradecyl	3.77	4.38	4.34	0.04	4.20	0.18
Pentadecyl	4.27	4.28	4.30	– 0.02	4.24	0.04
Hexadecyl	4.77	4.12	4.15	– 0.03	4.19	– 0.07
Heptadecyl	5.27	3.97	3.95	0.02	4.05	– 0.08

[a]Calculated from Eq. 4.37.
[b]Calculated from Eq. 4.38.

Table 4.4. log(βP + 1) values for different log β values [20]

log P	log(βP + 1) for log β =							
	– 4.50	– 4.00	– 3.50	– 3.00	– 3.60	– 3.55	– 3.56	– 3.54
0.27	0.0000	0.0001	0.0003	0.0008	0.0002	0.0002	0.0002	0.0002
0.77	0.0001	0.0003	0.0008	0.0025	0.0006	0.0007	0.0007	0.0007
1.27	0.0003	0.0008	0.0025	0.0080	0.0020	0.0023	0.0022	0.0023
1.77	0.0008	0.0025	0.0080	0.0248	0.0064	0.0071	0.0070	0.0073
2.27	0.0025	0.0080	0.0248	0.0742	0.0199	0.0222	0.0217	0.0227
2.77	0.0080	0.0248	0.0742	0.2011	0.0599	0.0667	0.0653	0.0681
3.27	0.0248	0.0742	0.2011	0.4567	0.1666	0.1832	0.1798	0.1867
3.77	0.0742	0.2011	0.4567	0.8381	0.3943	0.4248	0.4186	0.4311
4.27	0.2011	0.4567	0.8381	1.2927	0.7541	0.7957	0.7874	0.8042
4.77	0.4567	0.8381	1.2927	1.7773	1.1984	1.2454	1.2360	1.2548
5.27	0.8381	1.2927	1.7773	2.2723	1.6792	1.7282	1.7184	1.7380

calculation that revealed the regression model as given by Eq. 4.37. Equation 4.38 is the Hansch parabolic model, which is given for comparison. As obvious, the bilinear model represents a much better fit than Hansch model

$$\log(1/C) = 0.963\ (\pm\ 0.04) \log P - 1.406\ (\pm\ 0.12) \log(\beta P + 1) \\ + 1.304\ (\pm\ 0.09)$$

$$n = 11,\ r = 0.999,\ s = 0.050,\ F = 1268.80 \tag{4.37}$$

$$\log(1/C) = 1.521\ (\pm\ 0.25)\ \log P - 0.179\ (\pm\ 0.04)\ (\log P)^2 + 1.009\ (\pm\ 0.30)$$
$$n = 11,\ r = 0.992,\ s = 0.142,\ F = 234.84 \tag{4.38}$$

Sometimes, a different formulation of bilinear model (e.g. Eq. 4.39a) is used if the physicochemical parameter is already in the logarithmic scale, but the model of the type as expressed by Eq. 4.39b, often seen in the literature, should not be preferred.

$$\log(1/C) = a\ \pi - b\ \log(\beta \cdot 10^{\pi} + 1) + c \tag{4.39a}$$

$$\log(1/C) = a\ \log P - b\ \log(\beta \cdot 10^{\log P} + 1) + c \tag{4.39b}$$

In Eq. 4.39b, the term $10^{\log P}$ is equivalent to P.

4.4 Principal Component Analysis

The principal component analysis (PCA) is a method which is used to reduce the number of descriptors (dimensionality) of a data set when there are significant correlations between some or all of the descriptors. The PCA provides a new set of variables, called *principal components*, which are simply the linear combinations of original descriptors. The principal components have some special properties. They are much more convenient for graphical data display and analysis. It is often found that much of the variations in the data set can be explained by a small number of these principal components.

The principal components are calculated using standard matrix techniques. The first step is to calculate the variance-covariance matrix. If there are n compounds with p variables, then the data set can be expressed as a matrix $\mathbf{A}$ of $n \times p$ dimension (n rows and p columns). A multiplication of this matrix by its transpose matrix $\mathbf{A}^{\mathrm{T}}$ leads to the variance-covariance matrix $\mathbf{B}$ of $n \times n$ dimension

$$\mathbf{B} = \mathbf{A}\mathbf{A}^{\mathrm{T}} \tag{4.40}$$

The matrix $\mathbf{B}$ is then diagonalized, generating the eigenvalue and eigenvector matrices (as we do in HMO calculation). The first principal component (PC_1) then corresponds to the largest eigenvalue and the second principal component (PC_2) to the second largest eigenvalue, and so on. If the eigenvalues are labeled λ_i, then the ith principal component PC_i would account for a proportion of the total variance in the data set equal to $\lambda_i / \sum_{j=1} \lambda_j$ and the fraction f of the total variance that can be accounted for by m principal components will be given by

$$f = \sum_{i=1}^{m} \lambda_i / \sum_{j=1} \lambda_j \tag{4.41}$$

The number of principal components that can be calculated is equal to the smaller of the number of data points (molecules) or the number of variables (descriptors) in the original data set. All principal components are orthogonal to each other. Although, in order to account for whole of the variance in the data, we may include all the *PC*'s obtained, inclusion of only a first few that may account for a significant proportion of the variance would be sufficient. As a widely applied rule of thumb, it is common to consider as meaningful only those principal components which have eigenvalues greater than 1.

If the eigenvector matrix is represented by **C**, then a principal component will be given by

$$PC_i = \sum_{j=1}^{p} c_{ij}\, x_j \tag{4.42}$$

The first principal component is defined as the vector of weighting coefficient c_{ij} which maximizes the variance subject to the restriction that sum of the squares for the c_{ij} equals a constant, which conventionally has been taken equal to 1.

As an example of principal component analysis, Table 4.5 gives some descriptors of a set of amino acids studied by El Tayar et al. [21]. The descriptors are [21, 22]:

LCE and LCF: two lipophilicity constants of amino acid side chains
FET: free energy of transfer of amino acid side chains from organic solvent into water
POL: a polarity parameter
VOL: molecular volume of the amino acid
ASA: solvent-accessible surface area of the amino acid

Table 4.6 shows the correlations among these descriptors. As obvious from the table, many of them are mutually well correlated. A principal component analysis of the data was, therefore, performed and the resulting first three components out of a total of six were as follows. The other three were not so significant.

$$\begin{aligned} PC_1 &= 0.514\ \text{LCE} + 0.506\ \text{LCF} - 0.489\ \text{FET} + 0.371\ \text{POL} \\ &\quad + 0.202\ \text{VOL} + 0.248\ \text{ASA} \\ &\quad \lambda_1 = 74.84,\ v = 62\% \end{aligned} \tag{4.43}$$

$$\begin{aligned} PC_2 &= -\,0.013\ \text{LCE} - 0.076\ \text{LCF} + 0.108\ \text{FET} - 0.477\ \text{POL} \\ &\quad + 0.638\ \text{VOL} + 0.590\ \text{ASA} \\ &\quad \lambda_2 = 40.06,\ v = 33\% \end{aligned} \tag{4.44}$$

Table 4.5. Descriptors of amino acids and amino acid side chains [21, 22]

Name	LCE	LCF	FET	POL	VOL	ASA
Ala	0.23	0.31	– 0.55	– 0.02	82.20	254.20
Arg	– 0.79	– 1.01	2.00	– 2.56	163.00	363.40
Asn	– 0.48	– 0.60	0.51	– 1.24	112.30	303.60
Asp	– 0.61	– 0.77	1.20	– 1.08	103.70	287.90
Cys	0.45	1.54	– 1.40	– 0.11	99.10	282.90
Gln	– 0.11	– 0.22	0.29	– 1.19	127.50	335.00
Glu	– 0.51	– 0.64	0.76	– 1.43	120.50	311.60
Gly	0.00	0.00	0.00	0.03	65.00	224.90
His	0.15	0.13	– 0.25	– 1.06	140.60	337.20
Ile	1.20	1.80	– 2.10	0.04	131.70	322.60
Leu	1.28	1.70	– 2.00	0.12	131.50	324.00
Lys	– 0.77	– 0.99	0.78	– 2.26	144.30	336.60
Met	0.90	1.23	– 1.60	– 0.33	132.30	336.30
Phe	1.56	1.79	– 2.60	– 0.05	155.80	366.10
Pro	0.38	0.49	– 1.50	– 0.31	106.70	288.50
Ser	0.00	– 0.04	0.09	– 0.40	88.50	266.70
Thr	0.17	0.26	– 0.58	– 0.53	105.30	283.90
Trp	1.85	2.25	– 2.70	– 0.31	185.90	401.80
Tyr	0.89	0.96	– 1.70	– 0.84	162.70	377.80
Val	0.71	1.22	– 1.60	– 0.13	115.60	295.10

Table 4.6. Correlation matrix for amino acid data [22]

Name	LCE	LCF	FET	POL	VOL	ASA
LCE	1.00	0.97	– 0.93	0.74	0.37	0.46
LCF	0.97	1.00	– 0.92	0.77	0.28	0.38
FET	– 0.93	– 0.92	1.00	– 0.74	– 0.26	– 0.28
POL	0.74	0.77	– 0.74	1.00	– 0.35	– 0.18
VOL	0.37	0.28	– 0.26	– 0.35	1.00	0.89
ASA	0.46	0.38	– 0.28	– 0.18	0.89	1.00

$$\begin{aligned} PC_3 &= 0.081\ \text{LCE} + 0.074\ \text{LCF} + 0.597\ \text{FET} + 0.373\ \text{POL} \\ &\quad - 0.365\ \text{VOL} + 0.600\ \text{ASA} \\ &\quad \lambda_3 = 3.47,\ v = 2\% \end{aligned} \tag{4.45}$$

In these equations, v refers to the variance explained by the PC's. The first two components together account for 95% of the variance.

The relative contribution of each descriptor to a principal component can be assessed by their weighting coefficients. Thus, PC_1 is shown to have reasonably significant contributions from all six descriptors, while PC_2 has the significant contribution only from POL, VOL and ASA. To calculate the fraction of contribution, the square term of the weighting coefficient is taken and it can be verified that the sum of the square of the weighting coefficients of a principal component is equal to 1, i.e.

$$\sum_{j=1}^{p} c_{ij}^{2} = 1$$

Figure 4.3 shows a scores plot showing the distribution of amino acids in the first two components. This shows that similar amino acids are grouped roughly together: the charged and polar amino acids (e.g., Arg, Lys, Glu, Asp) in one region, the small hydrophobic amino acids (e.g., Ala, Pro, Val) in another region, and aromatic amino acids (e.g., Phe, Trp) in a third region,

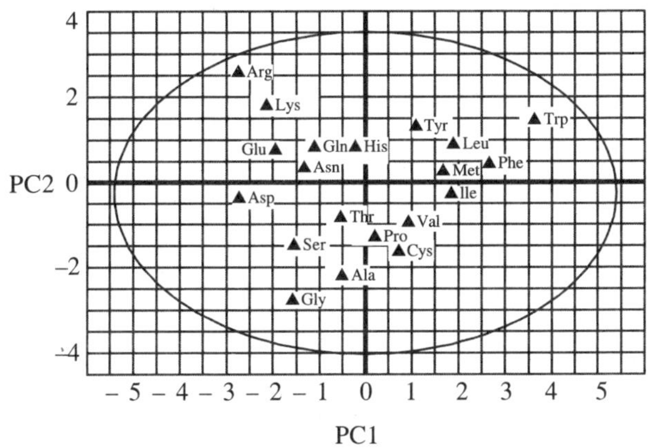

Fig. 4.3. Scores plot showing distribution of amino acids in the first two principal components. Reprinted with permission from [22]. Copyright 2003 Kluwer Academic Publishers.

4.5 Principal Component Regression (PCR)

After the principal components are obtained for a set of descriptors, they can be used as variables in the multiple regression analysis to correlate the biological activity y as

$$y = a_1\ PC_1 + a_2\ PC_2 + a_3\ PC_3 + ... + c \tag{4.46}$$

In this correlation, it is however not necessary that the most significant principal component will be a significant variable, because the principal components are selected according to their ability to explain the variance in the independent variables and not to explain the variation in the dependent variable. However, more often than not, the first few (usually two) principal components are found to account for the maximum in the variation of the dependent variable. Usually, after first two principal components, if an extra term is added in the QSAR, the regression coefficients do not change. It is simply because of their orthogonality, but they can add to the proportion of the variance already explained in the dependent variable by the terms already used. The PCR, however, is unable to point out which of the molecular properties are actually controlling the variation in the dependent variable. This is in fact a drawback of the PCR.

4.6 Partial Least Squares

The partial least squares (PLS) method, also known as *projection to latent structures technique*, is very much similar to PCR, in which the quantities calculated to explain the variation in the dependent variables as well as independent variables are not called principal components but *latent variables* (t). These latent variables are obtained exactly in the same manner as principal components in PCA, and thus a t_i, like a PC_i, is also a linear combination of independent variables as

$$t_i = b_{i1} x_1 + b_{i2} x_2 + b_{i3} x_3 + \ldots\ldots + b_{ip} x_p \qquad (4.47)$$

These t_i's are then used in regression analysis to express the dependent variable y as

$$y = a_1 t_1 + a_2 t_2 + a_3 t_3 + \ldots\ldots + a_n t_n \qquad (4.48)$$

As in PCA, here also the number of latent variables is equal to the smaller of the number of descriptors p and the number of observations n.

Using Eq. 4.48 the values of y can be calculated, which are better called as *predicted values*. The differences between the observed and the predicted values are often referred to as the *residuals*, which represent the variation not explained by the model. The quality of a PLS model can be assessed graphically by plotting the predicted values against the measured ones. In a perfect match, all the points would lie on a straight line obtained.

In PLS model also, all the latent variables may not be significant, only a first few may be important. The predictive ability of a PLS model is judged by the values of cross-validated R^2 (Q^2) as defined by Eq. 4.20. The fit of the model r^2 can always be enhanced by the addition of more latent variables, but Q^2 will typically show such an improvement only in initial stages. Otherwise, it either passes through a maximum or else reaches a plateau. The maximum in Q^2 corresponds to the most appropriate number of latent variables to include. The parameters S_{PRESS} (Eq. 4.22) can also be used for the selection of latent variables. As a guideline, we should use the smallest number of latent variables that gives a reasonably high Q^2 and a reasonably low S_{PRESS} [23]. Each latent variable added should produce at least a fall of 5% in value of S_{PRESS} [23].

Another related parameter, often used to assess the predictive ability of the PLS model, is SDEP (standard error of prediction) defined as

$$\text{SDEP} = (\text{PRESS}/n)^{1/2} \qquad (4.49)$$

which differs from S_{PRESS} (Eq. 4.22) only in that it has in the denominator only n instead of $(n - k - 1)$ (in PLS model k would be the number of latent variables used in the model). Thus, SDEP would not penalize an increased number of variables and thus a model selected on the basis of SDEP may have more components than the one selected on the basis of S_{PRESS}.

An early and simple example of PLS analysis is the study of Dunn et al. [24] for the toxicity of eight halogenated hydrocarbons. In this analysis, eleven descriptors related to hydrophobic, electronic, and steric properties were used. For seven of the compounds, analysis revealed three significant components, which were then used to predict the activity of the eighth compound.

4.7 Discriminant Analysis

Discriminant analysis in drug design is applied when any biological or pharmacological activity of a series of molecules is only qualitatively reported and no numerical data are given. By this method, we can find a linear combination of variables that will best discriminate between two groups. To weigh the importance of these variables and to indicate their positive or negative effect, a desired discriminant function Y is obtained, which is of the form

$$Y = a_1 X_1 + a_2 X_2 + \ldots\ldots + a_n X_n \tag{4.50}$$

where $a_1, a_2, \ldots, a_n$ are the weighting coefficients of the variables or descriptors $X_1, X_2, \ldots, X_n$, respectively. This discriminant function is found as follows.

Suppose there is a series of compounds where any biological assay of the compounds is reported only in terms of 'active' or 'inactive'. This series then can be divided into two groups: Group A containing all active compounds and Group B containing all inactive compounds. Now, if four descriptors have been obtained to account for their activity, we can construct two tables such as Tables 4.7a and 4.7b. From these two tables we calculate the difference of means d for each descriptor

$$d_1 = \bar{X}_1^a - \bar{X}_1^b; \quad d_2 = \bar{X}_2^a - \bar{X}_2^b; \quad d_3 = \bar{X}_3^a - \bar{X}_3^b; \quad d_4 = \bar{X}_4^a - \bar{X}_4^b$$

These d's form a column vector $\boldsymbol{d}$, which is used to generate a column vector $\boldsymbol{a}$ of weighting coefficients a's using the equation

$$\boldsymbol{a} = \boldsymbol{C}^{-1} \boldsymbol{d} \tag{4.51}$$

where $\boldsymbol{C}^{-1}$ is the inverse of within-groups variance-covariance matrix $\boldsymbol{C}$. The elements of matrix $\boldsymbol{C}$ can be calculated as (Eqs. 4.52 and 4.53)

$$c_{ii} = \frac{\sum_{k=1}^{n}\left(x_{ki} - \bar{X}_i\right)_a^2 + \sum_{k=1}^{m}\left(x_{ki} - \bar{X}_i\right)_b^2}{(n + m - 2)} \tag{4.52}$$

Table 4.7a. Group A (active compounds) and some descriptors

Compd.	X_1	X_2	X_3	X_4
1	x_{11}	x_{12}	x_{13}	x_{14}
2	x_{21}	x_{22}	x_{23}	x_{24}
3	x_{31}	x_{32}	x_{33}	x_{34}
:	:	:	:	:
:	:	:	:	:
n	x_{n1}	x_{n2}	x_{n3}	x_{n4}
Mean	$\bar{X}_1$	$\bar{X}_2$	$\bar{X}_3$	$\bar{X}_4$

Table 4.7b. Group B (inactive compounds) and some descriptors

Compd.	X_1	X_2	X_3	X_4
1	x_{11}	x_{12}	x_{13}	x_{14}
2	x_{21}	x_{22}	x_{23}	x_{24}
3	x_{31}	x_{32}	x_{33}	x_{34}
:	:	:	:	:
:	:	:	:	:
m	x_{m1}	x_{m2}	x_{m3}	x_{m4}
Mean	$\bar{X}_1$	$\bar{X}_2$	$\bar{X}_3$	$\bar{X}_4$

$$c_{ij} = \frac{\sum_{k=1}^{n}\left(x_{ki} - \bar{X}_i\right)_a \left(x_{kj} - \bar{X}_j\right)_a + \sum_{k=1}^{m}\left(x_{ki} - \bar{X}_i\right)_b \left(x_{kj} - \bar{X}_j\right)_b}{n+m-2} \quad (i \neq j) \qquad (4.53)$$

In both Eqs. 4.52 and 4.53, i and j will take the values from 1 to the number of descriptors (4 here). Now, Eq. 4.51 can be written as

$$\begin{bmatrix} a_1 \\ a_2 \\ a_3 \\ a_4 \end{bmatrix} = \begin{bmatrix} c_{11} & c_{12} & c_{13} & c_{14} \\ c_{21} & c_{22} & c_{23} & c_{24} \\ c_{31} & c_{32} & c_{33} & c_{34} \\ c_{41} & c_{42} & c_{43} & c_{44} \end{bmatrix}^{-1} \begin{bmatrix} d_1 \\ d_2 \\ d_3 \\ d_4 \end{bmatrix} \qquad (4.54)$$

If the inverse of $\boldsymbol{C}$ is taken and its elements are represented as c^{ij}, then Eq. 4.54 will be of the form

$$\begin{bmatrix} a_1 \\ a_2 \\ a_3 \\ a_4 \end{bmatrix} = \begin{bmatrix} c^{11} & c^{12} & c^{13} & c^{14} \\ c^{21} & c^{22} & c^{23} & c^{24} \\ c^{31} & c^{32} & c^{33} & c^{34} \\ c^{41} & c^{42} & c^{43} & c^{44} \end{bmatrix} \begin{bmatrix} d_1 \\ d_2 \\ d_3 \\ d_4 \end{bmatrix} \qquad (4.55)$$

which will give

$$\begin{aligned} a_1 &= d_1\, c^{11} + d_2\, c^{12} + d_3\, c^{13} + d_4\, c^{14} \\ a_2 &= d_1\, c^{21} + d_2\, c^{22} + d_3\, c^{23} + d_4\, c^{24} \\ a_3 &= d_1\, c^{21} + d_2\, c^{22} + d_3\, c^{33} + d_4\, c^{34} \\ a_4 &= d_1\, c^{41} + d_2\, c^{42} + d_3\, c^{43} + d_4\, c^{44} \end{aligned} \qquad (4.56)$$

Multiplying Eq. 4.51 by $\boldsymbol{C}$ on both sides will give

$$\boldsymbol{C}\,\boldsymbol{a} = \boldsymbol{C}\,\boldsymbol{C}^{-1}\,\boldsymbol{d} = \boldsymbol{d} \qquad (4.57)$$

which will give four (equal to the number of descriptors) simultaneous equations as

$$\begin{aligned} a_1 c_{11} + a_2 c_{12} + a_3 c_{13} + a_4 c_{14} &= d_1 \\ a_1 c_{21} + a_2 c_{22} + a_3 c_{23} + a_4 c_{24} &= d_2 \\ a_1 c_{31} + a_2 c_{32} + a_3 c_{33} + a_4 c_{34} &= d_3 \\ a_1 c_{41} + a_2 c_{42} + a_3 c_{43} + a_4 c_{44} &= d_4 \end{aligned} \tag{4.58}$$

The solution of these simultaneous equations will lead to the values of a's.

After evaluating the values of a's, the mean values of the discriminant function are obtained for both the groups using the means of the descriptors in the groups, i.e.

$$\bar{Y}^a = a_1 \bar{X}_1^a + a_2 \bar{X}_2^a + a_3 \bar{X}_3^a + a_4 \bar{X}_4^a \tag{4.59a}$$

$$\bar{Y}^b = a_1 \bar{X}_1^b + a_2 \bar{X}_2^b + a_3 \bar{X}_3^b + a_4 \bar{X}_4^b \tag{4.59b}$$

These mean values of discriminant function are then used to find the cut-off point Y_c as

$$Y_c = \frac{1}{2}\left(\bar{Y}^a + \bar{Y}^b\right) \tag{4.60}$$

Now from Eq. 4.50, the discriminant function can be calculated for each compound in both the groups using the value of each descriptor given for a compound. Any individual having a discriminant function less than Y_c would be classified into Group A and the one having that greater than Y_c will be classified into Group B (Fig. 4.4). The proportion of individuals actually belonging to Group B that would be misclassified by being assigned to Group A would be represented by the area under Group B to the left of Y_c in Fig. 4.4 and vice-versa.

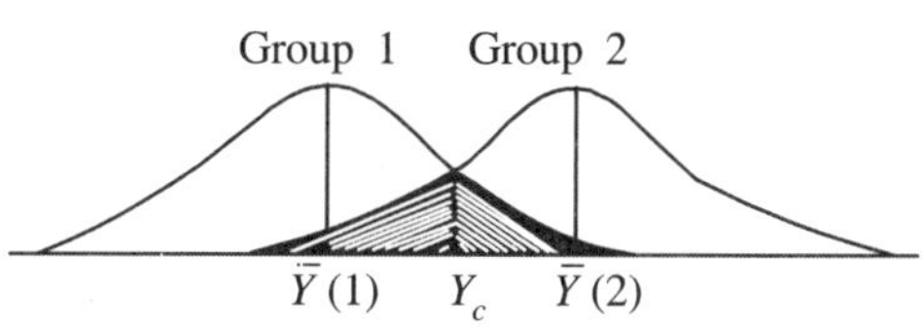

Fig. 4.4. Schematic diagram of distribution of discriminant function scores in two groups showing error of misclassifications.

A variance of the discriminant function $V(y)$ within each group is calculated by

$$V(y) = \boldsymbol{d}'\boldsymbol{C}^{-1}\boldsymbol{d} \tag{4.61}$$

where $\boldsymbol{d'}$ is the row vector of mean differences. Then this $V(y)$ is used to find the Z-scores, using Eq. 4.62, which lead to find the probability of misclassification of individuals in the assigned group

$$Z = \frac{y - \bar{y}}{\sqrt{V(y)}} \tag{4.62}$$

We cite here an example of discriminant analysis of a series of carcinogenic aromatic amines [25]. Compounds were divided into two groups as shown in Table 4.8. The descriptors were two molecular orbital parameters, E_{HOMO} and E_{LUMO}, and two structural parameters N_B and N_{NH2}, where the former refers to the number of benzene rings and the latter to the number of NH_2 substituents in a molecule. While N_B was assigned a value of 1 if the molecule had only one benzene ring and 2 if the molecule had more than one benzene ring, the value of N_{NH2} was taken exactly equal to the number of NH_2 groups in the molecule, which was normally 1 or 2. The E_{HOMO} and E_{LUMO} were calculated by simple Hückel approximation. With all the four descriptors, the discriminant function obtained was

$$\begin{gathered} Y = 4.63\,E_{HOMO} + 3.09\,E_{LUMO} - 3.97N_B + 1.52N_{NH_2} \\ F_{4,21} = 4.41\,[F_{4,21}(0.01) = 4.37] \end{gathered} \tag{4.63}$$

In this equation, N_{NH2} had a very low weighting coefficient, hence it could be neglected and a new discriminant function was obtained (Eq. 4.64)

$$\begin{gathered} Y = 3.33\,E_{HOMO} + 2.36\,E_{LUMO} - 3.46N_B \\ F_{3,22} = 4.41\,[F_{3,22}(0.01) = 4.37] \end{gathered} \tag{4.64}$$

Though Eq. 4.64 had a smaller F-value than Eq. 4.63, it was as competent to discriminate a carcinogenic amine from a noncarcinogenic one as Eq. 4.63 (Table 4.8). Thus, primarily three factors, E_{HOMO}, E_{LUMO} and N_B could be said to control the activity. Some important functions of discriminant analysis obtained from both Eqs. 4.63 and 4.64 are given in Table 4.9. This analysis had led the authors to propose that the polycyclic nature of the amine will favor its carcinogenic activity and that the compounds would form the charge-transfer complexes with DNA to elicit their effect.

Table 4.8. Descriptors of aromatic amines and a DF analysis of their animal carcinogenicity [25]

Compound	E_{HOMO} (β)	E_{LUMO} (β)	N_B	N_{NH_2}	Y (Eq. 4.63)	Y (Eq. 4.64)
Group A (Carcinogens)						
2,4-Xylidine	0.739	− 0.990	1	1	− 2.09*	− 3.32*
2,4-Diaminotoluene	0.697	− 1.013	1	2	− 0.84*	− 3.52*
2,5-Xylidine	0.756	− 0.980	1	1	− 1.98*	− 3.25*
1-Naphthyl amine	0.526	− 0.645	2	1	− 5.98	− 6.53
2-Naphthyl amine	0.572	− 0.628	2	1	− 5.72	− 6.48
5-Amino-naphthacene	0.273	− 0.306	2	1	− 6.11	− 6.73
Benzidine	0.545	− 0.747	2	2	− 4.69	− 6.86
3,3'-Dimethoxybenzidine	0.518	− 0.751	2	2	− 4.83	− 6.96
3,3'-Dichlorobenzidine	0.553	− 0.731	2	2	− 4.60	− 6.79
4,4'-Methylene-bis-2-methylaniline	0.719	− 0.989	2	2	− 4.63	− 6.85
4,4'-Methylene-bis-2-chloroaniline	0.732	− 0.954	2	2	− 4.46	− 6.72
Group B (Indefinite or noncarcinogens)						
Aniline	0.774	− 1.000	1	1	− 1.96	− 3.23
o-Toluidine	0.761	− 0.990	1	1	− 1.99	− 3.25
Anthranilic acid	0.786	− 0.439	1	1	− 0.17	− 1.87
Cinnamylanthranilide	0.717	− 0.267	1	1	− 0.04	− 1.70
m-Phenylenediamine	0.720	− 1.017	1	2	− 0.74	− 3.45
p-Phenylenediamine	0.634	− 1.000	1	2	− 1.09	− 3.70
p-Aminobenzoic acid	0.800	− 0.442	1	1	− 0.11	− 1.83
2,5-Diaminotoluene	0.600	− 0.991	1	2	− 1.22	− 1.79
2,4-Diamino-5-nitrotoluene	0.697	− 0.132	1	2	− 1.89	− 1.45
1,2-Diamino-4-nitrobenzene	0.639	− 0.074	1	2	− 1.80	− 1.50
4-Amino-2-nitrophenol	0.724	− 0.139	1	1	− 0.47	− 1.37
p-Chloro-o-toluidine	0.777	− 0.983	1	1	− 1.89	− 3.18
2,5-Diaminoanisole	0.610	− 1.003	1	2	− 1.21	− 3.78
2,4-Diaminodiphenyl	0.565	− 0.737	2	2	− 4.57*	− 6.77*
4,4'-Methylenediaminobenzidine	0.657	− 0.704	2	2	− 4.89*	− 6.38*

*Values show misclassification of the compounds

Table 4.9. Some important functions of DF analysis obtained from Eqs. 4.63 and 4.64 [25]

Equation	Mean of DF		Cut-off point	Variance of DF	Z_c-score
	$\overline{Y}^a$	$\overline{Y}^b$	Y_c	$V(Y)$	Z_c
4.63	− 4.17	− 0.99	− 2.58	3.18	± 0.89
4.64	− 5.83	− 3.15	− 4.49	2.68	± 0.82

4.8 Neural Networks

The application of neural networks in the field of chemistry, biology and medicinal chemistry has grown considerably since their first applications were described in process control [26] and in protein secondary structure determination [27, 28]. The neural network is a computer-based system derived from simplified picture of the brain in which a number of nodes, called processing elements or neurons, are interconnected in a netlike framework [29]. This artificial neural network (ANN) has been shown by many workers to be of great value in QSAR studies [30-35]. Besides, the ANN represents a unified and general purpose method for solving pattern recognition and functional mapping problems, providing satisfactory solution in cases where there are no viable alternatives.

The usefulness of neural networks in QSAR lies in their capability of nonlinear feature extraction and modeling complex polynomial surfaces. Functions of several variables represent surfaces or hypersurfaces over the space of independent variables. Even if we take a simplest case in which the activity depends on only two physicochemical properties, the Hansch model will reveal the activity to be a function where it is linear in both variables, linear in one variable and parabolic in other, or parabolic in both the variables, which will correspond, respectively, to three possible surface shapes: Plane (Fig. 4.5a), parabolically curved plane ("barn roof", Fig. 4.5b), and paraboloid of revolution ("eggshell", Fig. 4.5c).

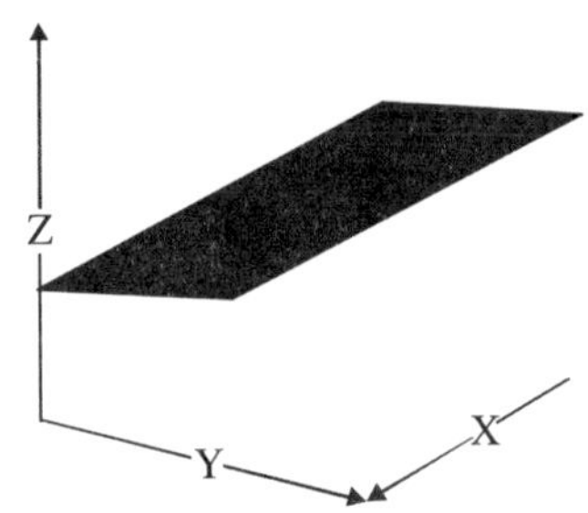

(a)

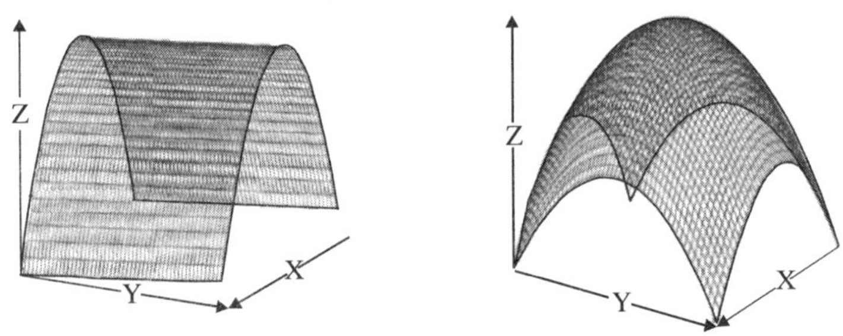

(b) (c)

Fig. 4.5. Biological activity surfaces possible from a Hansch model where the activity may depend on only two variables: (a) a plane, exhibiting the activity being linear in both the variables, (b) a parabolically curved plane "barn roof", exhibiting the activity being linear in one variable and parabolic in other and (c) paraboloid of revolution "eggshell", exhibiting the activity being parabolic in both the variables. Reprinted with permission from [31]. Copyright 1991 American Chemical Society.

The Hansch model has limited flexibility. In this, the only adjustable degrees of freedom are the statistically calculated coefficients which can determine the heights of surfaces, tilts of the planes, curvature of the parabolas, and the location of their maxima. Any further undulation of these surfaces is not possible from this model since it does not incorporate the third or any higher order terms of the variables, nor does it take into account any cross product terms. The absence of the cross product terms suggests that the dependence of the function on a particular variable is invariant to the changes in other variables. For example, if a function is parabolic in π and linear in E_s and σ, the curvature of the parabola and the location of its maximum will be invariant to the changes in the values of E_s and σ.

Outliers are the result of such weaknesses in the Hansch model, which Hansch et al. tried to adjust using indicator variables, which in certain cases become several in numbers and account for a major part of the variance in the activity. An artificial neural network circumvents the need for such *ad hoc* indicator variables and leads to the elucidation of nonlinear and cross-products effects that correspond to trade-offs between physicochemical properties in their effects on biological activity.

An artificial neural network consists of layers of brain-like neurons with feed-forward and feed-backward interconnections [29, 36]. Among the several ANN paradigms developed so far, the back propagation network [BPN] [29] has been the simplest one. Topologically, it consists of an input layer, a hidden layer and an output layer of neurons or nodes connected by bonds as shown in Fig. 4.6. Each of the input and hidden layers has an

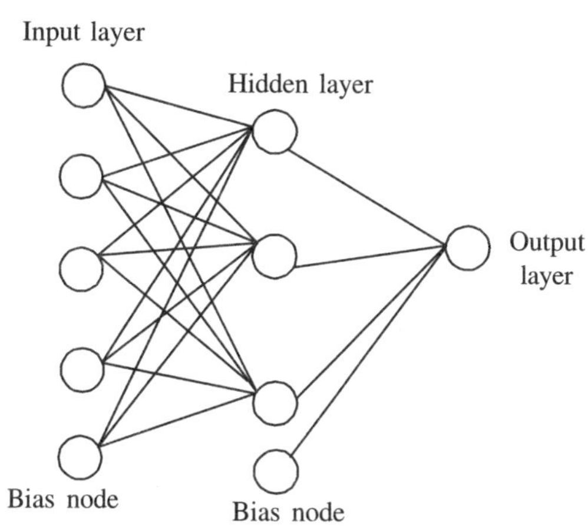

Fig. 4.6. A three-layer BPN technology.

additional node, called a 'bias node', whose internal state is assigned a value of 1. The values of the internal state of other nodes in input, hidden and output layers are calculated as follows.

The internal state of a node i in input layer S_i is given by

$$S_i = 0.8\left(\frac{V_i - V_{i,\min}}{V_{i,\max} - V_{i,\min}}\right) + 0.1 \tag{4.65}$$

where V_i is a value of the ith independent variable, $V_{i,\min}$ and $V_{i,\max}$ are its minimum and maximum values, respectively. Thus, each input layer node corresponds to a single independent variable with the exception of the bias node.

The state S_h of each hidden unit is calculated by a squashing function as

$$S_h\,(\Phi_h) = \frac{1}{\left(1 + e^{-\Phi_h}\right)} \tag{4.66a}$$

$$\Phi_h = \sum_i W_{hi} S_i + \theta_h \tag{4.66b}$$

where W_{hi} is the weight of the bond that connects a hidden unit h with an input unit i and θ_h the weight of the bond connecting hidden unit h to the input layer 'bias unit'. The state of the output unit m, O_m, is calculated as

$$O_m(\Phi_m) = \frac{1}{\left(1 + e^{-\Phi_m}\right)} \tag{4.67a}$$

$$\Phi_m = \sum_h W_{mh} S_h + \theta_m \tag{4.67b}$$

where W_{mh} is the weight of the bond that connects an output unit m to a hidden unit h and θ_m the weight of the bond that connects output unit m to the hidden layer 'bias unit'. Thus, each output layer node corresponds to a dependent variable. The ANN calculated values for O_m fall in the range (0, 1).

4.8.1 Training of Neural Networks

To get the desired results, the neural networks are first to be trained. The training methods are of two types, viz. supervised and unsupervised. The supervised method follows the principle of minimization of the error between the desired value and network output value. The aim is to determine a set of bond weights (W_{hi}, W_{mh}) which minimizes the error. Initially, these bond weights are given the arbitrary values. This process is iterated until the weights are optimized such that the overall error is minimized.

In the unsupervised method, the input patterns are presented once into the network and the network settles to a final state. At present, however, it is not well understood and is still the subject of thorough investigation. On the other hand, the supervised method has been quite successful in practical applications.

The best and the simplest supervised method follows the back-propagation algorithm of Owens and Filkin [37], which seems to be the best for solving the pattern recognition problems. It consists of two phases, viz. forward and backward phases. The forward phase occurs when the input is presented and propagated forward through the network to compute, according to Eq. 4.67a, b, an output value for each processing element based on its current set of weights. The backward phase is a recurring computation of an error function E in a backward direction. This error function is a measure of the difference between the desired result (experimentally measured value) and the output value as a function of the bond weight $\{W_{hi}, W_{mh}\}$. It is properly defined as

$$E = \sum_p E_p = 0.5 \sum_p \sum_m \left(A_{pm} - O_{pm}\right)^2 \tag{4.68}$$

where E_p is the error of the pth training pattern, defined as the set of the independent and dependent variables corresponding to the pth data point or chemical compound. A_{pm} corresponds to the experimentally measured value a_{pm} of the mth dependent variable, say biological activity, of the pth pattern, scaled by

$$A_{pm} = 0.8 \left(\frac{a_{pm} - a_{m,\,\min}}{a_{m,\,\max} - a_{m,\,\min}} \right) + 0.1 \tag{4.69}$$

$a_{m,\,\min}$ and $a_{m,\,\max}$ are the minimum and maximum values of A_{pm} over the dataset.

The training of the neural network by this back propagation is completed by minimizing this error function. It is minimized by following its gradient with respect to the weights given by

$$-\frac{\partial E}{\partial W_{mh}} = -\sum_p \frac{\partial E_p}{\partial W_{mh}} \tag{4.70a}$$

$$-\frac{\partial E}{\partial W_{hi}} = -\sum_p \frac{\partial E_p}{\partial W_{hi}} \tag{4.70b}$$

Using the chain rule, we can have

$$-\frac{\partial E_p}{\partial W_{mh}} = -\sum_m \frac{\partial E_p}{\partial O_{pm}} \frac{\partial O_{pm}}{\partial W_{mh}} = \sum_m \left(A_{pm} - O_{pm}\right) O_{pm} \left(1 - O_{pm}\right) S_{ph} \tag{4.71a}$$

$$\begin{aligned} -\frac{\partial E_p}{\partial W_{hi}} &= -\sum_m \frac{\partial E_p}{\partial O_{pm}} \frac{\partial O_{pm}}{\partial W_{hi}} \\ &= \sum_m \left(A_{pm} - O_{pm}\right) O_{pm} \left(1 - O_{pm}\right) W_{mh} S_{ph} (1 - S_{ph}) S_{pi} \end{aligned} \tag{4.71b}$$

The derivatives with respect to θ_h and θ_m are calculated in a similar fashion.

The most common and simplest method, however, to minimize the error function E is to follow the delta rule [29] where the bond weights are iteratively changed from their initially assigned small random values following the equations

$$W_{mh}^{n+1} = W_{mh}^{n} - \eta \frac{\partial E}{\partial W_{mh}} \tag{4.72a}$$

$$W_{hi}^{n+1} = W_{hi}^{n} - \eta \frac{\partial E}{\partial W_{hi}} \tag{4.72b}$$

where the superscripts n and $n+1$ designate consecutive iterations in the minimization sequence and η is the learning rate with values typically much less than 1. Similar equations are used to calculate the values of θ_h and θ_m.

Following the algorithm of Owens and Filkin [37], we can minimize E using the equations

$$\frac{dW_{mh}}{dt} = -\frac{\partial E}{\partial W_{mh}} \tag{4.73a}$$

$$\frac{dW_{hi}}{dt} = -\frac{\partial E}{\partial W_{hi}} \tag{4.73b}$$

where t corresponds to the sequential training iterations. These two equations are simply the replacement of Eqs. 4.71a and b. Equations 4.72a and b are solved by the Gear algorithm [38].

After the neural network has been trained, it can be used to predict the activity of any new compound. The predictive ability of a trained NN can be judged by cross-validation check, using either leave-one-out (LOO) or leave-n-out (LNO) procedure. Though the LNO procedure takes less time than the LOO, the former is slightly less preferred because it has the complication of the choice of the compounds.

Another, and perhaps more useful method of testing the predictive ability of an NN, is to divide the whole data set into two groups, viz. training set and the test set. The training set should be used to train the NN and then after the training is over, the NN should be utilized to predict the activity of the compounds in the test set and the predicted and observed activities should be compared. That is what we also do to test the predictive ability of traditional QSAR model.

To derive statistically a sound NN model, however, a precaution must be taken to take the number of nodes in the hidden layers that fix the number of bonds (connections) whose weights are the adjustable parameters of the models. In traditional regression model, it is desirable to have at least five data points for each parameter or variable. No corresponding rule of thumb exists for NN models except that the ratio ρ of number of data points to the number of bonds must be greater than 1. In a three-layer NN model, if the number of units (nodes) in input, hidden and output layers be i, h and o, respectively then there would be $h\ (i + o)$ connections and $(h + o)$ biases (i.e., bonds connected to bias nodes). Thus, the total number of adjustable parameters P will be $h\ (i + o) + (h + o)$, i.e.

$$P = h\ (i + o) + (h + o) = (i + 1)\ h + (h + 1)\ o \tag{4.74}$$

and then ρ for a three-layer NN model can be given as

$$\rho = \frac{\text{Number of data points in the training set}}{(i + l)\,h + (h + l)\,o} \tag{4.75}$$

In their work, Andrea and Kalayeh [31] had suggested that the optimal NN models may have the values of ρ between 1.8 and 2.2. Models with $\rho > 2.2$ were found to be unable to extract all the relevant features and to give poor predictions and those with $\rho \approx 1$ were found to over fit the training set and unable to accurately predict the test set. It is claimed that with $\rho \ll 1.0$ the network simply memorizes the data and with $\rho \gg 3.0$ it is not able to generalize.

4.8.2 Strengths and Weaknesses of Neural Network Models

The most advantageous strengths of NN models relative to regression models are enhanced prediction accuracy and accounting for most of the outliers without any indicator variables. Among the weaknesses of the NN models, the first is that they cannot assess the importance or contribution of individual parameters and that they cannot show the statistical significance of any parameter, and thus there are dangers of chance effects. The other weakness is that the NN model cannot describe the mechanism of drug-receptor interaction, or that they cannot explain the forces involved in the interaction of drug molecules with the receptors. Another aspect of serious concern is the time involved in training a neural network, and the choice of number of hidden units is quite critical. Thus, disadvantages of the NN models seem to overweigh their advantages, at least for the feed-forward-back propagation model applied by many workers so far. However, we may hope that in future there can be further improvement in NN methodology to offset these weaknesses. Ajay [33] proposed a unified framework for using neural networks to build QSARs. This framework explicitly separates the linear and nonlinear contributions to the biological activity. To facilitate the use of neural networks as a regular tool, Ajay demonstrated that: (1) a perception with linear output units is equivalent to multiple linear regression and (2) one hidden unit at a time can be added to the network so that QSAR data can be modeled by everything from the simplest linear hyperspaces to complicated ones. He suggested that significant improvements can be made in the model by using the weight decay. In Ajay's framework, an NN model can be of the type

$$O = 0.77 - 0.74\pi - 1.45MR + \frac{7.62}{1 + \exp[3.36 - 6.09\pi - 6.58MR]} + \frac{5.43}{1 + \exp[-3.92 + 0.05\pi + 18.34MR]} \quad (4.76)$$

which he derived using two hidden units and the weight decay for 3-X-triazine inhibition of cultured L1210 leukemia cells sensitive to methotrexate.

References

[1] Grim, H., In *Biostatics in Pharmacology*, Vol. 2, 1st Edition, Delaunois, A.L. (Ed.), Pergamon Press, Oxford (1973), 771.

[2] Hansch, C., In *Biological Activity and Chemical Structure* (Proceedings of the Conference on Chemical Structure-Biological Activity, Relationships: Quantitative Approaches, Prague, 1973), *Experentia Suppl.*, ***23***, Birkhaüser Verlag, Basel (1976), 47.

[3] Kubinyi, H., *QSAR: Hansch Analysis and Related Approaches*, Vol. 1, VCH, Weinheim (1993).

[4] Hansch, C., Hatheway, G.J., Quin, F.R. and Greenberg, N.J., *J. Med. Chem.*, ***21*** (1978), 574.

[5] Hansch, C., *Drug Dev. Res.*, ***1*** (1981), 267.

[6] Singh, and Gupta, S.P., *J. Pharm. Sci.*, ***67*** (1973), 706.

[7] Albert, A., Rubbo, S. and Goldacre, R., *Nature* (*London*), ***147*** (1941), 332.

[8] Albert, A., Rubbo, S., Goldacre, R., Davey, M. and Stone, J., *Br. J. Exp. Pathol.*, ***26*** (1945), 160.

[9] Albert, A., In *Drug Design*, Vol. III, Ariëns, E.J. (Ed.), Academic Press, New York (1972).

[10] Albert, A., *Selective Toxicity*, Chapman and Hall, London, England (1973).

[11] Sinha, J., Kurup, A., Paleti, A. and Gupta, S.P., *Bioorg. Med. Chem.*, ***7*** (1999), 1127.

[12] Gupta, S.P., *Current Pharm. Des.*, ***8*** (2002), 111.

[13] Fukunaga, J.Y., Hansch, C. and Steller, E.E., *J. Med. Chem.*, ***19*** (1976), 605.

[14] Free, S.M., Jr. and Wilson, J.W., *J. Med. Chem.*, ***7*** (1964), 395.

[15] Kubinyi, H., *Quant. Struct.-Act. Relat.*, ***7*** (1988), 121.

[16] Fujita, T. and Ban, T., *J. Med. Chem.*, ***14*** (1971), 148.

[17] Kubinyi, H., *Arzneim.-Forsch/Drug Res.*, ***26*** (1976), 1991.

[18] Kubinyi, H., *J. Med. Chem.*, ***20*** (1977), 625.

[19] McFarland, J.W., *J. Med. Chem.*, ***13*** (1970), 1192.

[20] Kubinyi, H. and Kehrhahn, O.-H., *Arzneim-Forsch./Drug Res.*, ***28*** (1978), 598.

[21] El Tayar, N., Tsai, R.S., Carrupt, P.A. and Testa, B., *J. Chem. Soc. Perkin Trans.*, ***2*** (1992), 79.

[22] Leach, A.R. and Gillet, V.J., *An Introduction to Chemoinformatics*, Kluwer Academic Publishers, The Netherlands (2003).

[23] Wold, S., Johansson, E. and Cocchi, M., In *3D QSAR in Drug Design*, Kubinyi, H. (Ed.), Leiden, ESCOM (1993), 523.

[24] Dunn III, W.J., Wold, S., Edlund, U., Hellberg, S. and Gasteiger, J., *Quant. Struct.-Act. Relat.*, ***3*** (1984), 131.

[25] Gupta, S.P., *Indian J. Chem.*, ***30B*** (1991), 122.

[26] Hoskins, J.C. and Himmelblau, D.M., *Comput. Chem. Eng.*, ***12*** (1988), 881.

[27] Qian, N. and Sejnowski, T.J., *J. Mol. Biol.*, ***202*** (1988), 865.

[28] Bohr, H., Bohr, J., Brunak, S., Cotterill, R., Lautrup, B., Norskov, L., Olsen, O. and Peterson, S., *FEBS Lett.*, ***241*** (1988), 223.

[29] For example: Rumehart, D.E. and McClellan, J.L. (Eds.), *Parallel Distributed Processing Exploration in Microstructure of Cognition*, MIT Press, Cambridge, M.A., ***Vols. 1 and 2*** (1986).

[30] Aoyama, T., Suzuki, Y. and Ichikawa, H., *J. Med. Chem.*, ***33*** (1990), 905.

[31] Andrea, T.A. and Kalayeh, H., *J. Med. Chem.*, ***34*** (1991), 2824.

[32] So, S.S. and Richards, W.G., *J. Med. Chem.*, ***35*** (1992), 3201.

[33] Ajay, *J. Med. Chem.*, ***36*** (1993), 3565.

[34] Ghosal, N., Mukhopadhayay, S.N., Ghosal, T.K. and Achari, B., *Indian J. Chem.*, ***32B*** (1993), 1045.

[35] Manallack, D.T., Ellis, D.D. and Livingstone, D.J., *J. Med. Chem.*, ***37*** (1994), 3758.

[36] Hertz, J., Krogh, A. and Palmer, R.G., *Introduction to the Theory of Neural Computation*, Addison-Wesley Publishing Co., Reading, MA (1991).

[37] Owens, A.J. and Filkin, D.L., *Joint IEEE/INNS International Joint Conference of Neural Networks*, Washington, D.C., June 11 (1989), 381.

[38] Gear, C.W., *Numerical Initial Value Problems in Ordinary Differential Equations*, Prentice Hall, Englewood Cliffs, New Jersey (1971).

5

Three-dimensional (3D) QSAR Approaches: Molecular Modeling

Before we discuss three-dimensional QSAR or molecular modeling, it is essential to define *lead molecule* and *pharmacophore*.

5.1 Lead Molecule

A *lead molecule* refers to a compound that is active in an appropriate assay, i.e., it possesses some activity against a disease. It may be only marginally useful and possess severe side effects. In fact, a *lead compound* has its name because it provides a starting point from where some modifications, refinements can be made to enhance its potency and selectivity, to ensure that neither it nor any of its metabolites is toxic, and to provide appropriate transport characteristic to enable it to pass through all membranes and reach its targets. Thus a *lead molecule* is novel bioactive molecule having scope of structure modification for the improvement in bioactivity, selectivity and transport, and the reduction in the toxic effects.

However, finding a lead compound is difficult. The advent of combinatorial chemistry and high throughput screening enabled the medicinal chemists to synthesize and screen much larger number of compounds but it did not lead to any significant improvement in the identification of lead compounds. This problem led to the development of a new idea of *drug-likeness* [1, 2] and people started to determine which features of the drug molecules confer their biological activity and distinguish them from general organic compounds. A generic algorithm was used to build a scoring scheme for "drug-likeness" [3], which was based on molecular weight, a shape index (kappa-alpha 2 index [4]), and the number of hydrogen-bond donors, hydrogen-bond acceptors, rotatable bonds, and aromatic rings. The consideration of some of these properties led Lipinski et al. [5] to formulate a *rule of five* (the phrase derived from the fact that it involves number 5 and its multiple). The rule predicts that poor absorption and permeability of potential drugs is more likely if

1. the molecular weight is more than 500.
2. the log *P* is more than 5.
3. there are more than 5 H-bond donors (defined as the sum of OH and NH groups).
4. there are more than 10 H-bond acceptors (defined as the sum of N and O atoms).

This rule also addresses the question of "drug-likeness".

As a distinct concept from drug-likeness, a concept of *lead-likeness* was developed from the idea that during the lead modification to give the final drug there is an increase in the molecular complexity as measured by the properties such as molecular weight, the number of H-bond donors and acceptors, and log *P*. Therefore, it has been advised that we should use "lead-like" criteria when performing virtual screening (discussed later) at that stage rather than the "drug-like" criteria which has to follow the rule of five [6, 7].

5.2 Pharmacophore

The crucial parts of a drug molecule that interact with the receptor (or target) constitute the *pharmacophore* of the compound. The pharmacophore is involved in the key interaction responsible for the biological response. The role of the molecular modeling is to suggest the compounds that contain the required functional groups of the pharmacophore and thus to suggest the compounds that would be expected to interact favorably with the receptor.

In a series of drug molecules, there can be a common pharmacophore. The typical features of a pharmacophore may be H-bond donors and acceptors, positively and negatively charged groups, and hydrophobic groups. These features are referred to as *pharmacophoric groups*. In a three-dimensional (3D) pharmacophore, the spatial relationships between the key features are specified, usually in terms of distances or distance ranges. However, sometimes angles and planes can also be taken into account. The determination of possible 3D pharmacophores for a series of active compounds is called *pharmacophore mapping*. If molecules are not completely rigid, the pharmacophore mapping takes into account the conformational properties of the molecules. There can be several combinations of pharmacophoric groups that are common to the molecules and can be positioned in a similar orientation in space. Thus, there can be more than one pharmacophore. Some algorithms can generate hundreds of possible pharmacophores, but then we have to find which fits the data best.

Several methods have been suggested to perform pharmacophore mapping, of which the most commonly used are constrained systematic search, clique detection, the maximum likelihood method, and the genetic algorithm approach. In this book, we describe only the constrained systematic search approach, which is the simplest. For other approaches, the reader may refer [8, 9].

5.2.1 Constrained Systematic Search Approach for Pharmacophore Mapping

This approach involves the determination of the conformation of the molecules in which each molecule can position its pharmacophoric groups in identical relative position in the space. First, identify the pharmacophoric groups that will be overlaid in the final pharmacophore. The most rigid molecule is then taken and its conformational space explored. During the conformational search the distances between all pairs of the selected pharmacophoric groups are recorded. Then, for other molecules, one has to find the conformations that would enable their pharmacophoric groups to be positioned in the same locations that have already been found for the most rigid molecule. In the constrained systematic search approach, Dammkoehler et al. [10] then suggested that constraints on the values permitted to each of the torsion angles of any molecule can be derived and the only torsion angle values explored for the rotatable bonds in the molecule are those that may permit it to match the pharmacophore distances found first for the most rigid molecule.

The best example of the application of constrained systematic search approach cited by Leach [8, 9] is the determination of the 3D pharmacophores for the inhibitors of angiotension converting enzyme (ACE), an enzyme involved in the regulation of blood pressure. Typical ACE inhibitors contain a zinc-binding group such as a thiol or carboxylic group, a terminal carboxylic group (believed to interact with a basic residue in the enzyme), and an amido carbonyl group which acts as hydrogen-bond acceptor. Figure 5.1 shows three examples of such ACE inhibitors that possess these pharmacophoric groups. For all such ACE inhibitors possessing these pharmacophoric groups, the distance ranges between these groups, as shown in Fig. 5.2, were derived that were accessible to all inhibitors in low energy conformations. These distance ranges represented the pharmacophores of the ACE inhibitors and two such pharmacophores were finalized with different sets of *d*-values.

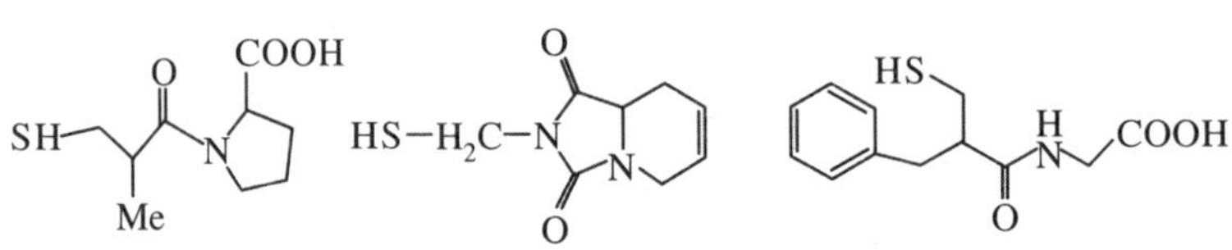

Fig. 5.1. Some typical examples of ACE inhibitors [8].

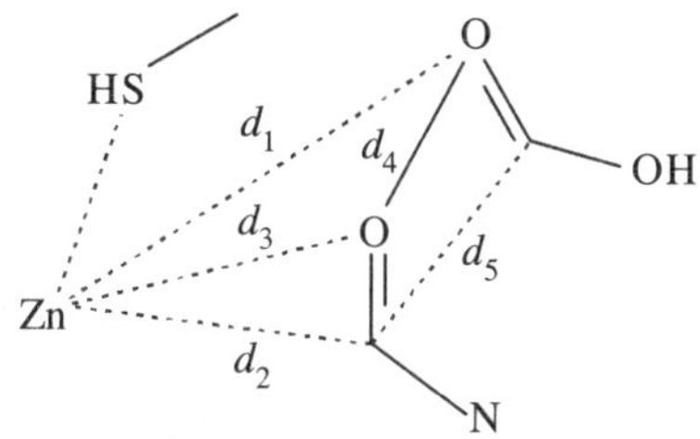

Fig. 5.2. Representation of two pharmacophores found for ACE inhibitors exemplified in Fig. 5.1. For pharmacophore 1, d_1 = 8.5-8.78 Å, d_2 = 4.75-5.25 Å, d_3 = 3.75-4.0 Å, d_4 = 5.25-5.5 Å and d_5 = 4.0-4.25 Å. For pharmacophore 2, d_1 = 5.75-6.25 Å, d_2 = 2.75-3.0 Å, d_3 = 3.75-4.0 Å, d_4 = 3.25-3.75 Å and d_5 = 4.0-4.25 Å. Reprinted with permission from [8]. Copyright 1996 Addison Wesley Longman.

5.3 Molecular Modeling

After a lead compound or a pharmacophore has been found, a mathematical simulation of drug-receptor interaction is done to predict a final most active drug molecule. This is known as *molecular modeling*. It adopts graphical visualization techniques in order to provide a plausible three-dimensional representation of drug molecule, their targets, and the interaction between them. After the advancement in the crystallographic studies, the 3D structures of several target molecules (proteins, enzymes) have been delineated which have greatly facilitated the molecular modeling studies and the drug design. Some of the strategies adopted in molecular modeling studies to design the drugs are as follows:

1. The *de novo* Ligand Design
2. Structure-Based Ligand Design
3. Docking
4. Molecular Similarity
5. Comparative Molecular Field (CoMFA) Analysis
6. Virtual Screening

5.3.1 The *de novo* Ligand Design

In *de novo* design the 3D structure of the receptor or the 3D pharmacophore is used to design new molecules. In the receptor, the search is made for certain important binding sites, such as hydrogen-bond donor and acceptor sites, and the hydrophobic sites which may be aliphatic or aromatic in nature. Also a survey is made of the regions where other groups of the drug molecules can be favorably positioned. A program called LUDI [11] has been used for this. After these sites are located, the favorable positions of the interacting groups are generated, as shown in Fig. 5.3a, and a database is searched for possible ligands. The next step is to generate a hit-list of the molecules that may have optimal interactions with these sites (Fig. 5.3b). This hit-list then can be further modified, as shown in Fig. 5.3c, by adding some small fragments to have additional interactions [12].

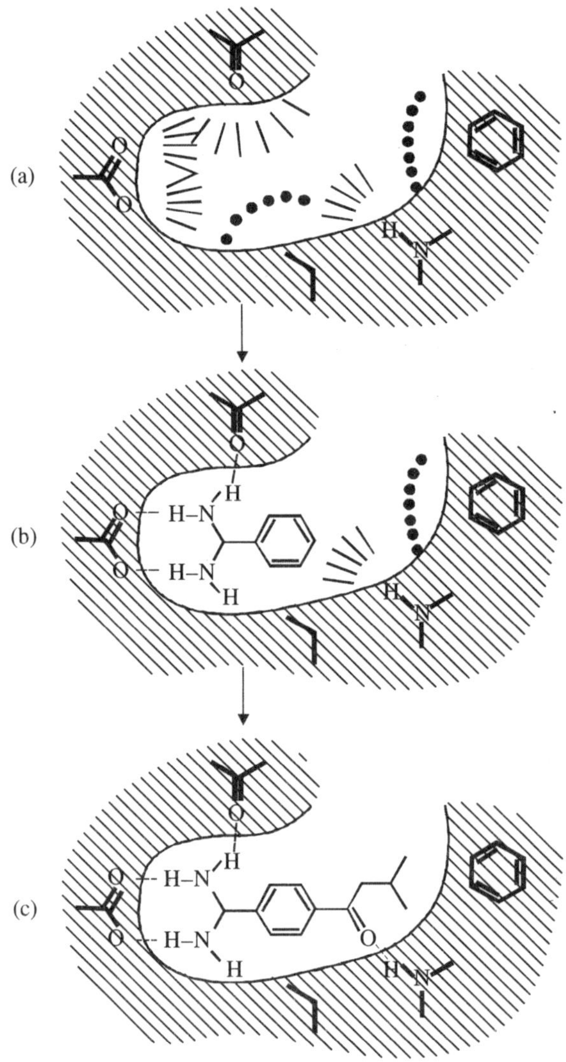

Fig. 5.3. Concept of the program LUDI for *de novo* design of enzyme inhibitors. The program automatically identifies hydrogen bond donor, acceptor, and lipophilic aliphatic and lipophilic aromatic groups within a predefined area, e.g., the active site of an enzyme. In the next step favorable positions of interacting groups are generated (a) and a database is searched for possible ligands. Then a hit-list of molecules optically interacting with these sites is generated (b). This hit-list can be further modified, including additional interactions (c). Reprinted from [12] with permission from original source: Wermuth, C.G. (Ed.), *Trends in QSAR and Molecular Modelling 92*, ESCOM Science Publishers, Leiden, 1993. Copyright 1993 ESCOM.

There are two types of *de novo* design methods, viz. *outside in* and *inside out*. In the "outside in" method, first the binding sites in the receptor are analyzed and then the specific functional groups that can interact with the binding sites are thought of. These functional groups are then connected together to give molecular skeletons, from which the real molecules are designed. In the "inside out" method, the molecules are developed within the binding region of the receptor, calculating the energy for each step.

5.3.2 Structure-Based Ligand Design

This approach is based on 3D databases of the chemical compound which takes into account the conformational properties of the molecules. From these databases, attempts are made to find the molecules that satisfy the chemical and the geometrical requirements of the receptors. This strategy, however, requires the 3D structural information of the target or the receptor molecules. We can search a database for compounds either by matching a 3D pharmacophore or by generating orientation of each molecule within the binding site of the receptor using a programme such as DOCK [13-15].

In a 3D database search, the information about the 3D structures of the molecules is required, which can be had from the Cambridge structural database that contains experimental X-ray structures of thousands of compounds. For the compounds for which the X-ray data are not available, some structure generation programs, such as CONCORD [16], can be used. CONCORD uses a knowledge-based approach combined with energy minimization to generate 3D structures. Another similar programme is CORINA [17].

A single minimization energy conformation generated for a molecule by any program may or may not correspond to the conformation adopted by the molecule when it binds with the receptor. To overcome this problem, we should either take into account the conformational flexibility of the molecules during the 3D database search, or explore the conformational space for each molecule during the search. There are the methods that rapidly identify one or more conformations which satisfy the constraints of the pharmacophore or the chemical and geometrical requirements of the receptor.

One of the best examples of the structure-based drug design can be cited of the investigation of an HIV protease inhibitor (**1**) by Lam et al. at DuPont Merck [18]. The HIV protease is a dimer with C_2 symmetry. The pharmacophore of the inhibitors of this enzyme was found to have two hydrophobic groups and a hydrogen-bond donor or acceptor group that could interact with the two hydrophobic sites S_1 and S'_1 of the enzyme and the catalytic aspartate residues in it, respectively. Therefore, Lam et al. started with the initial molecule (**2**), which was also based on Merck's discovery of a series of peptide-based diols, where diol's functionality was important. These peptide-based diols were potent HIV inhibitors but had poor oral bioavailability. Docking of this molecule into the enzyme required further modification to fulfill the optical stereochemistry and the optimal interaction requirements. This led finally to molecule **(1)**.

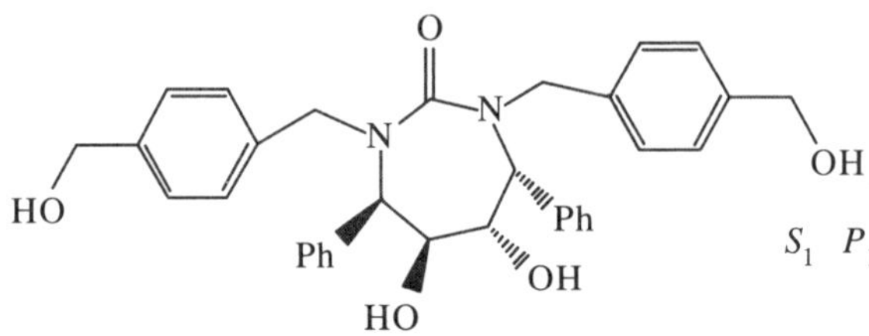

(1)

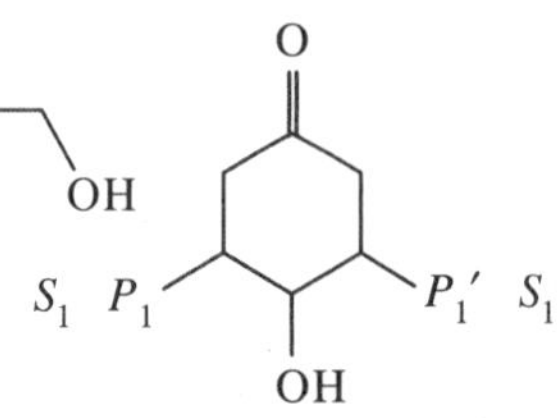

(2)

5.3.3 Molecular Docking

Molecular docking is a computational technique for exploration of the possible binding modes of a substrate or inhibitor to a given enzyme or receptor to give the optimal interactions. To perform a docking, the first requirement is to have the 3D structure of the receptor or protein of interest which can be determined by X-ray crystallography or NMR spectroscopy. This protein structure and a 3D database of potential ligands serve as input to a docking programme. The success of a docking programme depends on two components, viz. the search algorithm and the scoring function.

Search Space

The search space involves finding all possible conformations of the receptor molecule and all possible rotational and translational orientations of the ligand relative to the receptor with a given structure. Most docking programs in use account for a flexible ligand, and several are being used to model a flexible protein receptor. The search space consists of all possible orientations and conformations of the receptor molecule paired with the ligand. Each 'snapshot' of the pair is called a *pose*.

Most of the methods that attempt to include only the conformational degrees of freedom consider the conformational space of the ligand and the receptor to be rigid. In a *Monte Carlo* procedure, which consists of randomly sampling the conformational space of a molecule, the internal conformation of the ligand is changed by rotating about a bond, or the entire molecule is randomly translated or rotated. The energy of the ligand within the binding site is calculated using *molecular mechanics* and the situation is then accepted or rejected using the standard Metropolis criterion. Genetic algorithm, which is an optimization technique based on the mechanisms of Darwinian evolution that uses random mutation, crossover and selection procedures to breed better models or solutions from an originally random starting population or sample, can also be used to perform molecular docking [19-22]. Another method that can be used for molecular docking is Crippen's distance geometry method [23], but in this, we have to find the way to generate the conformations of the ligand within the binding site of the receptor. However, the ideal docking method would be the one which would permit both ligand and receptor to explore their conformational degrees of freedom. A molecular dynamics simulation of the ligand-receptor complex probably can achieve this objective but its use is limited by the complexity of the computation.

Scoring Function

The scoring function is a measure of the degree of the favorable binding of the ligand with the receptor. It takes a *pose* as input and returns a number that indicates how far a *pose* represents a favorable ligand-receptor binding. Most scoring functions involve molecular mechanics force fields that evaluate the energy of the *pose*. A likely binding interaction is indicated by a low (negative) energy.

Most of the scoring functions depend on the minimization of the free energy of the binding (ΔG_{bind}) [24], which comes from the various phenomena that the formation of ligand-protein complex may involve [25], such as interaction of ligand, protein, and ligand-protein complex with the solvent molecules ($\Delta G_{solvent}$), the conformational changes in the ligand and the protein molecules (ΔG_{conf}), interactions between the ligand and the protein molecules (ΔG_{int}), freezing internal rotations of protein and ligand (ΔG_{rot}), loss in translational and rotational degrees of freedom when the ligand-protein complex is formed ($\Delta G_{t/r}$), changes in the vibrational modes of the ligand and protein (ΔG_{vib}). Thus

$$\Delta G_{bind} = \Delta G_{solvent} + \Delta G_{conf} + \Delta G_{int} + \Delta G_{rot} + \Delta G_{t/r} + \Delta G_{vib} \qquad (5.1)$$

Later Böhm proposed that this free energy change in the binding can also be evaluated by calculating the free energy changes in hydrogen bonding, ionic interactions, lipophilic interactions, and the loss of the internal conformational freedom of the ligand [26].

An alternative approach is to use a large database of protein-ligand complexes and evaluate the fit of the *pose*. These databases actually provide the data for high affinity ligands bound with the proteins. Since low affinity ligands do not stay bound with protein for long enough, the data available for their complexes are very few. The available databases are used to train the scoring functions, which when trained can correctly dock high affinity ligands. However, they can also give plausible dock conformations for some inactive ligands. This gives a large number of *false-positive* hits, i.e., ligands predicted to bind that really do not.

5.3.4 Docking in a Rigid Target

Kuntz [13] initially developed the DOCK algorithm to identify molecules with a high degree of shape complementarity to the binding site in a receptor that has rigid structure. For such a system, DOCK first generates the "negative image" of the binding site of the receptor by rolling a series of spheres of varying radii on the molecular surface of the receptor (Fig. 5.4). Each sphere should touch the surface just at two points. Then a matching operation is performed between the centers of the atoms and those of the spheres and an attempt is made such that within some tolerance, the distances between the atoms equal the distances between the corresponding sphere centers. Then a translation-rotation operation is performed on the ligand to enable it to acquire the optimum shape complementarity, avoiding any unacceptable steric interactions. If this orientation of the ligand is acceptable, then the ligand-receptor interaction energy is calculated to give the score for that binding mode. This entire operation can be repeated for matching different sets of atoms with the sphere centers and each time a new score can be obtained for a new orientation. The top scoring orientations can be presented for further analysis.

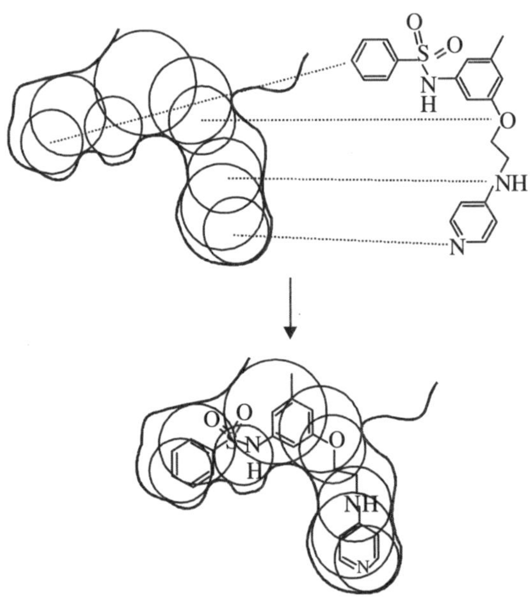

Fig. 5.4. Docking in a rigid target using DOCK algorithm. The DOCK first generates the negative image of the binding site of the target by rolling a series of spheres of varying radii on the molecular surface of the target and then ligand atoms are matched to the sphere centers, enabling the ligand conformation to be oriented within the active site for subsequent scoring. Reprinted with permission from [9]. Copyright 2003 Kluwer Academic Publishers.

5.4 Virtual Screening

The matter described so far falls under virtual screening. Virtual screening refers to theoretical approaches that help the medicinal chemists to decide which compound to screen, which library to synthesize, and which compound to purchase from an external source. Virtual screening is a theoretical aspect of biological screening that can score, rank and/or filter a set of structures using one or more computational techniques as described above.

5.5 Comparative Molecular Field Analysis

Comparative molecular field analysis (CoMFA) is not any molecular modeling scheme, but it comes under 3D QSAR methodologies because it takes into account the 3D shape of molecules in QSAR analysis. It was developed by Cramer et al. [27] to correlate the biological activity of a series of molecules with their 3D shape and their electrostatic and steric characteristics. This method was earlier called *dynamics lattice-oriented molecular modeling system* (DYLOMMS) and was not so popular.

In the application of CoMFA, the first important step is to find a common pattern of receptor binding so that all the molecules can be put in that pattern. For this, the superimposable conformation of each molecule would be required, so that all the molecules can be overlaid upon each other in their common binding mode. These conformations are presumed to represent the biologically active structures of the molecules. In the second step, molecules are placed in a box of points (called grid or lattice) and the interaction energy is calculated between the molecules and a series of probe groups placed at each point. Originally, only steric and electrostatic interactions were calculated, but Kim [28] extended the method to also include the hydrophobic interaction. The original CoMFA programme uses an sp^3-hybridized carbon atom with a unit positive charge to calculate the steric and electrostatic fields. The steric potential is calculated using Lennard-Jones (L-J) potential function and the electrostatic potential using Coulomb's law. Kim, however, used CH_3, H^+ and H_2O as probes to calculate steric, electrostatic, and hydrophobic interactions, respectively. One can also calculate and include in CoMFA analysis the hydrogen bond energy using a hydrogen-bond donor or acceptor as a probe. The results of these energy calculations are put in a data matrix, in which each row corresponds to one molecule and each column corresponds to the interaction energy of a particular probe at a specific lattice point. If there are l lattice points and p probe groups (P's), then there would be $l \times p$ such columns. A final column in the data matrix is added to list the activities of the molecules. Thus, for example, if we take only 3 probe groups to calculate steric (S), electrostatic (E) and hydrophobic (H) energies, then the matrix will have the form

Compound	S_1	$S_2 \ldots S_l$		E_1	$E_2 \ldots E_l$		H_1	$H_2 \ldots H_l$		Activity
1	.	.	.	.	.	.	.	.	.	a_1
2	.	.	.	.	.	.	.	.	.	a_2
3	.	.	.	.	.	.	.	.	.	a_3
.	.	.	.	.	.	.	.	.	.	.
.	.	.	.	.	.	.	.	.	.	.
.	.	.	.	.	.	.	.	.	.	.
.	.	.	.	.	.	.	.	.	.	.
n	S_{1n}	S_{2n}	S_{ln}	E_{1n}	E_{2n}	E_{ln}	H_{1n}	H_{2n}	H_{ln}	a_n

A regression analysis is then performed to correlate the biological activity with these interaction energy parameters. The general form of the correlation may be

$$\text{Activity} = C + \sum_{i=1}^{l} \sum_{j=1}^{p} c_{ij}\, P_{ij} \tag{5.2}$$

where c_{ij} is the coefficient of the energy parameter P_{ij} of a probe group P_j at the grid point i. Since there can be thousands of grid points and comparatively very less number of compounds, the problem is solved by using *partial least square* (PLS) method. The predictive ability of the PLS model is then checked by the *cross-validation* method. In fact, in PLS analysis a certain subgroup of molecules is selected which constitutes a training set to derive a PLS model. The residual molecules constitute a test set. The predictive ability of the model derived is then judged by predicting the activity of the molecules of this test set.

Care should be taken that in the training set the activities of the compounds should be more or less equally distributed and that the structures and all relevant properties of the test set compounds should not be too far from the training set compounds.

For calculating the electrostatic fields, the partial charges on atom are determined for all the molecules either before or after their preferred conformations are obtained, using a semi-empirical method such as AM1, PM3 or MNDO. The hydrophobic fields can be calculated using either HINT [29, 30] or GRID [29, 31] program. Hydrophobicity of the molecules (log P) can also be added as an additional parameter in the PLS analysis. Likewise, any other physiochemical parameters, such as MR, can be added in the analysis, but an appropriate scaling of all the parameters is then to be performed to give a comparable weight to all the fields and the additional parameters.

The results of CoMFA analysis are shown as color-coded contours around molecules, representing regions for favorable and unfavorable interactions with the receptor. Green and yellow colors are used for steric interactions and blue and red for electrostatic interactions. In steric interactions, green contours indicate the regions where an increase in steric bulk will enhance the activity, while yellow contours indicate the regions where an increase in steric bulk will reduce the activity. Likewise, in electrostatic interactions, the blue contours represent the regions where an increase in the positive charge will enhance the activity and the red contours the regions where an increase in the negative charge will do the same. An example of such contours is shown in Fig. 5.5 for a cyclic urea derivative acting as HIV-1 protease inhibitors [32].

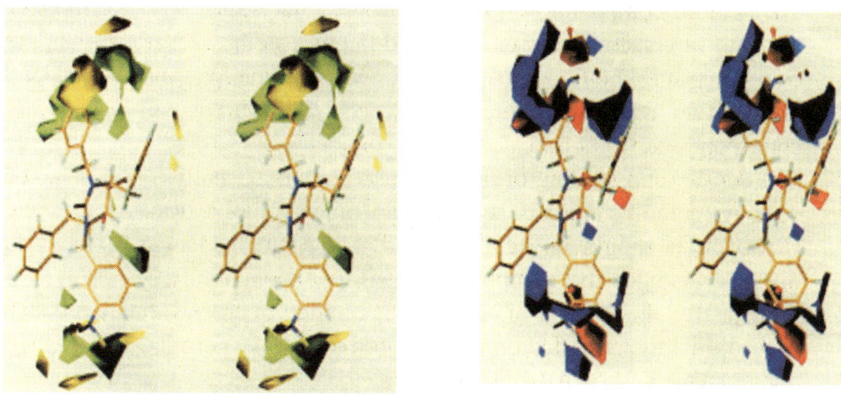

(a) (b)

Fig. 5.5. Stereoview of CoMFA contour plots for a cyclic urea derivative acting as an HIV-1 protease inhibitors: (a) steric fields (stdev* coeff) – the green polyhedra (80% contribution) represents areas where bulkier groups may enhance activity and the yellow polyhedra (20% contribution) indicate areas where bulky groups may have detrimental effects, (b) electrostatic fields (stdev* coeff) – the blue polyhedra (80% contribution) represent the favored electrostatic areas with positive charges and the red polyhedra (20% contribution) the favored electrostatic areas with negative charges. Reprinted with permission from [32]. Copyright 1999 American Chemical Society.

The major advantages of 3D QSAR using CoMFA are that it provides: (1) a fundamental understanding of the interactions of the ligands with the binding site of the receptor and (2) contour plots in relation to receptor site structure, whose critical analysis provides valuable insight into drug-receptor interactions.

Since its inception in 1988, the CoMFA methodology has seen its vast application leading to hundreds of publications [29, 33-39] and is now a most preferred approach for 3D QSAR analysis, and the appropriate software, Tripos CoMFA [40], has gained wide popularity. However, CoMFA approach has a number of shortcomings described as follows:

1. The most serious problem is related to the use of the conformations of the molecules determined *in vacuo* by any semi-empirical method. These conformations may be entirely different from those in the bound state at a receptor surface.
2. It does not take into account the fact that a subtle change in the substituents of a molecule may have the drastic change in the binding mode.
3. Of the several minimum energy conformations obtained for a molecule, only one conformation is considered for the analysis.
4. The fit of the compounds is not performed with the "rigid body" assumptions but with fit constraints. Even a small difference in the energy between the conformer after the fit and its minimal energy counterpart may correspond to manifold decrease in the activity, e.g., a difference of 4 kcal/mol corresponds to 1000-fold decrease in the activity.
5. The density and spacing of the grid also matters. Usually a grid distance of 2 Å (default value) is selected but other values can also be taken. However, it should be kept in mind that a small change in the grid distance changes the computational effort exponentially.
6. Statistically, the number of compounds omitted in cross-validation check is also an important factor. If the computer time permits, only leave-one-out check should be performed.
7. The predictive ability of the model largely depends on the selection of the training and test sets. Often, the better the training set is described, the worse is the prediction for the test set.
8. Different models can be obtained by different persons for given series of compounds.
9. The activity of new derivatives cannot be extrapolated from CoMFA models.
10. CoMFA models cannot provide any general information about the hydrophobic effects as does the simple QSAR. The optimum value of log P or π that simple QSAR can establish for a series of compounds is of great help in designing the new compounds. This type of result is not possible from CoMFA.
11. It is hard to interpret any role of physicochemical properties in the drug action from the latent variables used in the CoMFA model.

However, despite the above shortcomings, CoMFA has been widely accepted as it is the only approach that presently correlates the biological activity with 3D structures of the molecules and solves the problem of using the steric factors. Kim and Martin [28, 41-45] presented some interesting comparisons of CoMFA with simple QSAR. In general, the use of additional parameters has been found to give higher values of r.

The steric problems posed by the receptor could be solved by other methods also. Simon et al. [46] developed a method called minimum steric difference (MSD) and Hopfinger [47, 48] proposed a method called molecular shape analysis (MSA). The MSD is based on the assumption that the most active compound of a congeneric series gives an estimate of the shape of the receptor. The minimal steric difference between this compound and each of the other members in the series is then determined by counting the non-superimposable atoms. In MSA, first a set of most stable congeners is determined using molecular mechanics and then a reference compound is selected with which the total common overlap of the remaining molecules in the set is determined. This common overlap is designated as $V_o(s)$ and used as a steric parameter in QSAR. Another method to define the shape and character of a receptor is the *distance geometry approach* developed by Crippen and Ghosh [49-51].

5.6 Comparative Molecular Similarity Indices Analysis (CoMSIA)

The CoMFA method in its standard form uses only Lennard-Jones (L-J) and Coulomb potentials to map only the steric and electrostatic fields. No other fields, such as hydrophobic, hydrogen-bond acceptor, or hydrogen-bond donor field, are taken into account. Moreover, these two potentials used in the CoMFA produce significant variations in the energy for very small changes in position, for example, the L-J potential becomes very steep close to the van der Waals surface of the molecules (i.e., to a situation when the distance between the molecules approaches to the sum of their van der Waals radii). Therefore, an arbitrary cut-off is taken for both the fields that results in fragmented contour plots which are difficult to interpret. A modification in CoMFA was therefore needed which led to develop CoMSIA [39, 52]. CoMSIA is simply a modified version of CoMFA where Gaussian functions are used whose slopes are not as steep as those of Coulomb and L-J potentials. Thus, in CoMSIA no cut-offs need to be defined. CoMSIA calculates SEAL similarity fields, where probes are used to calculate their 'similarity indices' to the investigated molecules in different grid points. These fields are then correlated with the biological activities of the molecules as in CoMFA.

The similarity indices $A_{F,k}$ between the compound of interest and a probe atom can be calculated as [53]

$$A_{F,k}^{q}(j) = -\sum_{i=1}^{n} w_{\text{probe},k}\, w_{ik} \exp\left(-\alpha r_{iq}^{\;2}\right) \tag{5.3}$$

where the summation extends over all the atoms of a molecule j, w_{ik} is the actual value of the physicochemical property k of atom i, $w_{\text{probe},k}$ the physicochemical property k of the probe atom, and r_{iq} the mutual distance between the atom i and the probe atom at grid point q. In principle, any relevant physicochemical property can be considered in CoMSIA to calculate a field of similarity indices. Presently, five fields considered are steric, electrostatic, hydrophobic, hydrogen-bond donor, and hydrogen-bond acceptor. A common probe atom can be used to calculate all the fields, e.g., an atom with radius 1 Å, charge +1, hydrophobicity +1, hydrogen-bond donating property +1, and hydrogen-bond acceptor property +1 [39, 52, 54].

In Eq. 5.3, α is a constant called attenuation factor. Its large values result in a strong attenuation of the distance-dependent consideration of molecular similarity and lead to deeper Gaussian function. In this situation the global molecular similarity becomes less important. Global molecular features become more important, however, if small values of α are taken. Therefore, in most of the studies α has been set to 0.3 [39, 52, 54], which permits a reasonable local smearing of the molecular similarity indices and helps avoid extreme dependence on small change in mutual alignments.

5.7 Hologram QSAR (HQSAR)

HQSAR is a unique QSAR technique for SAR analysis that neither requires any physicochemical parameters that are needed for classical 2D QSAR nor faces any such problem like determination of 3D structure, putative binding conformation, or molecular alignment essential for 3D QSAR. It simply requires 2D structures of the molecules and their activity [55, 56].

In HQSAR, the molecule is converted to a characteristic molecular fingerprint that encodes the frequency of occurrence of various molecular fragment types. The molecular structure is broken down on the fly into all possible linear and branched fragments of connected atoms of a fixed size, usually in the range of 4 to 7 atoms. Each unique fragment is then assigned a specific large positive integral value by means of a cyclic redundancy check (CRC) algorithm. Each of these integers corresponds to a bin in an integer array called a *molecular hologram*. This hologram may be of a fixed length in the range of 50-500, in which the bin occupants become the molecular descriptors. If there are n compounds in a given series and l is the length of the hologram, then a matrix of $n \times l$ size is generated for HQSAR analysis. Standard PLS method is then applied for getting the results.

The molecular fragments in HQSAR can be distinguished based on the atoms, bonds, connections, number of hydrogen atoms, and chirality parameters. For example, for a molecular structure such as **(3)**, the three possible fragments (overlapping, linear, and branched) are as shown by **(3a)**, **(3b)**, **(3c)** [56]. The molecular hologram of l = 10 generated for this molecular structure is [56]

3	6	2	0	5	13	0	7	1	8

The hologram length, fragment size, and the fragment distinction are the important factors on which the HQSAR models really depend.

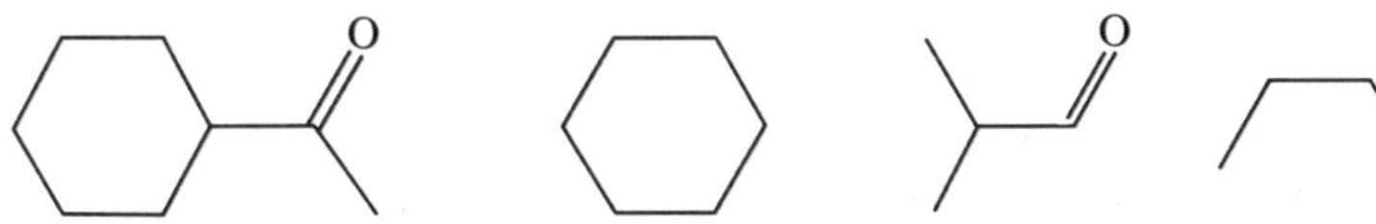

(3) (a molecular structure) **(3a)** (overlapping) **(3b)** (linear) **(3c)** (branched)

Fragments of (3)

5.8 Hypothetical Active Site Lattice (HASL) Approach

The HASL approach of QSAR was developed by Doweyko [57]. An HASL model depends on the mathematical construction of a hypothetical active site lattice that can simulate the enzyme-inhibitor interactions. This lattice provides predictive SAR model for a set of competitive inhibitors. Minimum energy conformations are calculated for all similar and dissimilar molecules in the set and the molecules are placed in a three-dimensional grid. A user-selected physicochemical property such as hydrophobicity or electron density is added to it as the fourth dimension. The resulting multidimensional lattices are automatically superimposed by an iterative fitting. Thus, a hypothetical active site lattice is formed which can predict the relative orientation and the affinities of the molecules.

In HASL modeling, the procedure starts with obtaining Cartesian coordinates of a molecule from an energy-minimization routine. These coordinates are then converted to a set of equally-spaced points such that all points lie within the van der Waals radii of the atoms present in the molecule. This framework of points is called *molecular lattice*. A 4D lattice can be constructed by adding a user-selected property. Such a 4D lattice for a selected molecule can be taken as a reference lattice and then lattices obtained in the same way for other molecules are matched. The degree of matching between two lattices is based on the degree of correspondence between the points of the two lattices, i.e., on the number of points being common in the two lattices. This degree of matching or "FIT' can be measured by

$$\text{FIT} = L\ (\text{common})/L\ (\text{ref}) + L\ (\text{common})/L\ (\text{molecule}) \quad (5.4)$$

where L is the number of lattice points. A value of 2 of FIT would correspond to a perfect match.

After the fit of 4D lattice of one molecule with that of other is obtained, a composite HASL is formed that contains all the points of both the lattices. In this composite HASL, however, all the information of both lattices is merged. This can be illustrated by two linear molecules A and B with biological activity (say pK_i or – log IC_{50}) values 3.0 and 6.0, respectively, whose lattices form a composite lattice C as shown in Fig. 5.6.

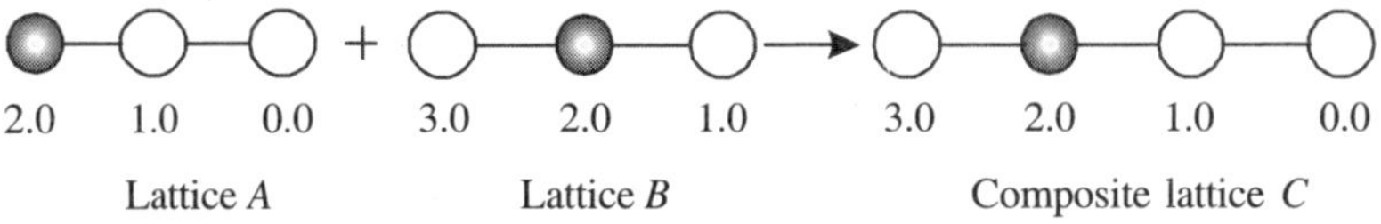

Fig. 5.6. Merging of two lattices *A* and *B* to give a composite lattice *C*. Below the lattices are the partial activity values of the lattice points. The shaded portion refers to the atom of different type, e.g. electron-rich or electron deficient. Adopted with permission from [57]. Copyright 1988 American Chemical Society.

In a lattice of a molecule, the total activity of the molecule is distributed to all the points of the lattice, which are called the partial activity values of the points. The distribution of the activity value as shown in Fig. 5.6 can be considered as the lattice description that the activity data of molecules *A* and *B* need to approach. Otherwise, as a first approximation, the total activity value of a molecule is evenly divided among its lattice points as shown in Fig. 5.7. From these averaged lattice point data, an averaged HASL is obtained, where the averaging is done among only the common points.

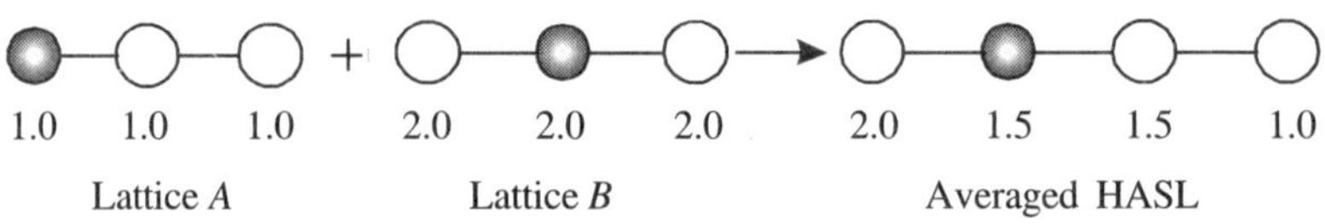

Fig. 5.7. Average distribution of activity data of molecules among the lattice points. In averaged HASL, only points 2 and 3 are common to lattices *A* and *B*, hence their average comes out to be 1.5 for each. Adopted with permission from [57]. Copyright 1988 American Chemical Society.

From this averaged HASL one can calculate the activity of the compounds by summing up the partial activity values of points that belong to a particular lattice. Thus, in Fig. 5.7, points 2, 3 and 4 of averaged HASL belong to lattice *A*, whose partial activity data on summing up leads to a value of 4.0 for molecule *A*. Similarly, a sum of partial activity data of points 1, 2 and 3, which belong to lattice *B*, gives the activity for molecule *B* as 5.0. Both these calculated values are quite different from the corresponding observed values 3.0 and 6.0, respectively. To minimize these differences, an iterative procedure is adopted where initially averaged HASL is taken as a starting point.

To start the iteration, two correction factors, referred to as 'IN' and 'OUT', are calculated from the difference in observed and predicted activities (referred to as 'Error'). 'IN' is defined as expressed by Eq. 5.5a and 'OUT' as expressed by Eq. 5.5b.

$$\mathrm{IN} = \mathrm{Error/NI} \tag{5.5a}$$
$$\mathrm{OUT} = -\ \mathrm{Error/NO} \tag{5.5b}$$

where NI refers to the number of lattice points in the overlap and NO to those outside the overlap. Figure 5.8 shows how the iteration starts from averaged HASL of Fig. 5.7 and goes to the final step to get an averaged HASL that makes the prediction with least error.

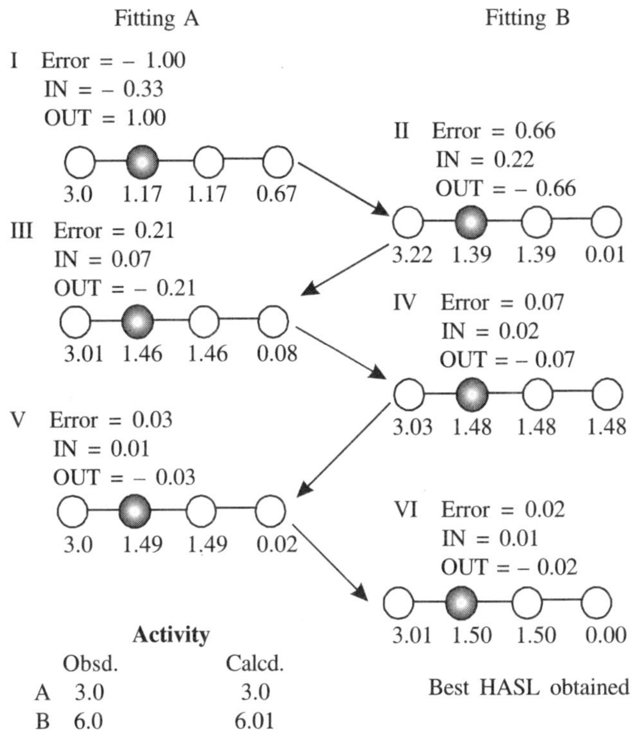

Fig. 5.8. Example of iterative procedure to obtain the best HASL, capable of giving the best prediction [57]. Reprinted with permission from [57]. Copyright 1988 American Chemical Society.

5.9 The 3D Molecular Similarity and QSAR

Structurally similar molecules may have similar physicochemical properties and may bind in a similar fashion with the receptor, eliciting similar biological effects. The difference in their binding with the receptors, and consequently the difference in their biological effects will, however, depend on the extent of the similarity in their 3D structures. If it can be measured in a quantitative term, it can be used as an important variable in classical QSAR.

One of the earliest methods to measure molecular similarity was to calculate a similarity index S based on field-based alignment of the molecules [58]. Carbó et al. [58] defined this index in terms of superposed electron density maps as

$$S_{AB} = \frac{\int P_A P_B dv}{\left(\int P_A^2 dv\right)^{\frac{1}{2}} \left(\int P_B^2 dv\right)^{\frac{1}{2}}} \tag{5.6}$$

where P_A and P_B are electron densities of molecules A and B, respectively. The numerator measures the degree of overlap between the two molecules and the denominator is a normalization term. Thus, the Carbó index is based on the degree of overlap and does not measure the magnitude of the fields. To account for the magnitude of the fields, Hodgkin [59] defined the index as

$$S_{AB} = \frac{2\int P_A P_B dv}{\int P_A^2 dv + \int P_B^2 dv} \tag{5.7}$$

Equations 5.6 and 5.7, however, have been applied to compare any structural properties P_A and P_B of two molecules.

A refinement in Carbó's index (Eq. 5.6) was, however, made by using the molecular electrostatic potential (MEP) $P_{\mathbf{r}}$ inside a grid which is measured as

$$P_{\mathbf{r}} = \sum_{i=1}^{N} \frac{q_i}{|\mathbf{r} - \mathbf{R}_i|} \tag{5.8}$$

where q_i is the point charge on atom i at position $\mathbf{R}_i$ from the grid point $\mathbf{r}$. The summation extends to all the atoms N in the molecule. Now in terms of this $P_{\mathbf{r}}$, the similarity index was defined as

$$S_{AB} = \frac{\sum_{r=1}^{n} P_{A,r} P_{B,r}}{\left(\sum_{r=1}^{n} P_{A,r}^2\right)^{\frac{1}{2}} \left(\sum_{r=1}^{n} P_{B,r}^2\right)^{\frac{1}{2}}} \tag{5.9}$$

where all the summations extend to all grid points n. In Eq. 5.9, one can also use steric and hydrophobic fields that can be calculated in the same manner as electrostatic potential.

The electrostatic potential and field at certain points on a grid can be calculated using a program called automatic similarity package (ASP) [60, 61]. This program has been modified to use Gaussian function approximations rather than grid to calculate electrostatic potential and similarity indices [62-64]. Molecular similarity indices are optimized in this program by fixing one molecule and translating and rotating the other molecule until their similarity reaches an optimum. These similarity indices can be successfully used in 3D QSAR analyses. In a preliminary study on a series of nitromethylene insecticides, Hodgkin and Richards [59] have shown a nice linear correlation between the activity of the molecules and their MEP similarity indices calculated for all molecules in comparison with the most active compound. The current version of ASP, however, uses $N \times N$ matrices, N being the number of molecules in the data set, where a matrix element S_{ij} $(i \neq j)$ refers to the similarity index between two molecules i and j. A quantitative analysis of these matrices in relation to the activity of the molecules can be performed using neural network. A number of examples of the use of similarity indices in QSAR analysis have been cited in [12].

References

[1] Clark, D.E. and Pickett, S.D., *Drug Discov. Today*, ***5*** (2000), 49.

[2] Walter, W.P. and Murcko, M.A., *Adv. Drug Deliv. Rev.*, ***54*** (2002), 255.

[3] Gillet, V.J., Willet, P. and Bradshaw, J., *J. Chem. Inform. Comput. Sci.*, ***38*** (1998), 165.

[4] Hall, L.H. and Kier, L.B., *Rev. Comput. Chem.*, ***2*** (1991), 367.

[5] Lipinski, C.A., Lombardo, F., Dominy, B.W. and Feeny, P.J., *Adv. Drug Deliv. Rev.*, ***23*** (1997), 3.

[6] Teague, S.J., Davis, A.M., Leeson, P.D. and Opera, T., *Angew. Chem.* (*Int. Ed. Eng.*), ***38*** (1999), 3743.

[7] Hann, M.M., Leach, A.R. and Harper, G., *J. Chem. Inform. Comput. Sci.*, ***41*** (2001), 856.

[8] Leach, A.R., *Molecular Modelling Principles and Applications*, Addison Wesley Longman Ltd., England (1996); Second edition, Pearson Education, Harlow (2001).

[9] Leach, A.R. and Gillet, V.J., *An Introduction to Chemoinformatics*, Kluwer Academic Publishers, The Netherlands (2003).

[10] Dammkoehler, R.A., Karasek, S.F., Shands, E.F.B. and Marshall, G.R., *J. Comput-Aided Mol. Des.*, ***3*** (1989), 3.

[11] Bohm, H.-J., *J. Comput-Aided Mol. Des.*, ***6*** (1992), 61; LUDI, BIOSYM Technologies, Inc., San Diego, C.A., USA.

[12] Kubinyi, H., *QSAR: Hansch Analysis and Related Approaches*, VCH, New York (1993).

[13] Kuntz, I.D., Blaney, J.M., Oatley, S.J., Langridge, R. and Ferrin, T.E., *J. Mol. Biol.*, ***161*** (1982), 269.

[14] Kuntz, I.D., *Science*, ***257*** (1992), 1078.

[15] Kuntz, I.D., Meng, E.C. and Shoichet, B.K., *Acc. Chem. Res.*, ***27*** (1994), 117.

[16] Rosinko, A. III, Skell, J.M., Balducci, R., McGarity, C.M. and Pearlman, R.S., *CONCORD*, the University of Texas at Austin and Tripos Associates, St. Louis, MO (1988).

[17] Gasteiger, J., Rudolph, C. and Sadowski, J., *Tetrahedran Computer Methodology*, ***3*** (1990), 537.

[18] Lam, P.Y.S., Jadhav, P.K., Eyermann, C.E. et al., *Science*, ***263*** (1994), 380.
[19] Judson, R.S., Jaeger, E.P. and Treasurywala, A.M., *J. Mol. Struct. (Theochem.)*, ***114*** (1994), 191.
[20] Jones, G., Willet, P. and Glen, R.C., *J. Mol. Biol.*, ***245*** (1995), 43.
[21] Gehlhaar, D.K., Verkhivker, G.M., Rejto, P.A., Sherman, C.J., Fogel, D.B., Fogel, L.J. and Freer, S.T., *Chem. Biol.*, ***2*** (1995), 317.
[22] Oshiro, C.M., Kuntz, I.D. and Dixon, J.S., *J. Comput.-Aided Mol. Des.*, ***9*** (1995), 113.
[23] Crippen, G.M. and Havel, T.F., *Distance Geometry and Molecular Conformation*, Wiley, New York (1988).
[24] Bohm, H.-J. and Klebe, G., *Angew. Chem.* (*Int. Ed. Eng.*), ***35*** (1996), 2588.
[25] Ajay and Murcko, M.A., *J. Med. Chem.*, ***38*** (1998), 4951.
[26] Bohm, H.J., *J. Comput.-Aided Mol. Des.*, ***8*** (1994), 243.
[27] Cramer, R.D. III, Patterson, D.E. and Bunce, J.D., *J. Am. Chem. Soc.*, ***110*** (1988), 5959.
[28] Kim, K.H., *Med. Chem. Res.*, ***1*** (1991), 259.
[29] Kubinyi, H. (Ed.), *3D QSAR in Drug Design: Theory, Methods and Applications*, ESCOM, Leiden (1993).
[30] Klebe, G., Mietzner, T. and Weber, F., *J. Comput.-Aided Mol. Des.*, ***8*** (1994), 758.
[31] Wireko, F.C., Kellog, G.E. and Abraham, D.J., *J. Med. Chem.*, ***34*** (1991), 758.
[32] Debnath, A.K., *J. Med. Chem.*, ***42*** (1999), 249.
[33] Kubinyi, H., *Chemie in Unserver Zeit*, ***23*** (1994), 281.
[34] Green, S.M. and Marshall, G.R., *Trends Pharm. Sci.*, ***16*** (1995), 285.
[35] Kim, K.H., In *Molecular Similarity in Drug Design*, Dean, P.M. (Ed.), Chapman and Hall, New York (1995), 291.
[36] Martin, Y.C. and Lin, C.T., In *The Practice of Medicinal Chemistry*, Wermuth, C.G. (Ed.), Academic Press, London (1996), 459.
[37] Blankley, C.J., In *Structure-Property Correlations in Drug Research*, Waterbeemd, van de H. (Ed.), Academic Press, Austin, TX (1996), 111.
[38] Martin, Y.C., Kim, K.H. and Lin, C.T., In *Advances in Quantitative Structure-Property Relationships*, Vol. 1; Charton, M. (Ed.), JAI Press, Greenwich, CT (1996), 1.
[39] Kubinyi, H., Folkers, G. and Martin, Y.C. (Eds.), *3D QSAR*, Vols. 2 and 3, Kluwer, Dordrecht (1998).
[40] SYBYL/QSAR, *Molecular Modelling Software*, Tripos Inc., 1699S, Hanley Road, St. Louis, MO 63944, USA.
[41] Kim, K.H., In Ref. [29], 169.
[42] Kim, K.H., *J. Comput.-Aided Mol. Des.*, ***7*** (1993), 71.
[43] Kim, K.H. and Martin, Y.C., *J. Med. Chem.*, ***34*** (1991), 2056.
[44] Kim, K.H., *Med. Chem. Res.*, ***2*** (1992), 22.
[45] Kim, K.H., *Quant. Struct.-Act. Relat.*, ***11*** (1992), 127.
[46] Simon, Z., Chiriac, A., Holban, S., Ciubotaru, D. and Mihalas, G.I., *Minimum Steric Difference: The MTD Method for QSAR Studies*, Research Studies Press, Letchworth, UK (1984).
[47] Hopfinger, A.J., *J. Am. Chem. Soc.*, ***102*** (1980), 7196.
[48] Hopfinger, A.J., *J. Med. Chem.*, ***26*** (1983), 990.

[49] Ghosh, A.K. and Crippen, G.M., In *Comprehensive Medicinal Chemistry, **Vol. 4**, Quantitative Drug Design*, C. Hansch, P.G. Sammes and J.B. Taylor (Eds.), C.A. Ramsden (Series Ed.), Pergamon Press, Oxford (1990), 715.

[50] Crippen, G.M., *J. Med. Chem.*, ***22*** (1979), 988.

[51] Crippen, G.M., In *Distance Geometry and Conformational Calculations: Chemometric Research Studies*, ***Vol. 1***, Bawden, D. (Ed.), Wiley, Chichester, UK (1981).

[52] Klebo, G., Abraham, U. and Mietzner, T., *J. Med. Chem.*, ***37*** (1994), 4130.

[53] Malinowski, E.R. and Howery, D.G., *Factor Analysis in Chemistry*, Wiley, New York (1980).

[54] Suh, M.-E., Park, S.-Y. and Lee, H.J., *Bull. Korean Chem. Soc.*, ***23*** (2002), 417.

[55] HQSAR is the product of Tripos, Inc., St. Louis, MO (1997).

[56] Lowis, D.R., *Tripos Technical Notes*, ***1*** (1997), 1.

[57] Doweyko, A.M., *J. Med. Chem.*, ***31*** (1988), 1396.

[58] Carbo, R., Leydo, L. and Arnau, M., *Int. J. Quantum Chem.*, ***17*** (1980), 1185.

[59] Hodgkin, E.E. and Richards, W.G., *Int. J. Quantum Chem., Quantum Biol. Symp.*, ***14*** (1987), 105.

[60] Burt, C., Richards, W.G. and Huxley, P.G., *J. Comput. Chem.*, ***11*** (1990), 1139.

[61] *Automated Similarity Package*, Oxford Molecular Ltd., Oxford, UK.

[62] Good, A.C., So, S.-S. and Richards, W.G., *J. Med. Chem.*, ***36*** (1993), 433.

[63] Good, A.C., Hodgkin, E.E. and Richards, W.G., *J. Chem. Inform. Comput. Sci.*, ***32*** (1992), 188.

[64] Good, A.C. and Richards, W.G., *J. Chem. Inform. Comput. Sci.*, ***33*** (1993), 112.

6

ADMET Studies

6.1 Introduction

The necessity for the prediction of ADMET (absorption, distribution, metabolism, excretion (or elimination) and toxicity) properties of the drugs has increased as the capacity for biological screening and chemical synthesis have dramatically increased. For a drug molecule it is not just sufficient to have studied *in vitro* that it has strong interactions with its receptor. It must also be able to reach its site of action *in vivo*, which depends on its ability to cross some physiological barriers such as cell membrane or blood-brain barrier. Further, the molecule must remain in the body for an appropriate period of time to give the desired effect but must ultimately be removed from body by metabolism, excretion, or other pathways. Finally, neither the drug nor its metabolites should be toxic. Therefore, a detailed pharmacokinetic study of a drug is desired before it is recommended for the use. A pharmacokinetic study is the kinetic study of all four ADME process, i.e., adsorption, distribution, metabolism and excretion [1]. Pharmacokinetic parameters are derived from the measurement of the drug concentrations in blood or plasma.

Because of the convenience and compliance, most drugs are given orally which have to pass the intestinal cell membrane to get into the blood circulation. The percentage of the drug reaching the blood circulation is called the *bioavailability*. Thus, for oral bioavailability the major requirement of a drug is its permeability through the intestinal cell membrane. Another physiological barrier is the blood-brain barrier between the systematic circulation and the brain.

After a drug molecule gets into blood circulation, it is distributed to various tissues and organs of the body and finally reaches its molecular target with which it has to interact and produce the effect. Both its distribution and interaction with the target depend on its structural and physicochemical properties.

Drugs, that cannot pass through the cell membrane or blood-brain barrier passively, involve the transport mechanisms which actively promote (or reduce) the absorption of the substances across these barriers, e.g., P-glycoprotein (PGP) efflux pump [2]. For oral bioavailability, however, the aqueous solubility of the drug is of prime importance.

The metabolism is also an important factor for the oral bioavailability of a drug. For its bioavailability, the drug should be able to withstand degradation by intestinal and hepatic metabolizing enzyme, most notably cytochrome P450 (CYP450). In the meantime, drugs inhibiting CYP450 may result in undesirable drug-drug interactions and hepatotoxicity. Therefore, a good drug, except prodrugs, should neither be a substrate nor an inhibitor of any CYP450 enzyme. The CYP450 family of enzymes is composed of about 60 isoenzymes, but only a very few such as CYP3A4, CYP2D6 and CYP2C9 can be involved in the metabolism of drugs [3]. However, the most important aspect of the metabolism is the rate and extent of metabolism (turnover) that affects the clearance.

Finally, toxicity comes as the most challenging problem in the drug discovery whose prediction has been of great interest since long.

6.2 Prediction of ADMET Properties

Prediction of ADMET properties is now the most important area in the drug discovery. It requires large database of ADMET properties associated with structures to build computational models that link structural changes with changes in response, from which compounds with improved properties can be predicted and designed. However, a common problem with many ADMET properties is the paucity of experimental data, especially human *in vivo*. This creates a great problem in getting reliable models applicable to a wide variety of chemical classes. Therefore, there has been significant interest in the identification of *in vitro* systems that are surrogates for the real system. *Caco-2 cells*, derived from human intestinal cell-line, present such an example, which act as surrogate for the human absorption process and are used to measure permeability. Besides, Madin-Darby canine kidney (MDCK) monolayers are also used to make oral absorption estimates.

Human ADMET predictions can be attempted at both theoretical and experimental levels, but since experimental aspect is beyond the scope of this book, we shall describe here only theoretical level where *in silico* or computational models are obtained for the prediction. For *in silico* or computational models, however, we first have to find the ADMET parameters to account for the following properties.

6.2.1 Absorption

The passive permeability of a drug across a cell membrane can be estimated using single molecular properties such as log D (D is the distribution coefficient, for which an aqueous buffer at pH 7.4 (blood pH) or 6.5 (intestinal pH) is used in the experimental determination) or hydrogen-bonding capacity. The hydrogen-bonding capacity of a drug molecule has been recognized as very crucial factor of permeability because it promotes the binding of the drug with its aqueous environment which is unfavorable to its permeability and absorption. According to Lipinski's '*rule of five*' described in Sec. 5.1, the poor absorption and permeability of a potential drug is more likely if there are more than 5 H-bond donors and 10 H-bond acceptors.

A variety of methods have been adopted to estimate the H-bonding capacity that include simple heteroatoms (O and N) count, or the count of the number of H-bond donors and acceptors in the molecules, and measuring the (dynamic) polar surface area (PSA) [4]. The PSA is defined as the molecular surface arising from polar atoms (N and O atoms together with their attached hydrogens – some definitions also include *S* atoms and their attached hydrogen atoms). The PAS can be easily calculated, and it is now accepted that a single minimum energy conformation is sufficient to compute the PSA, instead of more computationally demanding and time consuming molecular dynamics simulations approach [4]. A fast fragment-based algorithm for PSA has been reported [5], which allows PSA calculations to be implemented in virtual screening approaches.

However, the above described factors are not the only ones that affect the permeability and absorption of drugs, but many drugs are also affected by some biological events such as transport and metabolism. Many drugs can act as substrates for the transporter molecules which can either promote or hinder the permeability. For example, a combined role of cytochrome P4503A4 (CYP3A4) and P-glycoprotein in the gut has been found to act as a barrier to drug absorption [6].

6.2.2 Blood-Brain Barrier Permeability

For the drugs acting in CNS, the blood-brain permeability is of prime importance. Several authors have discussed various factors that affect the uptake of drugs into the brain, and a variety of models for the prediction of uptake have been developed [7-11]. One of such models takes into account only three factors, namely, the calculated octanol/water partition coefficient, number of hydrogen-bond acceptors in the aqueous medium, and the polar surface area [9]. Another model considered simply a '*rule of five*' like hypothesis and proposed that molecules with a molecular weight < 450 Da or with PSA < 100 Å^2 are more likely to penetrate the blood-brain barrier [7]. Some models, such as Volsurf model, consider the 3D molecular field descriptors that are, however, finally transformed to 2D numerical descriptors for the use [10].

6.2.3 Bioavailability

Bioavailability depends on absorption and the first-pass metabolism through the liver. Since these two processes superpose upon each other and since absorption in turn depends on the solubility and permeability of the drug molecules as well as on the interaction with transporter and metabolizing enzymes in the gut wall, predicting bioavailability is not so easy. However, molecular flexibility, which can be accounted for by counting the number of rotatable bonds, has been found as a factor affecting the bioavailability [12]. A simple QSAR model for human oral bioavailability has been discussed by Yoshida and Topliss [13]. In a report, Podlogar et al. [14] have attempted to give another model, based on classification using the Soft Independent Modeling of Class Analogy (SIMCA) approach which seems as successful as Yoshida and Topliss QSAR model. A better model than that of Yoshida and Topliss has, however, been developed by Bains et al. [15], which is based on genetic programming, a specific form of evolutionary programming.

6.2.4 Metabolism

For predicting metabolism, QSAR and 3D QSAR approaches have been found to be very important [16]. A novel approach to predicting P450-mediated drug metabolism has been discussed by De Groot et al. [17] where a combined protein and pharmacophore model for CYP2D6 has been mentioned. Pharmacophore and 3D QSAR methods for modeling cytochrome P450 active site have also been discussed by Ekins et al. [18].

Several approaches based on databases are available or are under development to predict metabolism [19]. Examples are some expert systems such as MetabolExpert (compudrug) or Meteor (LHASA, Ltd.), the databases Metabolite (MDL), and Metabolism (Accelrys) [20].

6.2.5 Toxicity

Toxicity is the end-point and the most frustrating problem of the drug industry because many drugs, after completing a long journey facing ADME challenges, fail to reach market or are withdrawn from the market after being approved due to their toxicity. It has been estimated that approximately 20-40% of drug failures in investigational drug development can be attributed to toxicity problem.

Prediction of toxicity is a challenging problem since it can be related to a multitude of phenomena, such as carcinogenicity, mutagenicity, tetrotogenicity, irritation, sensitization, immunotoxicology, and neurotoxicity. Carcinogenicity and mutagenicity have, however, been chosen to build the models for toxicity prediction [21] and consequently the current software packages are related to only these two phenomena. Attempts, however, have also been made to try and predict more general toxicity. One of the most widely used methods is the DEREK (Deductive Estimation of Risk from Existing Knowledge) system [22]. DEREK is an expert- or rule-based system, where a set of rules derived from experts in the field and from the literature are employed. These rules are based on a list of chemical structures that can be related to specific toxic effects. The other models are CASE and MULTICASE [23] and TOPKAT [24]. TOPKAT is based on a more traditional QSAR approach using electropological descriptors.

Apart from these approaches that use the expert systems, there are methods that are primarily based on the generation of descriptors of chemical structures and correlating them with toxicological end-points. Some recent reviews have presented a comparative utility of some commercially available *in silico* toxicology softwares [21, 25, 26]. However, the limited availability of public-domain toxicology data has greatly limited the number of toxicological end-point to be forecasted.

References

[1] Smith, D.A., van de Waterbeemd, H. and Walker, D.K., *Pharmacokinetic and Metabolism in Drug Design*, Wiley-VCH, Weinheim, Germany (2001).

[2] Stouch, T.R. and Gudmundsson, A., *Adv. Drug. Deliv. Rev.*, ***54*** (2002), 315.

[3] Guengerich, F.P., *Chem. Res. Toxicol.*, ***14*** (2001), 611.

[4] Stenberg, P., Norinder, U., Luthmen, K. and Artursson, P., *J. Med. Chem.*, ***44*** (2001), 1927.

[5] Ertel, P., Rohde, B. and Selzer, P., *J. Med. Chem.*, ***43*** (2000), 3714.

[6] Cummins, C.L., Jacobson, W. and Benet, L.Z., *J. Pharmacol. Exp. Ther.*, ***300*** (2002), 1036.

[7] van de Waterbeemd, H., Camenisch, G., Folkers, G., Chretien, J.R. and Raevsky, O.A., *J. Drug Target*, ***6*** (1998), 151.

[8] Clark, D.E., *J. Pharm. Sci.*, ***88*** (1999), 815.

[9] Feher, M., Sourial, E. and Schmidt, J.M., *Int. J. Pharm.*, ***201*** (2000), 239.

[10] Crivoric, P., Cruciani, G., Carrupt, P.A. and Testa, B., *J. Med. Chem.*, ***43*** (2000), 2204.

[11] Kaznessis, Y.N., Snow, M.E. and Blankley, C.J., *J. Comput-Aided Mol. Des.*, ***15*** (2001), 697.

[12] Veber, D.F., Johnson, S.R., Cheng, S.Y., Smith, B.R., Ward, K.W. and Kopple, K.D., *J. Med. Chem.*, ***45*** (2002), 2615.

[13] Yoshida, F. and Topliss, J.G., *J. Med. Chem.*, ***43*** (2000), 2575.

[14] Podlogar, B.L., Muegge, I. and Brice, L.J., *Current Opin. Drug Disc. Dev.*, ***4*** (2001), 102.

[15] Bains, W., Gilbert, R., Sviridenko, L., Gasson, J.-M., Scoffin, R., Birchall, K., Harvey, I. and Caldwell, J., *Current Opin. Drug Disc. Dev.*, ***5*** (2002), 44.

[16] Ekins, S., Bravi, G., Binkley, S., Gillespie, J.S., Ring, B.J., Wikel, J.H. and Wrighton, S.A., *Drug Metab. Dispos.*, ***28*** (2000), 994.

[17] De Groot, M., Ackland, M.J., Horne, V.A., Alex, A.A. and Jones, B.C., *J. Med. Chem.*, ***42*** (1999), 1515.

[18] Ekins, S., De Groot, M. and Jones, J.P., *Drug Metab. Dispos.*, ***29*** (2001), 936.

[19] Langowski, J. and Long, A., *Adv. Drug Deliv. Rev.*, ***54*** (2002), 407.

[20] Ehrhardt, P.W. (Ed.), *Drug Metabolism Databases and High-Throughput Testing During Drug Design and Development*, IUPAC, Blackwell Science, Maiden, Massachusetts (1999).

[21] Richard, A.M. and Benigni, R., *SAR and QSAR Environ. Res.*, ***13*** (2002), 1.

[22] Sanderson, D.M. and Earnshaw, C.G., *Human Exp. Toxicol.*, ***10*** (1991), 261.

[23] Rosenkranz, H.S., Cunningham, A.R., Zhang, Y.P., Claycamp, H.G., Macina, O.T., Sussman, N.B., Grant, S.G. and Klopman, G., *SAR and QSAR Environ. Res.*, ***10*** (1999), 277.

[24] Gombar, V.K. and Enslein, K., *ACS Symp. Ser.*, ***589*** (*Computer-Aided Mol. Des.*) (1995), 236.

[25] Greene, N., *Adv. Drug Deliv. Rev.*, ***54*** (2002), 417.

[26] Durham, S.K. and Pearl, G.M., *Drug Disc. Dev.*, ***4*** (2001), 110.

7

High-Throughput Screening

7.1 Introduction

The high-throughput screening (HTS) is the screening of a large number of diverse chemical compounds to identify candidate '*hits*' rapidly and accurately. HTS, thus, has greatly facilitated the drug discovery and has become the backbone of the pharmaceutical industry. Over the past decade it has also greatly drawn the attention of academicia. Robotic methods, parallel processing, and miniaturization of biological assays have made it possible to screen large numbers of compounds very efficiently. Current HTS systems enable hundreds of thousands of compounds to be assayed in only few days [1].

As shown in Fig. 7.1, HTS is a large scale process in which just a single measurement of each compound's activity is obtained in an initial

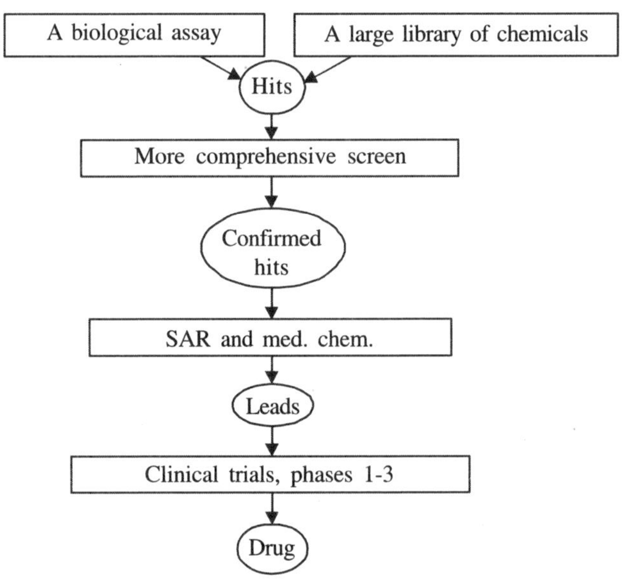

Fig. 7.1. A drug development chart from HTS process.

primary screen. The data set is then analyzed to identify a subset of compounds '*hits*' that are progressed to the next stage, in which a more comprehensive measure of the activity is performed. This comprehensive measure which is 'secondary screen' leads to '*confirmed hits*'. *Confirmed hits* with an established biological activity according to an SAR study and medicinal chemistry are termed '*leads*' that can develop into drug candidates for clinical testing.

For the HTS data analysis, the statistical methods described in Chapter 4 can be in principle applied. However, methods such as classical QSAR or Partial Least Squares (PLS) may be of little use, since such methods work best with small data sets comprising high-quality data, and where the compounds in a given set are analogs of each other and involve a common mechanism of action. In contrast, HTS data sets are characterized by their volumes, greater level of noise, which means that for single-shot data, in particular, the measured activity may not be accurate quantitative indication of the true biological activity, the diverse nature of the chemical classes, and the possibility of the presence of multiple binding modes.

For the analysis of HTS data, however, there are methods [2] based on data visualization and data reduction techniques. A data mining technique can correlate the chemical structure with biological activity. Most of the techniques, however, discussed below for the analysis of HTS data, can also be applied to smaller data sets.

7.2 Techniques for HTS Data Analysis

It is often more appropriate for HTS data analysis to classify a given set into 'active' and 'inactive' classes or 'high', 'medium' and 'low' activity classes. The following techniques can be adopted for HTS data analysis.

7.2.1 Free-Wilson Approach

The Free-Wilson approach as described in Sec. 4.2 can be successfully applied to analyze the HTS data. This can be called as *substructural analysis*. The Free-Wilson approach is based on the philosophy that each substructural fragment in a molecule makes a constant contribution to the activity, independent of the other fragments in the molecule. Thus, from Free-Wilson analysis of a given data set, we can find the activity contribution of each different substructural fragment present in the set and then derive a weight for each substructural fragment. One fairly simple formula to find the weight of a fragment i is

$$w_i = \frac{\text{act}_i}{\text{act}_i + \text{inact}_i} \tag{7.1}$$

where act_i refers to the number of active molecules in the set that contain i^{th} fragment and inact_i to the number of inactive molecules in the set that contain the ith fragment. The sum of weights for all the fragments in a new molecule then would decide the fate of a molecule whether it can be put in the active or inactive class. A decreasing rank order of the weights for a large series of new compounds will rank the molecule in decreasing probability of activity. In such analysis, however, there is a limitation of fragments. We can use only those fragments which are available in the given set. An alternative approach is to use an automated method to identify substructures that are relevant for a given data set. This is the base of CASE and MULTICASE algorithms [3, 4].

7.2.2 Discriminant Analysis

As discussed in Sec. 4.7, a discriminant analysis permits us to find a linear combination of physicochemical variables that can discriminate an active group from a non-active group. It is applied when any biological and pharmacological activity of a series of molecules is only qualitatively reported and no numerical data are given.

In discriminant analysis, a desired discriminant function Y is obtained which is of the form

$$Y = a_1X_1 + a_2X_2 + \ldots + a_nX_n \tag{7.2}$$

where a_1, a_2,... a_n are weighting coefficients of the variables X_1, X_2,... X_n, respectively. These weighting coefficients define the importance of the variables. A given set of compounds is already divided into two groups, viz. active and inactive. After evaluating the values of a's in Eq. 7.2, the mean values of Y are obtained for both the groups using the means of descriptors in the groups. From these mean values a cut-off point Y_c is obtained which decides for a new compound with a particular value of Y, calculated from Eq. 7.2, if this compound can be put in active or in inactive group.

7.2.3 Neural Network

Neural network has been discussed in detail in Sec. 4.8. Once a neural network has been trained for a set of data, it can be used to predict the activity values for new, unseen molecules.

All the three approaches described above come under '*Data Mining*' methods.

7.2.4 Non-Linear Mapping

The non-linear mapping comes under the '*Data Visualization*' approach. HTS data sets are usually multidimensional in nature in that they require descriptors which may include various physicochemical properties, fingerprints, the presence of substructural fragments, and a biological activity. The multidimensional data set, however, can be visualized if it is mapped to a lower dimensional space (2D or 3D). This is known as *non-linear mapping*.

A simple procedure for this non-linear mapping is *multidimensional scaling* [5, 6], which involves two stages. In the first stage, an initial set of random coordinates is generated in the low-dimensional space. In the second stage, this initial set of coordinates is modified by improving the correspondence between the distances in the low-dimensional space and original multidimensional space. For this, some mathematical optimization procedures can be applied that use an objective function such as defined by Eq. 7.3 or 7.4.

$$S = \frac{\sum_{i<j}^{N} \left(d_{ij} - D_{ij}\right)^2}{\sum_{i<j}^{N} d_{ij}^2} \tag{7.3}$$

$$S = \frac{\sum_{i<j}^{N} \left\{ \left(d_{ij} - D_{ij}\right)^2 / D_{ij} \right\}}{\sum_{i<j}^{N} D_{ij}} \tag{7.4}$$

The former is known as Kruskal's stress function [5] and the latter as Sammon's stress function [7]. In these equations, N refers to the number of data points, d_{ij} is the distance between two objects i and j in the low-dimensional space and D_{ij} the corresponding distance in the original multidimensional space. Now the optimization procedure continues until the value of the stress function falls below a threshold value. Thus, having the data set reduced to two or three dimensions, one may use graphics or other visual cues to identify structure-activity relationship, for example, by coloring the data points according to the biological activity.

Because of certain limitations in optimization procedure, however, the Kruskal or the Sammon function cannot be easily applied to large data sets, but several solutions that overcome this limitation have been devised [8, 9], making these techniques applicable to data sets containing tens of thousands of data points.

References

[1] Hertzberg, R.P. and Pope, A.J., *Curr. Opin. Chem. Biol.*, ***4*** (2000), 445.

[2] Bajorath, J., *Nature Reviews, Drug Dis.*, ***1*** (2002), 882.

[3] Klopman, G., *J. Am. Chem. Soc.*, ***106*** (1984), 7315.

[4] Klopman, G., *Quant. Struct-Act. Relat.*, ***11*** (1992), 176.

[5] Kruskal, J.B., *Psychometrika*, ***29*** (1964), 1.

[6] Cox, T.F. and Cox, M.A.A., *Multidimensional Scaling*, Chapman and Hall, London (1994).

[7] Sammon, J.W. Jr., *IEEE Transactions on Computers*, ***18*** (1969), 401.
[8] Xie, D., Tropsha, A. and Schlick, T., *J. Chem. Inf. Comput. Sci.*, ***40*** (2000), 167.
[9] Agrafiotis, D.K. and Lobanov, V.S., *J. Chem. Inf. Comput. Sci.*, ***40*** (2000), 1356.

Appendix I: Percentage Points of t-Distribution*

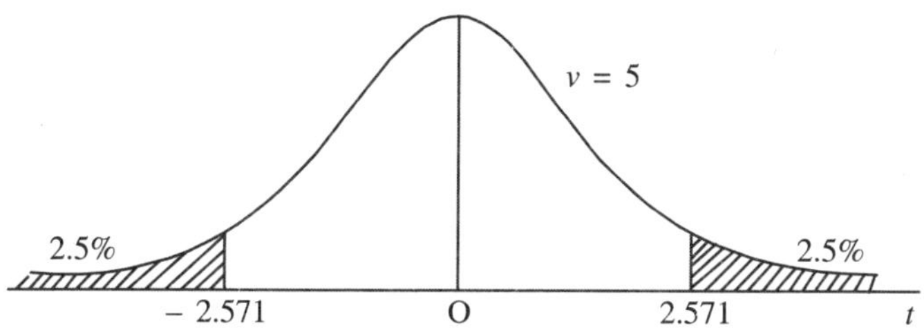

2.5% one sided test; 5% two sided test
Example ($\nu = 5$): $t_{0.025;5} = 2.571$, $t_{0.05/2;5} = 2.571$

ν \ α One-sided	0.25	0.2	0.15	0.1	0.05	0.025	0.01	0.005	0.0005
1	1.000	1.376	1.963	3.078	6.314	12.706	31.821	63.657	636.619
2	0.816	1.061	1.386	1.886	2.920	4.303	6.965	9.925	31.598
3	0.765	0.978	1.250	1.638	2.353	3.182	4.541	5.841	12.941
4	0.741	0.941	1.190	1.533	2.132	2.776	3.747	4.604	8.610
5	0.727	0.920	1.156	1.476	2.015	2.571	3.365	4.032	6.859
6	0.718	0.906	1.134	1.440	1.943	2.447	3.143	3.707	5.959
7	0.711	0.896	1.119	1.415	1.895	2.365	2.998	3.499	5.405
8	0.706	0.889	1.108	1.397	1.860	2.306	2.896	3.355	5.041
9	0.703	0.883	1.100	1.383	1.833	2.262	2.821	3.250	4.781
10	0.700	0.879	1.093	1.372	1.812	2.228	2.764	3.169	4.587
11	0.697	0.876	1.088	1.363	1.796	2.201	2.718	3.106	4.437
12	0.695	0.873	1.083	1.356	1.782	2.179	2.681	3.055	4.318
ν / α Two-sided	0.50	0.40	0.30	0.20	0.10	0.05	0.02	0.01	0.00

Contd.

*Reprinted with permission from Ref. 1 of Chapter 4. Copyright 1973 Pergamon.

Continued

ν \ α One-sided	0.25	0.2	0.15	0.1	0.05	0.025	0.01	0.005	0.0005
13	0.694	0.870	1.079	1.350	1.771	2.160	2.650	3.012	4.221
14	0.692	0.868	1.076	1.345	1.761	2.145	2.624	2.977	4.140
15	0.691	0.866	1.074	1.341	1.753	2.131	2.602	2.947	4.073
16	0.690	0.865	1.071	1.337	1.746	2.120	2.583	2.921	4.015
17	0.689	0.863	1.069	1.333	1.740	2.110	2.567	2.898	3.965
18	0.688	0.862	1.067	1.330	1.734	2.101	2.552	2.878	3.922
19	0.688	0.861	1.066	1.328	1.729	2.093	2.539	2.861	3.883
20	0.687	0.860	1.064	1.325	1.725	2.086	2.528	2.845	3.850
21	0.686	0.859	1.063	1.323	1.721	2.080	2.518	2.831	3.819
22	0.686	0.858	1.061	1.321	1.717	2.074	2.508	2.819	3.792
23	0.685	0.858	1.060	1.319	1.714	2.069	2.500	2.807	3.767
24	0.685	0.857	1.059	1.318	1.711	2.064	2.492	2.797	3.745
25	0.684	0.856	1.058	1.316	1.708	2.060	2.485	2.787	3.725
26	0.684	0.856	1.058	1.315	1.706	2.056	2.479	2.779	3.707
27	0.684	0.855	1.057	1.314	1.703	2.052	2.473	2.771	3.690
28	0.683	0.855	1.056	1.313	1.701	2.048	2.467	2.763	3.674
29	0.683	0.854	1.055	1.311	1.699	2.045	2.462	2.756	3.659
30	0.683	0.854	1.055	1.310	1.697	2.042	2.457	2.750	3.646
40	0.681	0.851	1.050	1.303	1.684	2.021	2.423	2.704	3.551
60	0.679	0.848	1.046	1.296	1.671	2.000	2.390	2.660	3.460
120	0.677	0.845	1.041	1.289	1.658	1.980	2.358	2.617	3.373
∞	0.674	0.842	1.036	1.282	1.645	1.960	2.326	2.576	3.291
ν / α Two-sided	0.50	0.40	0.30	0.20	0.10	0.05	0.02	0.01	0.00

Appendix II: A Model QSAR Calculation

Suppose there is a series of 24 compounds with different substituents with 4 independent variables (descriptions) X_1, X_2, X_3 and X_4 and one independent variable (activity) Y with their values for each compound as shown in Table 1.

Table 1

Compound No.	X_1	X_2	X_3	X_4	Y
1	0.000	0.206	0.103	0.000	7.610
2	0.000	0.668	0.103	0.000	7.840
3	0.000	0.890	0.103	0.000	8.090
4	0.000	0.890	0.103	0.000	8.040
5	0.000	1.260	0.103	0.000	8.220
6	– 0.020	0.260	0.787	0.000	7.750
7	0.000	1.574	0.787	0.000	8.100
8	0.000	0.896	0.103	0.000	8.400
9	0.000	2.494	0.103	0.000	8.570
10	0.710	1.574	0.103	0.000	9.270
11	0.000	1.748	0.103	0.000	7.840
12	0.000	1.072	0.103	1.000	9.230
13	0.710	1.574	0.103	1.000	9.800
14	0.860	1.574	0.103	1.000	9.700
15	– 0.280	1.574	0.103	1.000	9.160
16	– 1.230	1.574	0.103	1.000	9.020
17	0.000	1.574	1.394	1.000	8.120
18	0.000	1.574	0.736	1.000	8.550
19	0.000	1.574	0.542	1.000	8.890
20	0.000	0.195	0.092	1.000	9.050
21	0.000	0.184	0.103	1.000	8.470
22	0.000	0.879	0.103	1.000	9.420
23	0.000	0.605	0.103	1.000	8.910
24	0.000	1.130	0.103	1.000	9.060
25	0.000	1.574	0.103	1.000	9.860
Average	0.030	1.160	0.252	0.560	8.679

Now from the definition of a_{ii} in Eq. 4.8, we can form an **A** matrix according to Eq. 4.11 and then take its inverse matrix **C**. These two matrices would be of the forms

$$\mathbf{A} = \begin{pmatrix} 3.317 & 0.338 & -0.125 & -0.360 \\ 0.338 & 8.399 & 0.618 & 0.412 \\ -0.125 & 0.618 & 2.642 & 0.269 \\ -0.360 & 0.412 & 0.269 & 6.160 \end{pmatrix}$$

$$\mathbf{C} = \begin{pmatrix} 0.360 & -0.014 & 0.016 & 0.018 \\ -0.014 & 0.122 & -0.387 & -0.412 \\ 0.016 & -0.028 & 0.387 & -0.014 \\ 0.018 & -0.008 & -0.014 & 0.165 \end{pmatrix}$$

From this, the correlation equation comes out to be (this exercise is left to the readers):

$$Y = 0.508\ (\pm\ 0.388)\ X_1 + 0.354\ (\pm\ 0.226)\ X_2 - 0.818\ (\pm\ 0.402)\ X_3 + 0.973\ (\pm\ 0.263)\ X_4 + 7.914$$

$$n = 25,\ r = 0.907,\ s = 0.310,\ F_{4,20} = 23.19\ (4.43)$$

Here the figure in parenthesis for F is the literature value (1%) as shown in Appendix III for $v_1 = 4$ and $v_2 = 20$. With reference to Eq. 4.19, $v_1 = k$ and $v_2 = (n - k - 1)$.

Appendix III: Percentage Points of *F*-Distribution*

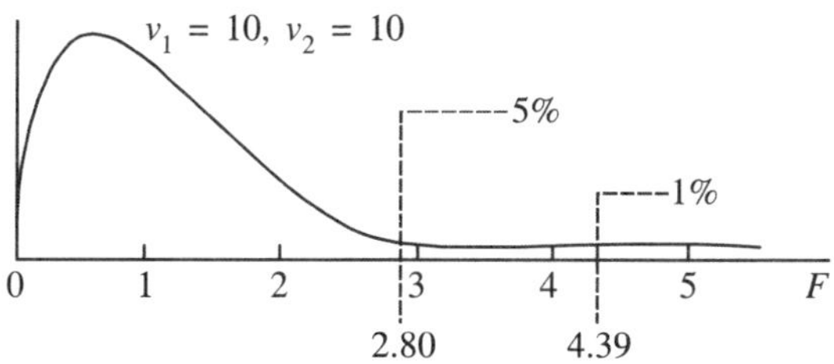

5% (First lines) and 1% (Second lines)

v_2	v_1 degrees of freedom**											
	1	2	3	4	5	6	7	8	9	10	11	12
1	161	200	216	225	230	234	237	239	241	242	243	244
	4.052	4.999	5.403	5.625	5.764	5.859	5.928	5.981	6.022	6.056	6.082	6.106
2	18.51	19.00	19.16	19.25	19.30	19.33	19.36	19.37	19.38	19.39	19.40	19.41
	98.49	99.00	99.17	99.25	99.30	99.33	99.34	99.36	99.38	99.40	99.41	99.42
3	10.13	9.55	9.28	9.12	9.01	8.94	8.88	8.84	8.81	8.78	8.76	8.74
	34.12	30.82	29.46	28.71	28.24	27.91	27.67	27.49	27.34	27.23	27.13	27.05
4	7.71	6.94	6.59	6.39	6.26	6.16	6.09	6.04	6.00	5.96	5.93	5.91
	21.20	18.00	16.69	15.98	15.52	15.21	14.98	14.80	14.66	14.54	14.45	14.37
5	6.61	5.79	5.41	5.19	5.05	4.95	4.88	4.82	4.78	4.74	4.70	4.68
	16.26	13.27	12.06	11.39	10.97	10.67	10.45	10.27	10.15	10.05	9.96	9.89
6	5.99	5.14	4.76	4.53	4.39	4.28	4.21	4.15	4.10	4.06	4.03	4.00
	13.74	10.92	9.78	9.15	8.75	8.47	8.26	8.10	7.98	7.87	7.79	7.72
7	5.59	4.74	4.35	4.12	3.97	3.87	3.79	3.73	3.68	3.63	3.60	3.57

Contd.

*Taken from Ref. 1 of Chapter 4. Reprinted with permission of the author and publishers of the original source: Snedecor, G.W., *Statistical Methods*, 5th Ed., The Iowa State University Press, Ames, Iowa (1956), 246-249, Copyright 1956 Iowa State University Press (now Wiley-Blackwell).

**With reference to Eq. 4.19, $v_1 = k$, $v_2 = (n - k - 1)$

Example: $v_1 = 4$, $v_2 = 20$, $F_{4, 20}$ (0.05) = 2.87, $F_{4, 20}$ (0.01) = 4.43

v_2	v_1 degrees of freedom											
	1	2	3	4	5	6	7	8	9	10	11	12
	12.25	9.55	8.45	7.85	7.46	7.19	7.00	6.84	6.71	6.62	6.54	6.47
8	5.32	4.46	4.07	3.84	3.69	3.58	3.50	3.44	3.39	3.34	3.31	3.28
	11.26	8.65	7.59	7.01	6.63	6.37	6.17	6.03	5.91	5.82	5.74	5.67
9	5.12	4.26	3.86	3.63	3.48	3.37	3.29	3.23	3.18	3.13	3.10	3.07
	10.56	8.02	6.99	6.42	6.06	5.80	5.62	5.47	5.35	5.26	5.18	5.11
10	4.96	4.10	3.71	3.48	3.33	3.22	3.14	3.07	3.02	2.97	2.94	2.91
	10.04	7.56	6.55	5.99	5.64	5.39	5.21	5.06	4.95	4.85	4.78	4.71
11	4.84	3.98	3.59	3.36	3.20	3.09	3.01	2.95	2.90	2.86	2.82	2.79
	9.65	7.20	6.22	5.67	5.32	5.07	4.88	4.74	4.63	4.54	4.46	4.40
12	4.75	3.88	3.49	3.26	3.11	3.00	2.92	2.85	2.80	2.76	2.72	2.69
	9.33	6.93	5.95	5.41	5.06	4.82	4.65	4.50	4.39	4.30	4.22	4.16
13	4.67	3.80	3.41	3.18	3.02	2.92	2.84	2.77	2.72	2.67	2.63	2.60
	9.07	6.70	5.74	5.20	4.86	4.62	4.44	4.30	4.19	4.10	4.02	3.96
14	4.60	3.74	3.34	3.11	2.96	2.85	2.76	2.70	2.65	2.60	2.56	2.53
	8.86	6.51	5.56	5.04	4.70	4.46	4.28	4.14	4.03	3.94	3.86	3.80
15	4.54	3.68	3.29	3.06	2.90	2.79	2.71	2.64	2.59	2.54	2.51	2.48
	8.68	6.36	5.42	4.89	4.56	4.32	4.14	4.00	3.90	3.81	3.73	3.67
16	4.49	3.63	3.24	3.01	2.85	2.74	2.66	2.59	2.54	2.49	2.45	2.42
	8.53	6.23	5.29	4.77	4.44	4.20	4.03	3.89	3.78	3.69	3.61	3.55
17	4.45	3.59	3.20	2.96	2.81	2.70	2.61	2.55	2.49	2.45	2.41	2.38
	8.40	6.11	5.18	4.67	4.34	4.10	3.93	3.79	3.68	3.59	3.52	3.46
18	4.41	3.55	3.16	2.93	2.77	2.66	2.58	2.51	2.46	2.41	2.37	2.34
	8.28	6.01	5.09	4.58	4.25	4.02	3.84	3.71	3.60	3.51	3.44	3.37
19	4.38	3.52	3.13	2.90	2.74	2.63	2.54	2.48	2.42	2.38	2.34	2.31
	8.18	5.93	5.01	4.50	4.17	3.94	3.77	3.63	3.52	3.43	3.36	3.30
20	4.35	3.49	3.10	2.87	2.71	2.60	2.51	2.45	2.39	2.35	2.31	2.28
	8.10	5.85	4.94	4.43	4.10	3.87	3.70	3.56	3.46	3.37	3.30	3.23
21	4.32	3.47	3.07	2.84	2.68	2.57	2.49	2.42	2.37	2.32	2.28	2.25
	8.02	5.78	4.87	4.37	4.04	3.81	3.64	3.51	3.40	3.31	3.24	3.17
22	4.30	3.44	3.05	2.82	2.66	2.55	2.46	2.40	2.34	2.30	2.26	2.23
	7.94	5.72	4.82	4.31	3.99	3.76	3.59	3.45	3.35	3.26	3.18	3.12
23	4.28	3.42	3.03	2.80	2.64	2.53	2.44	2.37	2.32	2.27	2.24	2.20
	7.88	5.66	4.76	4.26	3.94	3.71	3.54	3.41	3.30	3.21	3.14	3.07
24	4.26	3.40	3.01	2.78	2.62	2.51	2.42	2.36	2.30	2.25	2.22	2.18
	7.82	5.61	4.72	4.22	3.90	3.67	3.50	3.36	3.26	3.17	3.09	3.03
25	4.24	3.38	2.99	2.76	2.60	2.49	2.40	2.34	2.28	2.24	2.20	2.16
	7.77	5.57	4.68	4.18	3.86	3.63	3.46	3.32	3.22	3.13	3.05	2.99
26	4.22	3.37	2.98	2.74	2.59	2.47	2.39	2.32	2.27	2.22	2.18	2.15
	7.72	5.53	4.64	4.14	3.82	3.59	3.42	3.29	3.18	3.09	3.02	2.96
27	4.21	3.35	2.96	2.73	2.57	2.46	2.37	2.31	2.25	2.20	2.16	2.13
	7.68	5.49	4.60	4.11	3.79	3.56	3.39	3.26	3.15	3.06	2.98	2.93
28	4.20	3.34	2.95	2.71	2.56	2.45	2.36	2.29	2.24	2.19	2.15	2.12
	7.64	5.45	4.57	4.07	3.75	3.53	3.36	3.23	3.12	3.03	2.95	2.90
29	4.18	3.33	2.93	2.70	2.55	2.43	2.35	2.28	2.22	2.18	2.14	2.10
	7.60	5.42	4.54	4.05	3.73	3.50	3.33	3.20	3.09	3.01	2.92	2.87

Contd.

v_2	v_1 degrees of freedom											
	1	2	3	4	5	6	7	8	9	10	11	12
30	4.17	3.32	2.92	2.69	2.53	2.42	2.33	2.27	2.21	2.16	2.12	2.09
	7.56	5.39	4.51	4.02	3.70	3.47	3.30	3.17	3.07	2.98	2.90	2.84
32	4.15	3.30	2.90	2.67	2.51	2.40	2.32	2.25	2.19	2.14	2.10	2.07
	7.50	5.34	4.46	3.97	3.66	3.42	3.25	3.12	3.01	2.94	2.86	2.80
34	4.13	3.28	2.88	2.65	2.49	2.38	2.30	2.23	2.17	2.12	2.08	2.05
	7.44	5.29	4.42	3.93	3.61	3.38	3.21	3.08	2.97	2.89	2.82	2.76
36	4.11	3.26	2.86	2.63	2.48	2.36	2.28	2.21	2.15	2.10	2.06	2.03
	7.39	5.25	4.38	3.89	3.58	3.35	3.18	3.04	2.94	2.86	2.78	2.72
38	4.10	3.25	2.85	2.62	2.46	2.35	2.26	2.19	2.14	2.09	2.05	2.02
	7.35	5.21	4.34	3.86	3.54	3.32	3.15	3.02	2.91	2.82	2.75	2.69
40	4.08	3.23	2.84	2.61	2.45	2.34	2.25	2.18	2.12	2.07	2.04	2.00
	7.31	5.18	4.31	3.83	3.51	3.29	3.12	2.99	2.89	2.80	2.73	2.67
42	4.07	3.22	2.83	2.59	2.44	2.32	2.24	2.17	2.11	2.06	2.02	1.99
	7.27	5.15	4.29	3.80	3.49	3.26	3.10	2.96	2.86	2.77	2.70	2.64
44	4.06	3.21	2.82	2.58	2.43	2.31	2.23	2.16	2.10	2.05	2.01	1.98
	7.24	5.12	4.26	3.78	3.46	3.24	3.07	2.94	2.84	2.75	2.68	2.62
46	4.05	3.20	2.81	2.57	2.42	2.30	2.22	2.14	2.09	2.04	2.00	1.97
	7.21	5.10	4.24	3.76	3.44	3.22	3.05	2.92	2.82	2.73	2.66	2.60
48	4.04	3.19	2.80	2.56	2.41	2.30	2.21	2.14	2.08	2.03	1.99	1.96
	7.19	5.08	4.22	3.74	3.42	3.20	3.04	2.90	2.80	2.71	2.64	2.58
50	4.03	3.18	2.79	2.56	2.40	2.29	2.20	2.13	2.07	2.02	1.98	1.95
	7.17	5.06	4.20	3.72	3.41	3.18	3.02	2.88	2.78	2.70	2.62	2.56
55	4.02	3.17	2.78	2.54	2.38	2.27	2.18	2.11	2.05	2.00	1.97	1.93
	7.12	5.01	4.16	3.68	3.37	3.15	2.98	2.85	2.75	2.66	2.59	2.53
60	4.00	3.15	2.76	2.52	2.37	2.25	2.17	2.10	2.04	1.99	1.95	1.92
	7.08	4.98	4.13	3.65	3.34	3.12	2.95	2.82	2.72	2.63	2.56	2.50
65	3.99	3.14	2.75	2.51	2.36	2.24	2.15	2.08	2.02	1.98	1.94	1.90
	7.04	4.95	4.10	3.62	3.31	3.09	2.93	2.79	2.70	2.61	2.54	2.47
70	3.98	3.13	2.74	2.50	2.35	2.23	2.14	2.07	2.01	1.97	1.93	1.89
	7.01	4.92	4.08	3.60	3.29	3.07	2.91	2.77	2.67	2.59	2.51	2.45
80	3.96	3.11	2.72	2.48	2.33	2.21	2.12	2.05	1.99	1.95	1.91	1.88
	6.96	4.88	4.04	3.56	3.25	3.04	2.87	2.74	2.64	2.55	2.48	2.41
100	3.94	3.09	2.70	2.46	2.30	2.19	2.10	2.03	1.97	1.92	1.88	1.85
	6.90	4.82	3.98	3.51	3.20	2.99	2.82	2.69	2.59	2.51	2.43	2.36
125	3.92	3.07	2.68	2.44	2.29	2.17	2.08	2.01	1.95	1.90	1.86	1.83
	6.84	4.78	3.94	3.47	3.17	2.95	2.79	2.65	2.56	2.47	2.40	2.33
150	3.91	3.06	2.67	2.43	2.27	2.16	2.07	2.00	1.94	1.89	1.85	1.82
	6.81	4.75	3.91	3.44	3.14	2.92	2.76	2.62	2.53	2.44	2.37	2.30
200	3.89	3.04	2.65	2.41	2.26	2.14	2.05	1.98	1.92	1.87	1.86	1.80
	6.76	4.71	3.88	3.41	3.11	2.90	2.73	2.60	2.50	2.41	2.34	2.28
400	3.86	3.02	2.62	2.39	2.23	2.12	2.03	1.96	1.90	1.85	1.81	1.78
	6.70	4.66	3.83	3.36	3.06	2.85	2.69	2.55	2.46	2.37	2.29	2.23
1000	3.85	3.00	2.61	2.38	2.22	2.10	2.02	1.95	1.89	1.84	1.80	1.76
	6.66	4.62	3.80	3.34	3.04	2.82	2.66	2.53	2.43	2.34	2.26	2.20
∞	3.84	2.99	2.60	2.37	2.21	2.09	2.01	1.94	1.88	1.83	1.79	1.75
	6.64	4.60	3.78	3.32	3.02	2.80	2.64	2.51	2.41	2.32	2.24	2.19

Appendix IV: Glossary of Terms Used in Computational Drug Design*

***Ab Initio* Calculations:** *Ab initio* calculations are quantum chemical calculations using exact equations with no approximations which involve the whole electronic population of the molecule. Methods of quantum mechanical calculations independent of any experiment other than the determination of fundamental constants. The methods are based on the use of the full Schrödinger equation to treat all the electrons of a chemical system. In practice, approximations are necessary to restrict the complexity of the electronic wavefunction and to make its calculation possible.

AM1 Calculations: Semi-empirical molecular orbital calculations developed at the University of Austin in Texas (AM1 = Austin Model 1). These calculations involve the valence electrons of the atoms of the molecule. They are a further development of MNDO calculations [1] (see MNDO Calculations).

AMBER: A well-known molecular mechanics program for calculations on proteins and nucleic acids (see Molecular Mechanics).

Artificial Neural Networks: Artificial neural networks (ANN) are algorithms simulating the functioning of human neurons and may be used for pattern recognition problems, e.g., to establish quantitative structure-activity relationships.

Atomic Orbitals (AO): Mathematical functions (e.g. Gaussian or Slater functions) used in quantum chemical calculations. A set of atomic orbitals described by a defined function is the basis set of atomic orbitals (see Slater-Type Orbitals).

Basis Set: A set of mathematical functions used in molecular orbital (MO) calculations, e.g. the 6-31G* basis set used in *ab initio* calculations. 6-31G* and similar expressions refer to the type of mathematical function used (see molecular orbital (MO) calculations). It is a set of basis functions employed for the representation of molecular orbitals. One may distinguish the minimal basis set (includes one basis function for each self-consistent field (SCF) occupied atomic orbital with distinct principal and angular momentum quantum numbers); split valence basis set (includes two or more sizes of basis function for each valence orbital); double zeta (DZ) basis set (a split valence basis set that includes exactly twice as many functions as the minimal basis set); extended basis set (the set larger than the double zeta basis set); polarized basis set (incorporates basis functions of higher angular quantum number beyond what is required by the atom in its electron ground state; allows orbitals to change not only size, but also shape); basis set with diffuse functions and others.

---

*Source: van de Waterbeemd, H., Carter, R.E., Grassy, G., Kubinyi, H., Martin, Y.C., Tute, M.S. and Willet, P., *Ann. Rep. Med. Chem.*, ***33*** (1998), 397-409. Reprinted with permission from the original source: *Pure and Applied Chemistry*, ***69***, 1137-1152 (1997).

Chemometrics: It is the application of statistics to the analysis of chemical data (from organic, analytical or medicinal chemistry) and design of chemical experiments and simulations.
CLOGP Values: CLOGP values are calculated 1-octanol/water partition coefficients, frequently used in structure-property correlation or quantitative structure-activity relationship (SPC/QSAR) studies [2] (see structure-property correlations (SPC) and quantitative structure-activity relationships (QSAR)).
Cluster Analysis: Clustering (or grouping) of large data sets (e.g., chemical and/or pharmacological data sets) on the basis of similarity criteria for appropriately scaled variables that represent the data of interest. Similarity criteria (distance based, associative, correlative, probabilistic) among the several clusters facilitate the recognition of patterns and reveal otherwise hidden structures [3-5].
CNDO/2 Calculations: Semi-empirical molecular orbital (MO) calculations using complete neglect of differential overlap (see Molecular Orbital (MO) Calculations).
Comparative Molecular Field Analysis (CoMFA): It is a 3D QSAR method that uses statistical correlation techniques for the analysis of the quantitative relationship between the biological activity of a set of compounds with a specified alignment, and their three dimensional electronic and steric properties. Other properties, such as hydrophobicity and H-bonding can also be incorporated into the analysis [6, 7] (see 3D QSAR, Hydrophobicity).
Computational Chemistry: A discipline using mathematical methods for the calculation of molecular properties or for the simulation of molecular behavior. It also includes, e.g., synthesis planning, database searching, combinatorial library manipulation [8, 9].
Computer-Assisted Drug Design (CADD): This involves all computer-assisted techniques used to discover, design and optimize biologically active compounds with a putative use as drug (see Drug Design).
Computer-Assisted Molecular Design (CAMD): This involves all computer-assisted techniques used to discover, design and optimize compounds with desired structure and properties.
Computer-Assisted Molecular Modeling (CAMM): It is the investigation of molecular structures and properties using computational chemistry and graphical visualization techniques.
Computer Chemistry: Computer chemistry is often used as equivalent to computational chemistry, and can also refer to the use of computers in synthesis planning [9, 10].
Conformational Analysis: It consists of the exploration of energetically favorable spatial arrangements (shapes) of a molecule (conformations) using molecular mechanics, molecular dynamics, quantum chemical calculations or analysis of experimentally-determined structural data, e.g., NMR or crystal structures. Molecular mechanics and quantum chemical methods are employed to compute conformational energies, whereas systematic and random searches, Monte Carlo, molecular dynamics, and distance geometry are methods (often combined with energy minimization procedures) used to explore the conformational space (see Distance Geometry, Molecular Dynamics, Molecular Mechanics, Monte Carlo Technique, Quantum Chemical Calculations).
Conformationally Flexible Searching (CFS): A three dimensional-structure database search taking into account the flexibility of molecules.
Connolly Surface: An envelope traced out by the point of contact of a defined probe (e.g., a sphere) and a molecule of interest where they touch once, plus the van der Waal's surface of the probe where it touches twice or more (the re-entrant surface). It is used to visualize the molecular surface.
Craig Plot: A Craig plot is a plot of two substituent parameters (e.g., Hansch-Fujita π and Hammett σ values) used in analog design.
CSSR: The crystal structure search retrieval (CSSR) file format is one of several used

by the Cambridge crystal structure database (CSD) to store molecular structures. This format is used in many molecular modeling software packages.

***De Novo* Design:** The design of bioactive compounds by the incremental construction of a ligand model within the receptor or enzyme active site, the structure of which is known from X-ray or nuclear magnetic resonance (NMR) data.

Discriminant Analysis: Discriminant analysis is a statistical technique to find a set of descriptors which can be used to detect and rationalize separation between activity classes.

Distance Geometry: A mathematical method used to build three-dimensional (3D) molecular models from a set of approximate interatomic distances (e.g., nuclear Overhauser effect (NOE) experiments in nuclear magnetic resonance (NMR) suggest only ranges of distances). Distance geometry can be used to define a 3D pharmacophore starting from a set of molecules with the same mechanism of action, or for the generation of likely geometries for drug receptor complexes using intermolecular distance constraints [11].

Docking Studies: These are computational techniques for the exploration of the possible binding modes of a substrate to a given receptor, enzyme or other binding site.

D-optimal Design: D-optimal design is an experimental design technique based on the optimization of the determinant calculated from the variance-covariance matrix of the descriptors. It is used to maximize the efficiency of fractional (incomplete) factorial design (see Factorial Design, Fractional Factorial Design).

3D QSAR (Three-Dimensional Quantitative Structure-Activity Relationships): This involves the analysis of the quantitative relationship between the biological activity of a set of compounds and their three-dimensional properties using statistical correlation methods.

Drug Design: Drug design includes not only ligand design, but also pharmacokinetics and toxicity, which are mostly beyond the possibilities of structure- and/or computer-aided design. Nevertheless, appropriate chemometric tools, including experimental design and multivariate statistics, can be of value in the planning and evaluation of pharmacokinetic and toxicological experiments and results. Drug design is most often used instead of the correct term "Ligand design".

Electrostatic Field and Potential: These are properties of a molecule arising from the interaction between a charged probe, such as a positive unit point charge reflecting a proton, and a target molecule. These fields and potential are being used in three-dimensional quantitative structure-activity relationship (3D QSAR) studies and to compare or assess the similarity of a set of molecules. A physical property equal in magnitude to the electrostatic energy between the static charge distribution $r(r)$ of an atomic or molecular system and a positive unit point charge located at r. The electrostatic potential $V(r)$ that is produced at any point r by the electrons and nuclei A of the system is given by $V(r) = \Sigma Z_A/lR_A - rl$ − integral $(r(r')dr'/lr' - rl)$.

Energy Minimization: A mathematical procedure to locate the stable conformations of a molecule (energy minima), as determined by molecular mechanics or quantum mechanical calculations (see Molecular Mechanics, Quantum Chemical Calculations).

Experimental Design: It is the use of mathematical and statistical methods to select the minimum number of experiments or compounds for optimal coverage of descriptor or variable space.

Extended Hückel (EH) Calculations: These are low-level semi-empirical molecular orbital (MO) calculations. A semi-empirical all-valence electron quantum mechanical method which uses the same approximations, apart from π-approximation and neglect of overlap integrals, as those of Hückel molecular orbital theory. The method reproduces, relatively well, the shapes and order of energy levels of molecular orbitals. The account for overlap makes it possible to describe the net destabilization caused by interaction of two double occupied orbitals.

Extrathermodynamic Approach: A correlation between variables which, from a strictly thermodynamic standpoint, are not related. It is the basis of Hansch analysis used in traditional QSAR [12].

Factorial Design (FD): An experimental design technique in which each variable (factor or descriptor) is investigated at fixed levels. In a two level FD, each variable can take two values, e.g., high and low lipophilicity.

File Format: The (molecular) file format describes the layout of a computer data file. It is a set of instructions on how a molecule is encoded with respect to its connectivity, atom types, coordinates. and may also contain bibliographic data.

Force Field: The force field is a set of functions and parameterization used in molecular mechanics calculations. Within the molecular mechanics approach, a set of potential functions defining bond stretch, bond angle (both valence and dihedral) distortion energy of a molecule as compared with its nonstrained conformation (that characterized by standard values of bond lengths and angles). A set of transferable empirical force constants is preassigned and the harmonic approximation is usually employed. Some force fields may contain terms for interactions between non-bonded atoms, electrostatic, hydrogen bond and other structural effects as well as account for anharmonicity effects. In vibrational spectroscopy, the inverse problem is solved by determining a set of force constants and other parameters of a chosen potential energy functions which would match with the experimentally observed vibrational frequencies of a given series of congeneric molecules.

Fractional Factorial Design (FFD): It is an experimental design technique, using a reduction factor in order to limit the number of experiments to a lower number than obtained by factorial design.

Free Energy Perturbation Calculations: These are mathematical procedures used in molecular dynamics studies to gradually convert one chemical species to another in a thermodynamic cycle.

Free-Wilson (FW) Analysis: Free-Wilson analysis is a regression technique using the presence or absence of substituents or groups as the only molecular descriptors in correlations with biological activity [12].

Frontier Orbitals: The molecular orbitals that involve the highest occupied molecular orbital (HOMO) and the lowest unoccupied molecular orbital (LUMO) of a given molecular entity. In the case of an odd-electron molecular entity, when its HOMO is occupied by a single electron, such a molecular orbital is termed a singly occupied molecular orbital (SOMO). Depending on the properties of the reactive partner, the SOMO of a given species may function as either HOMO or LUMO. The special importance of the frontier orbitals is due to the fact that a broad variety of chemical reactions take place at a position and in a direction where the overlap of HOMO and LUMO of the respective reactants is maximal.

Gaussian-Type Orbitals (GTO): These are mathematical functions used in *ab initio* calculations. They have superceded Slater-type orbitals because of the greater computational efficiency that results (see Slater-Type orbitals).

Genetic Algorithm: A genetic algorithm is an optimization algorithm based on the mechanisms of Darwinian evolution which uses random mutation, crossover and selection procedures to breed better models or solutions from an originally random starting population or sample [13].

GOLPE: Generating optimal linear PLS estimations. It is an advanced variable selection technique in partial least squares (PLS) used in three-dimensional quantitative structure-activity relationships (3D QSAR) studies to handle very large data sets (see Partial Least Squares (PLS)).

GRID: This is a program for receptor/ligand mapping. It calculates interaction energies between probes and target molecules at interaction points on a 3D grid [14].

Hamiltonian: The Hamiltonian is a mathematical operator function used in molecular orbital calculations [1].

Hammett Constant σ: The Hammett constant is an electronic substituent descriptor reflecting the electron-donating or -accepting property of a substituent [15].
Hansch Analysis: It is the investigation of the quantitative relationship between the biological activity of a series of compounds and their physico-chemical substituent or global parameters representing hydrophobic, electronic, steric and other effects using multiple regression correlation methodology [12, 16].
Hansch-Fujita π Constant: The Hansch-Fujita π constant describes the contribution of a substituent to the lipophilicity of a compound [16].
Highest Occupied Molecular Orbital (HOMO) Energy: The HOMO energy is obtained by molecular orbital calculations and relates to the ionization potential of a molecule and its reactivity as a nucleophile (see Lowest Unoccupied Molecular Orbital (LUMO) Energy).
Homology Model: A homology model is a model of a protein, whose three dimensional structure is unknown, built from, e.g., the X-ray coordinate data of similar proteins or using alignment techniques and homology arguments.
Hydrophilicity: It is the tendency of a molecule to be solvated by water.
Hydrophobic Fragmental Constant (*f* or *f'*): The hydrophobic fragmental constant of a substituent or molecular fragment represents the lipophilicity contribution of that molecular fragment [17-19].
Hydrophobicity: Hydrophobicity is the association of non-polar groups or molecules in an aqueous environment which arises from the tendency of water to exclude non-polar molecules [20-22].
Indicator Variable: An indicator variable is a descriptor that can assume only two values indicating the presence (= 1) or absence (= 0) of a given condition. It is often used to indicate the absence or presence of a substituent or substructure. More broadly, it is a variable which can encode anything that the investigator chooses.
Ligand Design: It is the design of ligands using structural information about the target to which they should bind, often by attempting to maximize the energy of the interaction (see Docking Studies).
Linear Combination of Atomic Orbitals (LCAO): The LCAO is a mathematical method used in quantum chemical calculations. It expresses the approximation of the molecular orbital function as a linear combination of atomic orbitals chosen as the basis functions.
Lipophilicity: Lipophilicity represents the affinity of a molecule or a moiety for a lipophilic environment. It is commonly measured by its distribution behaviour in a biphasic system, either liquid-liquid (e.g. partition coefficient in 1-octanol/water) or solid-liquid (retention on reversed-phase high-performance liquid chromatography (RP-HPLC) or thin-layer chromatography (TLC) system).
Lowest Unoccupied Molecular Orbital (LUMO) Energy: The LUMO energy is obtained from molecular orbital calculations and represents the electron affinity of a molecule or its reactivity as an electrophile (see Highest Occupied Molecular Orbital (HOMO) Energy).
MINDO/3 Calculations: MINDO/3 (Modified Intermediate Neglect of Differential Overlap) calculations are semi-empirical MO calculations [23].
MM2 Calculations: These calculations involve molecular mechanical calculations using version 2 of the widely-distributed force field program MM2 [24].
MNDO Calculations: MNDO calculations are semi-empirical molecular orbital (MO) calculations, using a modified neglect of diatomic (differential) overlap approximation.
Molar Refractivity (MR): It is the molar volume corrected by the refractive index. It represents size and polarizability of a fragment or molecule.
MOL File Format: The MOL file format is used to encode chemical structures, substructures and conformations as text-based connection tables. It is used by MDL Information Systems Inc. (e.g., in their MACCS or ISIS programs) [25].

Molecular Connectivity Index: A molecular connectivity index is a numeric descriptor derived from molecular topology [26].
Molecular Descriptors: These are terms that characterize a specific aspect of a molecule [27].
Molecular Design: Molecular design is the application of all techniques leading to the discovery of new chemical entities with specific properties required for the intended application.
Molecular Dynamics: A simulation procedure consisting of the computation of the motion of atoms in a molecule or of individual atoms or molecules in solids, liquids and gases, according to Newton's laws of motion. The forces acting on the atoms, required to simulate their motions, are generally calculated using molecular mechanics force fields (see Molecular Mechanics).
Molecular Electrostatic Potentials (MEP): These are electrostatic properties of a molecule based on the charge density as calculated directly from the molecular wavefunction. The electrostatic potential (scalar with dimensions of energy) is calculated at a point in the vicinity of a molecule. The spatial derivative is the electric force (vector) acting on a unit positive charge at that point caused by the nuclei and the electrons of the molecule [28].
Molecular Graphics: A technique for the visualization and manipulation of molecules on a graphical display device.
Molecular Interaction Potentials (MIP): These are field properties arising from the interaction of a probe (e.g., methyl, proton or water) with a molecule. These are calculated in a space around the molecule.
Molecular Lipophilic Potentials (MLP): Molecular lipophilic potentials are properties on the van der Waal's or solvent accessible molecular surface or any other point in space (e.g., in a 3D grid for CoMFA studies) calculated from atomic lipophilicity contributions. They can be used for log *P* calculations, CoMFA and docking studies [29].
Molecular Mechanics: It is the calculation of molecular conformational geometries and energies using a combination of empirical force fields [30]. It is synonymous with force field method. It is a method of calculation of geometrical and energy characteristics of molecular entities on the basis of empirical potential functions (see force field), the form of which is taken from classical mechanics. The method implies transferability of the potential functions within a network of similar molecules. An assumption is made on "natural" bond lengths and angles, deviations from which result in bond and angle strain, respectively. Repulsive or attractive van der Waal's and electrostatic forces between nonbonded atoms are also taken into account.
Molecular Modeling: An investigation of molecular structures and properties using computational chemistry and graphical visualization techniques in order to provide a plausible three-dimensional representation under a given set of circumstances.
Molecular Orbital (MO) Calculations: These are quantum chemical calculations based on the Schrödinger equation, which can be subdivided into semiempirical and *ab initio* methods (see *ab initio* Calculations).
Molecular Orbital Theory: It is an approach to molecular quantum mechanics which uses one electron functions (orbitals) to approximate the full wavefunction.
Molecular Shape: The molecular shape is an attribute of a molecule dealing with spatial extension, form, framework, or geometry. It is often described, e.g., by principal axes, ovality, or connectivity indices.
Molecular (Dis-)Similarity: It is a number to express structural relatedness between pairs of molecules, e.g., the so-called Carbo, Hodgkin or Tanimoto coefficient [31, 32].
Molecular Topology: The description of the way in which the atoms in a molecule are bonded together (see Molecular Connectivity Index, Topological Index).
Molfile: A molfile is a table containing atom type, connectivity and a more or less arbitrary

2D or 3D information about a molecule. Well-known file formats include the MOLfile used by MDL Information Systems Inc. (e.g., in the database MACCS), the MOL2 file used by Tripo Associates (e.g., in the modeling package SYBYL), or the CSSR format.

Monte Carlo Technique: The Monte Carlo technique is a simulation procedure consisting of randomly sampling the conformational space of a molecule.

Mulliken Population Analysis: A method for allocating electrons to atoms in order to generate partial atomic charges. The results are strongly dependent on the basis set used. It involves a partitioning scheme based on the use of density and overlap matrices of allocating the electrons of a molecular entity in some fractional manner among its various parts (atoms, bonds, orbitals). As with other schemes of partitioning the electron density in molecules, Mulliken population analysis is arbitrary and strongly dependent on the particular basis set employed. However, comparison of population analyses for a series of molecules is useful for a quantitative description of intramolecular interactions, chemical reactivity and structural regularities.

Multivariate Statistics: A set of statistical tools to analyze data (e.g., chemical and biological) matrices using regression and/or pattern recognition techniques.

Neural Networks: See Artificial Neural Networks.

Non-Bonded Energy Terms: Non-bonded energy terms are potential energy functions describing van der Waal's, electrostatic and hydrogen bonding interactions in a force field.

Orbital (Atomic or Molecular): A wavefunction which depends explicitly on the spatial coordinates of only one electron.

Parameter Space: A multidimensional space spanned by the descriptors in a data set.

Partial Least Squares (PLS): Partial least squares projection to latent structures (PLS) is a robust multivariate generalized regression method using projections to summarize multitudes of potentially collinear variables [33].

Pattern Recognition: Pattern recognition is the identification of patterns in large data sets, using appropriate mathematical methodology, e.g., principal component analysis (PCA), SIMCA, partial least squares (PLS) and artificial neural networks (ANN) [3, 34, 35].

PCILO Calculations: Perturbative configuration interaction using localized orbitals (PCILO) calculations are semi-empirical molecular orbital calculations related to CNDO/2 and MNDO calculations.

PDB: The protein data bank (PDB), which is maintained at Brookhaven National Library, Upton, New York, contains X-ray structures of several hundreds of proteins (see PDB File).

PDB File: An ASCII (American Symbolic Code for Information Interexchange = text) file used to store the atomic coordinates of a molecule, usually a protein or nucleic acid (see PDB).

Pharmacophore Generation: It is a procedure to extract the most important common structural features relevant for a given biological activity from a series of molecules with a similar mechanism of action.

PM3: A widely used semi-empirical molecular mechanics program (see Molecular Mechanics).

Principal Components Analysis (PCA): It is a data reduction method using mathematical techniques to identify patterns in a data matrix. The main element of this approach consists of the construction of a small set of new orthogonal, i.e., non-correlated, variables derived from a linear combination of the original variables.

Principal Properties: These are scales of substituent or amino acid values derived by principal components analysis from a large matrix of structure descriptor variables, and are useful in series design and data analysis.

Quantitative Structure-Activity Relationships (QSAR): The QSAR are mathematical relationships linking chemical structure and pharmacological activity in a quantitative manner for a series of compounds. Methods which can be used in QSAR include various regression and pattern recognition techniques. QSAR is often taken to be equivalent to chemometrics or multivariate statistical data analysis. It is sometimes used in a more limited sense as equivalent to Hansch analysis. QSAR is a subset of the more general term SPC [12].

Quantum Chemical Calculations: These are molecular property calculations based on the Schrödinger equation, which takes into account the interactions between electrons in the molecule.

Receptor: A receptor is a protein or a protein complex in or on a cell that specifically recognizes and binds to a compound acting as a molecular messenger (neurotransmitter, hormone, lymphokine, lectin, drug, etc.). In a broader sense, the term receptor is often used as a synonym for any specific (as opposed to non-specific such as binding to plasma proteins) drug binding site, also including nucleic acids such as DNA.

Receptor Mapping: A technique used to describe the geometric and/or electronic features of a binding site when insufficient structural data for this receptor or enzyme are available. Generally, the active site cavity is defined by comparing the superposition of active to that of inactive molecules.

Regression Analysis: Regression analysis is the use of statistical methods for modeling a set of dependent variables *Y* in terms of combinations of predictors *X*. It includes methods such as multiple linear regression (MLR) and partial least squares (PLS).

Semi-empirical Methods: These are molecular orbital calculations using various degrees of approximation and using only valence electrons.

Semi-empirical Quantum Mechanical Methods: These are the methods which use parameters derived from experimental data to simplify computations. The simplification may occur at various levels: simplification of the Hamiltonian (e.g. as in the Extended Hückel method), approximate evaluation of certain molecular integrals (see, e.g., Zero Differential Overlap), simplification of the wave function (e.g., use of π-electron approximation as in Pariser-Parr-Pople).

Sequential Simplex Method: This is an experimental design method used for the rapid optimization of properties.

SIMCA: The SIMCA (SIMple Classification Analysis or Soft Independent Modeling of Class Analogy) method is a pattern recognition and classification technique [36].

Simulated Annealing: A procedure used in molecular dynamics simulations, in which the system is allowed to equilibrate at high temperatures, and then cooled down slowly to remove kinetic energy and to permit trajectories to settle into local minimum energy conformations.

Slater-Type Orbitals (STO): These are mathematical functions involving exponential functions, used in *ab initio* quantum chemical calculations. These functions mimic the electronic distribution in atoms and were used in *ab initio* calculations, but have now been superceded by Gaussian-type orbitals (see Gaussian-type orbitals). The exponential function on an atom, its radial dependence, is given by Nr_{n-1} $\exp(-\zeta r)$, where n is the effective principal quantum number and ζ the orbital exponent (screening constant) derived from empirical considerations. The angular dependence is usually introduced by multiplying the radial one by a spherical hammonic $Y_{lm}(\theta, \Phi)$.

SMILES: Simplified Molecular Input Line Entry System (SMILES) is a string notation used to describe the nature and topology of molecular structures.

Solvent-Accessible Surface: It is described as the surface traced out by a probe molecule, e.g., water, rolling over the van der Waal's surface of a molecule. These are of two types: (a) the surface formed by the locii of the centre of a spherical probe rolled around a molecule in the van der Waal's contact and (b) the contact surface (or Connolly/Richards surface) (see Connolly Surface).

STO-3G Basis Set: A STO-3G basis set is a set of Gaussian-type orbitals (GTO), each of which uses three Gaussian functions to approximate a Slater-type orbital (STO). More extended modern basis sets include STO-3-21 G or STO-KG.

Structure-Based Design: It is a design strategy for new chemical entities based on the three-dimensional (3D) structure of the target obtained by X-ray or nuclear magnetic resonance (NMR) studies, or from protein homolog models.

Structure-Property Correlations (SPC): The SPC refer to all statistical mathematical methods used to correlate any molecular property (intrinsic, chemical or biological) to any other property, using statistical regression or pattern recognition techniques [37].

Swain-Lupton Parameters (*F* and *R*): The Swain and Lupton parameters (*F* and *R*) are electronic field and resonance descriptors derived from Hammett constants [18].

Taft Steric Parameter (Es): A relative reaction parameter encoding the reaction rate retardation due to the size of a substituent group.

Three-dimensional Database Searching: It is a lead finding technique using three-dimensional structures of compounds stored in a database.

Topliss Tree: An operational scheme for analog design [38].

Topological Index: A numerical value associated with chemical constitution for correlation of chemical structure with various physical properties, chemical reactivity or biological activity (see molecular connectivity). The numerical basis for topological indices is provided (depending on how a molecular graph is converted into a numerical value) by either the adjacency matrix or the topological distance matrix. In the latter, the topological distance between two vertices is the number of edges in the shortest path between them.

United Atom Approach: The united atom approach is a simplification used by molecular mechanics programs such as AMBER and CHARMM, which approximates the influence of groups of atoms or molecular fragments by treating them as single atoms.

Verloop STERIMOL Parameters: The STERIMOL parameters defined by Verloop are a set of substitutent length and width parameters [39].

References

[1] Wylie, W.A., In *Molecular Modeling and Drug Design*, Vinter, J.G. and Gardner, M. (Eds.), Macmillan, London (1994).

[2] Leo, A.J., *Chem. Rev.*, ***93*** (1993), 1281.

[3] Rouvray, D.H., In *Concepts and Applications of Molecular Similarity*, Johnson, A. M. and Maggiora, G.M. (Eds.), Wiley, New York (1990), 15.

[4] Willett, P., *Similarity and Clustering in Chemical Information Systems*, John Wiley, New York (1987).

[5] Willett, P., *Three-dimensional Chemical Structure Handling*, John Wiley, New York (1991).

[6] Cramer III, R.D., Patterson, D.E. and Bunce, J.D., *J. Amer. Chem. Soc.*, ***110*** (1988), 5959.

[7] Kubinyi, H., *3D-QSAR in Drug Design: Theory, Methods and Applications*, Escom, Leiden (1993).

[8] Hopfinger, A.J., *J. Med. Chem.*, ***24*** (1981), 229.

[9] Ugi, I., Wochner, M., Fontain, E., Bauer, J., Gruber, B. and Karl, R. In *Concepts and Applications of Molecular Similarity*, Johnson, A.M. and Maggiora, G.M. (Eds.), Wiley, New York (1990), 239.

[10] Boyd, D.B. (Ed.), *Reviews in Computational Chemistry*, ***Vol. 1*** (1990).

[11] Crippen, G.M. and Havel, T.F., *Distance Geometry and Molecular Conformation*, Wiley, New York (1988).

[12] Kubinyi, H., *QSAR: Hansch Analysis and Related Approaches (1993), Vol. 1 of Methods and Principles in Medicinal Chemistry*, Mannhold, R. et al. (Eds.), VCH, Weinheim (1993).

[13] Rogers, D. and Hopfinger, A.J., *J. Chem. Inf. Comp. Sci.*, ***34*** (1994), 854.

[14] Goodford, P.J., *J. Med. Chem.*, ***28*** (1985), 849.

[15] Hansch, C., Leo, A. and Hoekman, D., *Exploring QSAR*, American Chemical Society, Washington (1995).

[16] Hansch, C. and Fujita, T., *J. Amer. Chem. Soc.*, ***86*** (1964), 1616.

[17] Rekker, R.F. and De Kort, H.M., *Eur. J. Med. Chem.*, ***14*** (1979), 479.

[18] Hansch, C. and Leo, A., *Substituent Constants for Correlation Analysis in Chemistry and Biology*, Wiley, New York (1979).

[19] Rekker, R.F. and Mannhold, R., *Calculation of Drug Lipophilicity*, VCH, Weinheim (1992).

[20] Martin, Y.C., *Quantitative Drug Design*, Marcel Dekker, New York (1978).

[21] Martin, Y.C., Theoretical Basis of Medicinal Chemistry: Structure-Activity Relationships and Three-Dimensional Structures of Small and Macromolecules, In *Modern Drug Research: Paths to Better and Safer Drugs*, Martin, Y.C., Austel, V. and Kutter, E. (Eds.), Marcel Dekker, New York (1989), 161.

[22] Dean, P.M., In *Concepts and Applications of Molecular Similarity*, Johnson, A.M. and Maggiora, G.M. (Eds.), Wiley, New York (1990), 211.

[23] Bingham, R.C., Dewar, M.J.S. and Lo, D.H., *J. Amer. Chem. Soc.*, ***97*** (1975), 1285.

[24] Allinger, N.L., *J. Amer. Chem. Soc.*, ***99*** (1977), 8127.

[25] Dalby, A., Nourse, J.G., Hounsell, W.D., Gushurst, A.K.I., Grier, D.L., Leland, B.A. and Laufer, J., *J. Chem. Inf. Comput. Sci.*, ***32*** (1992), 244.

[26] Kier, L.B. and Hall, L.H., *Molecular Connectivity in Chemistry and Drug Research*, Academic Press, London (1976).

[27] van de Waterbeemd, H. and Testa, B., *Adv. Drug Res.*, ***16*** (1987), 85.

[28] Williams, D.E., *Rev. Comp. Chem.*, ***2*** (1991), 226.

[29] Gaillard, P., Carrupt, P.A., Testa, B. and Boudon, A., *J. Comput.-Aided Mol. Des.*, ***8*** (1994), 83.

[30] Burkert, U. and Allinger, N.L., *Molecular Mechanics*, ACS Monograph (1982), 177.

[31] Good, A.C., *J. Mol. Graph.*, ***10*** (1992), 144.

[32] Willett, P. and Winterman, V., *Quant. Struct.-Act. Relat.*, ***5*** (1986), 18.

[33] Wold, S., Johansson, E. and M. Cocchi, M., In *3D-QSAR in Drug Design: Theory, Methods and Applications*, H. Kubinyi (Ed.), Escom, Leiden (1993), 523.

[34] van de Waterbeemd, H. (Ed.), *Chemometric Methods in Molecular Design: Vol. 2 of Methods and Principles in Medicinal Chemistry*, Mannhold, R. et al. (Eds.), VCH, Weinheim (1995).

[35] van de Waterbeemd, H., (Ed.), *Advanced Computer-Assisted Techniques in Drug Discovery, Vol. 3 of Methods and Principles in Medicinal Chemistry*, Mannhold, R. et al., (Eds.), VCH, Weinheim (1995).

[36] Dunn, W.J. and Wold, S., In *Chemometric Methods in Molecular Design*, van de Waterbeemd, H. (Ed.), VCH, Weinheim (1995), 179.

[37] van de Waterbeemd, H., *Quant. Struct.-Act. Relat.*, ***11*** (1992), 200.

[38] Topliss, J.G., *J. Med. Chem.*, ***15*** (1972), 1006.

[39] Verloop, A., *The STERIMOL Approach to Drug Design*, Marcel Dekker, New York (1987).

Appendix V: Glossary of Terms Used in Medicinal Chemistry*

Active Transport: Active transport is the carriage of a solute across a biological membrane from low to high concentration that requires the expenditure of (metabolic) energy.
Address-message Concept: Address-message concept refers to compounds in which part of the molecule is required for binding (address) and part for the biological action (message).
ADME: Abbreviation for Absorption, Distribution, Metabolism and Excretion (see also Pharmacokinetics; Drug Disposition).
Affinity: Affinity is the tendency of a molecule to associate with another. The affinity of a drug is its ability to bind to its biological target (receptor, enzyme, transport system, etc.). For pharmacological receptors it can be thought of as the frequency with which the drug, when brought into the proximity of a receptor by diffusion, will reside at a position of minimum free energy within the force field of that receptor. For an agonist (or for an antagonist) the numerical representation of affinity is the reciprocal of the equilibrium dissociation constant of the ligand: receptor complex denoted K_A, calculated as the rate constant for offset (k_{-1}) divided by the rate constant for onset (k_1).
Agonist: An agonist is an endogenous substance or a drug that can interact with a receptor and initiate a physiological or a pharmacological response characteristic of that receptor (contraction, relaxation, secretion, enzyme activation, etc.).
Allosteric Binding Sites: Allosteric binding sites are contained in many enzymes and receptors. As a consequence of the binding to allosteric binding sites, the interaction with the normal ligand may be either enhanced or reduced.
Allosteric Enzyme: Allosteric enzyme is an enzyme that contains a region to which small, regulatory molecules ("effectors") may bind in addition to and separate from the substrate binding site and thereby affect the catalytic activity. On binding the effector, the catalytic activity of the enzyme towards the substrate may be enhanced, in which case the effector is an activator, or reduced, in which case it is a de-activator or inhibitor.
Allosteric Regulation: Allosteric regulation is the regulation of the activity of allosteric enzymes (see also Allosteric Binding Sites; Allosteric Enzyme).
Analog: An analog is a drug whose structure is related to that of another drug but whose chemical and biological properties may be quite different (see also Congener).
Antagonist: An antagonist is a drug or a compound that opposes the physiological effects of another. At the receptor level, it is a chemical entity that opposes the receptor-associated responses normally induced by another bioactive agent.

---

*Source: Reprinted with permission from Wermuth, C.G., Ganellin, C.R., Lindberg, P. and Mitscher, L.A., *Pure and Applied Chemistry*, ***70*** (1998), 1129-1143.

Antimetabolite: An antimetabolite is a structural analog of an intermediate (substrate or coenzyme) in a physiologically occurring metabolic pathway that acts by replacing the natural substrate thus blocking or diverting the biosynthesis of physiologically important substances.

Antisense Molecule: An antisense molecule is an oligonucleotide or analog thereof that is complementary to a segment of RNA (ribonucleic acid) or DNA (deoxyribonucleic acid) and that binds to it and inhibits its normal function.

Autacoid: An autacoid is a biological substance secreted by various cells whose physiological activity is restricted to the vicinity of its release; it is often referred to as local hormone.

Autoreceptor: An autoreceptor, present at a nerve ending, is a receptor that regulates, via positive or negative feedback processes, the synthesis and/or release of its own physiological ligand (see also Heteroreceptor).

Bioassay: A bioassay is a procedure for determining the concentration, purity and/or biological activity of a substance (e.g., vitamin, hormone, plant growth factor, antibiotic, enzyme) by measuring its effect on an organism, tissue, cell, enzyme or receptor preparation compared to a standard preparation.

Bioisostere: A bioisostere is a compound resulting from the exchange of an atom or of a group of atoms with another, broadly similar, atom or group of atoms. The objective of a bioisosteric replacement is to create a new compound with similar biological properties to the parent compound. The bioisosteric replacement may be physicochemically or topologically based (see also Isosteres).

Bioprecursor Prodrug: A bioprecursor prodrug is a prodrug that does not imply the linkage to a carrier group, but results from a molecular modification of the active principle itself. This modification generates a new compound, able to be transformed metabolically or chemically, the resulting compound being the active principle.

Biotransformation: Biotransformation is the chemical conversion of substances by living organisms or enzyme preparations.

CADD: Abbreviation for Computer-Assisted Drug Design.

Carrier-Linked Prodrug (Carrier Prodrug): A carrier-linked prodrug is a prodrug that contains a temporary linkage of a given active substance with a transient carrier group that produces improved physicochemical or pharmacokinetic properties and that can be easily removed *in vivo*, usually by a hydrolytic cleavage.

Cascade Prodrug: A cascade prodrug is a prodrug for which the cleavage of the carrier group becomes effective only after unmasking an activating group.

Catabolism: Catabolism consists of reactions involving endogenous organic substrates to provide chemically available energy (e.g., ATP) and/or to generate metabolic intermediates used in subsequent anabolic reactions.

Catabolite: A catabolite is a naturally occurring metabolite.

Clone: A clone is a population of genetically identical cells produced from a common ancestor. Sometimes, "clone" is also used for a number of recombinant DNA (deoxyribonucleic acid) molecules all carrying the same inserted sequence.

Codon: A codon is the sequence of three consecutive nucleotides that occurs in mRNA which directs the incorporation of a specific amino acid into a protein or represents the starting or termination signals of protein synthesis.

Coenzyme: A coenzyme is a dissociable, low-molecular weight, non-proteinous organic compound (often nucleotide) participating in enzymatic reactions as acceptor or donor of chemical groups or electrons.

Combinatorial Synthesis: Combinatorial synthesis is a process to prepare large sets of organic compounds by combining sets of building blocks.

Combinatorial Library: A combinatorial library is a set of compounds prepared by combinatorial synthesis.
CoMFA: Abbreviation of Comparative Molecular Field Analysis.
Comparative Molecular Field Analysis (CoMFA): CoMFA is a 3D QSAR method that uses statistical correlation techniques for the analysis of the quantitative relationship between the biological activity of a set of compounds with a specified alignment, and their three-dimensional electronic and steric properties. Other properties such as hydrophobicity and hydrogen bonding can also be incorporated into the analysis (see also Three-Dimensional Quantitative Structure-Activity Relationship [3D QSAR]).
Computational Chemistry: Computational chemistry is a discipline using mathematical methods for the calculation of molecular properties or for the simulation of molecular behavior.
Computer-Assisted Drug Design (CADD): Computer-assisted drug design involves all computer-assisted techniques used to discover, design, and optimize biologically active compounds with a putative use as drugs.
Congener: A congener is a substance literally *con*-(with) *generated* or synthesized by essentially the same synthetic chemical reactions and the same procedures. Analogs are substances that are analogous in some respect to the prototype agent in chemical structure. Clearly congeners may be analogs or vice versa but not necessarily. The term congener, while most often a synonym for homologue, has become somewhat more diffuse in meaning so that the terms congener and analog are frequently used interchangeably in the literature.
Cooperativity: Cooperativity is the interaction process by which binding of a ligand to one site on a macromolecule (enzyme, receptor, etc.) influences binding at a second site, e.g. between the substrate binding sites of an allosteric enzyme. Cooperative enzymes typically display a sigmoid (S-shaped) plot of the reaction rate against substrate concentration. (see Allosteric Binding Sites).
3D QSAR: See Three-Dimensional Quantitative Structure-Activity Relationship.
***De novo* Design:** *De novo* design is the design of bioactive compounds by incremental construction of a ligand model within a model of the receptor or enzyme active site, the structure of which is known from X-ray or nuclear magnetic resonance (NMR) data.
Disposition: See Drug Disposition.
Distomer: A distomer is the enantiomer of a chiral compound that is less potent for a particular action. This definition does not exclude the possibility of other effect or side effect of the distomer (see also Eutomer).
Docking Studies: Docking studies are molecular modeling studies aimed at finding a proper fit between a ligand and its binding site.
Double-Blind Study: A *double-blind study* is a clinical study of potential and marketed drugs, where neither the investigators nor the subjects know which subjects will be treated with the active principle and which ones will receive a placebo.
Double Prodrug (or Pro-Prodrug): A double prodrug is a biologically inactive molecule which is transformed *in vivo* in two steps (enzymatically and/or chemically) to the active species.
Drug: A drug is any substance presented for treating, curing, or preventing disease in human beings or in animals. A drug may also be used for making a medical diagnosis or for restoring, correcting, or modifying physiological functions (e.g., the contraceptive pill).
Drug Disposition: Drug disposition refers to all processes involved in the absorption, distribution, metabolism, and excretion of drugs in a living organism.
Drug Latentiation: Drug latentiation is the chemical modification of a biologically active compound to form a new compound, which *in vivo* will liberate the parent compound. Drug latentiation is synonymous to prodrug design.

Drug Targeting: Drug targeting is a strategy aiming at the delivery of a compound to a particular tissue of the body.
Dual Action Drug: A dual action drug is a compound which combines two desired different pharmacological actions at a similarly efficacious dose.
Efficacy: Efficacy describes the relative intensity with which agonists vary in the response they produce even when they occupy the same number of receptors and with the same affinity. Efficacy is not synonymous to intrinsic activity. Efficacy is the property that enables drugs to produce responses. It is convenient to differentiate the properties of drugs into two groups, those which cause them to associate with the receptors (affinity) and those that produce stimulus (efficacy). This term is often used to characterize the level of maximal responses induced by agonists. In fact, not all agonists of a receptor are capable of inducing identical levels of maximal responses. Maximal response depends on the efficiency of receptor coupling, i.e., from the cascade of events, which, from the binding of the drug to the receptor, leads to the observed biological effect.
Elimination: Elimination is the process achieving the reduction of the concentration of a xenobiotic including its metabolism.
Enzyme: An enzyme is a macromolecule, usually a protein, that functions as a (bio) catalyst by increasing the reaction rate. In general, an enzyme catalyzes only one reaction type (reaction selectivity) and operates on only one type of substrate (substrate selectivity). Substrate molecules are transformed at the same site (regioselectivity) and only one or preferentially one of chiral substrates or racemates is transformed (enantioselectivity[special form of stereoselectivity]).
Enzyme Induction: Enzyme induction is the process whereby an (inducible) enzyme is synthesized in response to a specific inducer molecule. The inducer molecule (often a substrate that needs the catalytic activity of the inducible enzyme for its metabolism) combines with a repressor and thereby prevents the blocking of an operator by the repressor leading to the translation of the gene for the enzyme.
Enzyme Repression: Enzyme repression is the mode by which the synthesis of an enzyme is prevented by repressor molecules. In many cases, the end product of a synthesis chain (e.g., an amino acid) acts as a feed-back corepressor by combining with an intracellular aporepressor protein, so that this complex is able to block the function of an operator. As a result, the whole operation is prevented from being transcribed into mRNA, and the expression of all enzymes necessary for the synthesis of the end product enzyme is abolished.
Eudismic Ratio: Eudismic ratio is the potency of the eutomer relative to that of the distomer.
Eutomer: The Eutomer is the enantiomer of a chiral compound that is more potent for a particular action (see also Distomer).
Genome: A genome is the complete set of chromosomal and extrachromosomal genes of an organism, a cell, an organelle, or a virus; the complete DNA (deoxyribonucleic acid) component of an organism.
Hansch Analysis: Hansch analysis is the investigation of the quantitative relationship between the biological activity of a series of compounds and their physicochemical substituent or global parameters representing hydrophobic, electronic, steric and other effects using multiple regression correlation methodology.
Hapten: A hapten is a low molecular weight molecule that contains an antigenic determinant but which is not itself antigenic unless combined with an antigenic carrier.
Hard Drug: A hard drug is a nonmetabolizable compound, characterized either by high lipid solubility and accumulation in adipose tissues and organelles, or by high water solubility. In the lay press, the term "Hard Drug" refers to a powerful drug of abuse such as cocaine or heroin.

Heteroreceptor: A heteroreceptor is a receptor regulating the synthesis and/or the release of mediators other than its own ligand (see also Autoreceptor).
Homologue: The term homologue is used to describe a compound belonging to a series of compounds differing from each other by a repeating unit, such as a methylene group, a peptide residue, etc.
Hormone: A hormone is a substance produced by endocrine glands, released in very low concentration into the bloodstream, and which exerts regulatory effects on specific organs or tissues distant from the site of secretion.
Hydrophilicity: Hydrophilicity is the tendency of a molecule to be solvated by water.
Hydrophobicity: Hydrophobicity is the association of non-polar groups or molecules in an aqueous environment which arises from the tendency of water to exclude non-polar molecules (see also Lipophilicity).
IND: Abbreviation for Investigational New Drug.
Intrinsic Activity: Intrinsic activity is the maximal stimulatory response induced by a compound in relation to that of a given reference compound (see also Partial Agonist) This term has evolved with common usage. It was introduced by Ariëns as a proportionality factor between tissue response and receptor occupancy. The numerical value of intrinsic activity (alpha) could range from unity (for full agonists, i.e., agonist inducing the tissue maximal response) to zero (for antagonists), the fractional values within this range denoting partial agonists. Ariëns' original definition equates the molecular nature of alpha to maximal response only when response is a linear function of receptor occupancy. This function has been verified. Thus, intrinsic activity, which is a drug and tissue parameter, cannot be used as a characteristic drug parameter for classification of drugs or drug receptors. For this purpose, a proportionality factor derived by null methods, namely, relative efficacy, should be used. Finally, "intrinsic activity" should not be used instead of "intrinsic efficacy". A "partial agonist" should be termed "agonist with intermediate intrinsic efficacy" in a given tissue.
Inverse Agonist: An inverse agonist, also called as negative antagonist, is a drug which acts at the same receptor at which an agonist acts but produces an opposite effect.
Isosteres: Isosteres are molecules or ions of similar size containing the same number of atoms and valence electrons, e.g., O^{2-}, F^-, Ne (see also Bioisostere).
Latentiated Drug: See Drug Latentiation.
Lead Discovery: Lead discovery is the process of identifying active new chemical entities, which by subsequent modification may be transformed into a clinically useful drug.
Lead Generation: Lead generation is the term applied to strategies developed to identify compounds which possess a desired but non-optimized biological activity.
Lead Optimization: Lead optimization is the synthetic modification of a biologically active compound in order to fulfill all stereo-electronic, physicochemical, pharmacokinetic and nontoxic requirements for clinical usefulness.
Lipophilicity: Lipophilicity represents the affinity of a molecule or moiety for a lipophilic environment. It is commonly measured by its distribution behavior in a biphasic system, either liquid-liquid (e.g., partition coefficient in octan-1-ol/water) or solid/liquid (retention on reversed-phase high performance liquid chromatography (RP-HPLC) or thin-layer chromatography (TLC) system) (see also Hydrophobicity).
Medicinal Chemistry: Medicinal chemistry is a chemistry-based discipline, also involving aspects of biological, medical, and pharmaceutical sciences. It is concerned with the invention, discovery, design, identification, and preparation of biologically active compounds, the study of their metabolism, the interpretation of their mode of action at the molecular level, and the construction of structure-activity relationships.
Metabolism: The term metabolism comprises the entire physical and chemical processes involved in the maintenance and reproduction of life in which nutrients are broken down

to generate energy and to give simpler molecules (catabolism) which by themselves may be used to form more complex molecules (anabolism). In case of heterotrophic organisms, the energy evolving from catabolic processes is made available for use by the organism. In medicinal chemistry the term metabolism refers to the biotransformation of xenobiotics and particularly drugs (see also Biotransformation; Xenobiotic).

Metabolite: A metabolite is any intermediate or product resulting from metabolism.

Me-too Drug: A me-too drug is a compound that is structurally very similar to already known drugs, with only minor pharmacological differences.

Molecular Graphics: Molecular graphics is the visualization and manipulation of three-dimensional representations of molecules on a graphical display device.

Molecular Modeling: Molecular modeling is a technique for the investigation of molecular structures and properties using computational chemistry and graphical visualization techniques in order to provide a plausible three-dimensional representation under a given set of circumstances.

Mutagen: A mutagen is an agent that causes a permanent heritable change (i.e., a mutation) into the DNA (deoxyribonucleic acid) of an organism.

Mutual Prodrug: A mutual prodrug is the association in a unique molecule of two, usually synergistic, drugs attached to, and being the carrier of, each other.

NDA: Abbreviation for New Drug Application.

New Chemical Entity (NCE): A new chemical entity (NCE) is a compound not previously described in the literature.

Non-Classical Isostere: Same meaning as Bioisostere.

Nucleic Acid: A nucleic acid is a macromolecule composed of linear sequences of nucleotides that perform several functions in living cells, e.g., the storage of genetic information and its transfer from one generation to the next generation, the expression of this information in protein synthesis (mRNA, tRNA), and to act as functional components of subcellular units such as ribosomes (rRNA). RNA (ribonucleic acid) contains D-ribose and DNA (deoxyribonucleic acid) contains 2-deoxy-D-ribose as the sugar component.

Nucleoside: A nucleoside is a compound, without any phosphate groups, in which a purine or pyrimidine base is attached through its N-atom to C-1 atom of either 2-deoxy-D-ribose or D-ribose, replacing their hydroxy group (see also nucleotide). The common nucleosides in biological systems are adenosine, guanosine, cytidine, and uridine (which contain ribose) and deoxyadenosine, deoxyguanosine, deoxycytidine and thymidine (which contain deoxyribose).

Nucleotide: A nucleotide is a nucleoside in which the primary hydroxy group of either 2-deoxy-D-ribose or D-ribose is esterified by orthophosphoric acid (see also Nucleoside).

Oligonucleotide: An oligonucleotide is an oligomer resulting from a linear sequence of nucleotides.

Oncogene: An oncogene is a normal cellular gene which, when inappropriately expressed or mutated, can transform eukaryotic cells into tumour cells.

Orphan Drug: An orphan drug is a drug for the treatment of a rare disease for which reasonable recovery of the sponsoring firm's research and development expenditure is not expected within a reasonable time. The term is also used to describe substances intended for such uses.

Partial Agonist: A partial agonist is an agonist which is unable to induce maximal activation of a receptor population, regardless of the amount of drug applied (see also Intrinsic Activity).

Pattern Recognition: Pattern recognition is the identification of patterns in large data sets using appropriate mathematical methodologies.

Peptidomimetic: A peptidomimetic is a compound containing non-peptidic structural elements that is capable of mimicking or antagonizing the biological action(s) of a natural

parent peptide. A peptidomimetic does no longer have classical peptide characteristics such as enzymatically scissille peptidic bonds (see also Peptoid).
Peptoid: A peptoid is a peptidomimetic that results from the oligomeric assembly of N-substituted glycines.
Pfeiffer's Rule: Pfeiffer's rule states that in a series of chiral compounds the eudismic ratio increases with increasing potency of the eutomer.
Pharmacokinetics: Pharmacokinetics refers to the study of absorption, distribution, metabolism and excretion (ADME) of bioactive compounds in a higher organism (see also Drug Disposition).
Pharmacophore (Pharmacophoric Pattern): A pharmacophore is the ensemble of steric and electronic features that is necessary to ensure the optimal supramolecular interactions with a specific biological target structure and to trigger (or to block) its biological response. A pharmacophore does not represent a real molecule or a real association of functional groups, but a purely abstract concept that accounts for the common molecular interaction capacities of a group of compounds towards their target structure. The pharmacophore can be considered as the largest common denominator shared by a set of active molecules. This definition discards a misuse often found in the medicinal chemistry literature which consists of naming as pharmacophores simple chemical functionalities such as guanidines, sulfonamides or dihydroimidazoles (formerly imidazolines), or typical structural skeletons such as flavones, phenothiazines, prostaglandins or steroids.
Pharmacophoric Descriptors: Pharmacophoric descriptors are used to define a pharmacophore, including H-bonding, hydrophobic and electrostatic interaction sites, defined by atoms, ring centers and virtual points.
Placebo: A placebo is an inert substance or dosage form which is identical in appearance, flavor, and odor to the active substance or dosage form. It is used as a negative control in a bioassay or in a clinical study.
Potency: Potency is the dose of drug required to produce a specific effect of given intensity as compared to a standard reference. Potency is a comparative rather than an absolute expression of drug activity. Drug potency depends on both affinity and efficacy. Thus, two agonists can be equipotent, but have different intrinsic efficacies with compensating differences in affinity.
Prodrug: A prodrug is any compound that undergoes biotransformation before exhibiting its pharmacological effects. Prodrugs can thus be viewed as drugs containing specialized non-toxic protective groups used in a transient manner to alter or eliminate undesirable properties in the parent molecule (see also Double Prodrug).
QSAR: See Quantitative Structure-Activity Relationships.
Quantitative Structure-Activity Relationships (QSAR): Quantitative structure-activity relationships are mathematical relationships linking chemical structure and pharmacological activity in a quantitative manner for a series of compounds. Methods which can be used in QSAR include various regression and pattern recognition techniques.
Receptor: A receptor is a molecule or a polymeric structure in or on a cell that specifically recognizes and binds a compound acting as a molecular messenger (neurotransmitter, hormone, lymphokine, lectin, drug, etc.).
Receptor Mapping: Receptor mapping is the technique used to describe the geometric and/or electronic features of a binding site when insufficient structural data for this receptor or enzyme are available. Generally the active site cavity is defined by comparing the superposition of active to that of inactive molecules.
Second Messenger: A second messenger is an intracellular metabolite or ion increasing or decreasing as a response to the stimulation of receptors by agonists, considered as the "first messenger". This generic term usually does not prejudge the rank order of intracellular biochemical events.

Site-Specific Delivery: Site-specific delivery is an approach to target a drug to a specific tissue, using prodrugs or antibody recognition systems.
Soft Drug: A soft drug is a compound that is degraded *in vivo* to predictable non-toxic and inactive metabolites, after having achieved its therapeutic role.
SPC: Abbreviation for Structure Property Correlations.
Structure-Activity Relationship (SAR): Structure-activity relationship is the relationship between chemical structure and pharmacological activity for a series of compounds.
Structure-Based Design: Structure-based design is a drug design strategy based on the 3D structure of the target obtained by X-ray or NMR.
Structure-Property Correlations (SPC): Structure-property correlations refer to all statistical mathematical methods used to correlate any structural property to any other property (intrinsic, chemical, or biological), using statistical regression and pattern recognition techniques.
Systemic: Systemic means relating to or affecting the whole body.
Teratogen: A teratogen is a substance that produces a malformation in a foetus.
Three-Dimensional Quantitative Structure-Activity Relationship (3D QSAR): A three-dimensional quantitative structure-activity relationship is the analysis of the quantitative relationship between the biological activity of a set of compounds and their spatial properties using statistical methods.
Topliss Tree: A Topliss tree is an operational scheme for analog design.
Transition-State Analog: A transition-state analog is a compound that mimics the transition state of a substrate bound to an enzyme.
Xenobiotic: A xenobiotic is a compound foreign to an organism (*xenos* [greek] = foreign).

Suggestions for Further Reading

[1] Brown, R.D., Descriptors for Diversity Analysis, *Perspect. Drug Discov. Des.*, ***7/8*** (1997), 31-49.

[2] Cramer III, R.D. and Bunce, J.D., *QSAR in Drug Design and Toxicology*, Proceedings of the 6th European QSAR Symposium, Portoroz, 1986, Hadzi, D. and Jerman-Blazic, B. (Eds.), *Pharmacochem. Libr.*, ***10***, Elsevier, Amsterdam (1987), 3-12.

[3] Dean, P.M. (Ed.), *Molecular Similarity in Drug Design*, Blackie Academic and Professional, London (1995).

[4] Dean, P.M., *Molecular Foundations of Drug-Receptor Interaction*, Cambridge University Press, Cambridge (1987).

[5] Downs, G.M., Molecular Descriptors, In *Computational Medicinal Chemistry and Drug Discovery*, Bultinck, P., Winter, H.D., Langenaeker, W. and Tollenaere, J.P. (Eds.), Dekker Inc., New York (2003).

[6] Gedeck, P. and Willett, P., Visual and Computational Analysis of Structural-Activity Relationships in High-throughput Screening Data, *Curr. Opin. Chem. Biol.*, **5** (2001), 389-395.

[7] Ghose, A.K. and Viswanadhan, V.N. (Eds.), *Combinatorial Library Design and Evaluation: Principles, Software Tools and Applications in Drug Discovery,* Marcel Dekker, New York (2001).

[8] Golberg, L. (Ed.), *Structure-Activity Correlation as a Predictive Tool in Toxicology: Fundamentals, Methods and Applications*, Hemisphere, Washington (1983).

[9] Graham, R.C., *Data Analysis for the Chemical Sciences: A Guide to Statistical Techniques*, VCH Publishers, New York (1993).

[10] Greco, G., Novellino, E. and Martion, Y.C., Approaches to Three-Dimensional Quantitative Structure-Activity Relationships, *Rev. Comput. Chem.*, ***11*** (1997), 183-240.

[11] Johnson, M.A. and Maggiora, G.M. (Eds.), *Concepts and Applications of Molecular Similarity*, Wiley, New York (1990).

[12] Joliffe, I.T., *Principal Component Analysis*, Springer-Verlag, New York (1986).

[13] Karcher, W. and Devilers, J. (Eds.), Practical Application of Quantitative Structure-Activity Correlation (QSAR) in Environmental Chemistry and Toxicology, *Chemical and Environmental Sciences*, ***Vol. I***, Kluwer Academic Publishers for the European Communities, Dordrecht (1990).

[14] Kier, L.B. and Hall, L.H., *Molecular Connectivity in Stucture-Activity Analysis*, Research Studies Press, Letchworth (1986).

[15] Kohonen, T., *Self-Organizing Maps*, Third Edition, Springer, Berlin (2001).

[16] Kubinyi, H. (Ed.), *3D QSAR in Drug Design: Theory, Methods and Applications*, ESCOM Science Publishers, Leiden (1993).

[17] Kubinyi, H., QSAR and 3D QSAR in Drug Design, *Drug Discovery Today*, **2** (1997), 457-467 (Part 1) and 538-546 (Part 2).

[18] Kubinyi. H., From Narcosis to Hyperspace: The History of QSAR, *Quant. Struct-Act. Relat.*, ***21*** (2002), 348-356.

[19] Kubinyi, H. (Ed.), *3D QSAR in Drug Design: Theory, Methods and Applications*, ESCOM Science Publishers, Leiden (1993).

[20] Kuchar, M. (Ed.), *QSAR in Design of Bioactive Compounds*, Proceedings of the 1st Telesymposium on Medicinal Chemistry, Prous Science Publishers, Barcelona (1984).

[21] Lemmen, C. and Lengauer, T., Computational Methods for the Structural Alignment of Molecules, *J. Comput-Aided Mol. Des.*, ***14*** (2000), 215-232.

[22] Lewis, R.A., Pickett, S.D. and Clark, D.E., Computer-aided Molecular Diversity Analysis and Combinatorial Library Design, *Rev. Comput. Chem.*, ***16*** (2000), 1-51.

[23] Livingstone, D., The Characterization of Chemical Structures Using Molecular Properties: A Survey, *J. Chem. Inform. Comput. Sci.*, ***40*** (2000), 195-209.

[24] Livingstone, D., *Data Analysis for Chemists*, Oxford University Press, Oxford (1995).

[25] Martin, Y.C. and DeWitte, R.S. (Eds.), Hydrophobicity and Solvation in Drug Design, *Perspectives in Drug Discovery and Design, **Vol. 17***, Kluwer Academic Publishers, Dordrecht (1999).

[26] Martin, Y.C. and DeWitte, R.S. (Eds.), Hydrophobicity and Solvation in Drug Design, *Perspectives in Drug Discovery and Design, **Vol. 18***, Kluwer Academic Publishers, Dordrecht (2000).

[27] Martin, Y.C., *Quantitative Drug Design: A Critical Introduction,* Marcel Dekker, New York (1978).

[28] McGowan, J.C. and Mellors, A., *Molecular Volumes in Chemistry and Biology: Applications Including Partitioning and Toxicity*, Ellis Horwood Ltd., Chichester (1986).

[29] Zupan, J. and Gasteiger, J., *Neural Networks for Chemists*, Weinheim, Wiley-VCH (1999).

[30] Opera, T.I. and Waller, C.L., Theoretical and Practical Aspects of Three-Dimensional Quantitative Structure-Activity Relationships, *Rev. Comput. Chem.*, ***11*** (1997), 127-182.

[31] Otto, M., *Chemometrics: Statistics and Computer Application in Analytical Chemistry*, Wiley-VCH, New York (1998).

[32] Perun, T.J. and Propst, C.L., *Computer-Aided Drug Design: Methods and Applications*, Marcel Dekker, New York (1989).

[33] Purcell, W.P., Bass, G.E. and Clayton, J.M., *Strategy of Drug Design: A Molecular Guide to Biological Activity*, Wiley, New York (1973).

[34] Ramsden, C.A. (Ed.), *Quantitative Drug Design*, *Comprehensive Medicinal Chemistry: The Rational Design, Mechanistic Study and Therapeutic Application of Chemical Compounds*, Hansch, C., Sammes, P.G. and Taylor, J.B. (Eds.), ***4***, Pergamon Press, Oxford (1990).

[35] Rekker, R.F., The Hydrophobic Fragmental Constant – Its Derivation and Application: A Means of Characterizing Membrane Systems, *Pharmacochem. Libr.*, ***1***, Elsevier, Amsterdam (1977).

[36] Richards, W.G. (Ed.), *Computer-Aided Molecular Design*, IBC Technical Services, London (1989).

[37] Tute, M.S., History and Objectives of Quantitative Drug Design, In *Comprehensive Medicinal Chemistry*, Ramsden, C.A. (Ed.), ***4***, Pergamon Press, New York (1990), 1-31.

[38] van de Waterbeemd, H., Smith, D.A., Beaumont, K. and Walker, D.K., Property-Based Design: Optimization of Drug Absorption and Pharmacokinetics, *J. Med. Chem.*, ***44*** (2001), 1313-1333.

[39] van de Waterbeemd, H., In *Hydrophobicity of Organic Compounds: How to Calculate it by PC's*, Booksoft, Darvas, F. (Ed.), ***Vol. 1***, CompuDrug, Vienna (1986).

[40] Walters, W.P., Stahl, M.T. and Murcko, M.A., Virtual Screening: An Overview, *Drug Discovery Today*, ***3*** (1998), 160-178.

[41] Weise, M., *QSAR and Strategies in the Design of Bioactive Compounds*, Proceedings of the 5th European QSAR Symposium, Bad Segeberg, 1984, Seydel, J.K. (Ed.), VCH, Weinheim (1985), 19-29.

Index